Effective Assessment and The Improvement of Education — A Tribute to Desmond Nuttall

By

Roger Murphy
and
Patricia Broadfoot

 The Falmer Press

(A member of the Taylor & Francis Group)
London • Washington, D.C.

UK   The Falmer Press, 4 John Street, London WC1N 2ET
USA   The Falmer Press, Taylor & Francis Inc., 1900 Frost Road, Suite 101, Bristol, PA 19007

First published in 1995

A catalogue record for this book is available from the British Library

Library of Congress Cataloging-in-Publication Data are available on request

ISBN 0 7507 0374 1 cased
ISBN 0 7507 0375 X paper

Jacket design by Caroline Archer

Typeset in 11/13pt Bembo by
Graphicraft Typesetters Ltd., Hong Kong.

Printed in Great Britain by Burgess Science Press, Basingstoke on paper which has a specified pH value on final paper manufacture of not less than 7.5 and is therefore 'acid free'.

Effective Assessment and
The Improvement of Education —
A Tribute to Desmond Nuttall

Contents

Contents

Acknowledgments

We are grateful to the following for permission to reproduce copyright material:

The Longman Group for 'The case against examinations', *Education*, 152, 2, v–vi; 'A rare attempt to measure standards', *Education*, 154, 12, ii–iii; 'Will the APU rule the curriculum?' *Education*, 155, 21, ix–x; 'Did the secondary schools get a fair trial?' *Education*, 155, 46–51.

Times Newspapers Limited for 'Unnatural selection', *Times Educational Supplement*, 18 November 1983.

The University of London Institute of Education for 'Can graded assessment, records of achievement, modular assessment & the GCSE co-exist?', by H. Goldstein and D.L. Nuttall, in *The GCSE: An Uncommon Exam*, C.V. Gipps.

The British Educational Research Association for 'What can we learn from research on testing and appraisal? in *Appraising Appraisal*, Kendal, BERA.

Preface

Desmond Nuttall died tragically, at the age of 49, on 24 October 1993. He had by then had an enormously distinguished career as an educational researcher and was well known throughout the world amongst educationalists working in his field. Since his death there have been a large number of tributes to him including a special memorial conference organized by the British Educational Research Association in conjunction with the University of London Institute of Education on 10 June 1994.

In this book we have gathered together a set of twenty of his publications, which we think illustrate some of the major themes of his work as an educational researcher. Although these papers were written over a twenty year period there are many issues and themes contained within them that are highly pertinent now. We consider that this collection represents a classic statement of Desmond Nuttall's key ideas and viewpoints. His work has already had a major impact on national and international policy debates about education, and we hope that this collection will help to keep it in the mind's of those he wished to influence.

As two of his former friends and colleagues we have put together this collection as our tribute to someone we continue to think highly of and now miss. We hope that it will be used widely both by those who knew him and by others who missed out on that privilege.

Roger Murphy and
Patricia Broadfoot
September 1994

Section 1

A Great Record of Educational Achievement

A Great Record of Educational Achievement

Desmond Nuttall had a remarkable twenty-six year career in educational research, primarily as a researcher but also as a manager, an administrator and a policy adviser. His central concern was educational assessment, and through this interest he was closely involved in work focused upon improving the effectiveness of schools, teachers and pupil learning.

His own educational progress had always been outstanding. Starting his formal schooling at the Parents' National Education Union School at Desmoor, he went on to be awarded a scholarship to Bradfield College. From there he won an open exhibition, in 1963, to Trinity Hall, Cambridge, where he gained a First Class Honours Degree in Psychology, followed three years later by a PhD. His PhD thesis on 'Modes of thinking and their measurement' (Nuttall, 1971a, see also Paper 1) paved the way for his life's work, which was clearly fired by his interest in both the assessment of educational achievements and the promotion of educational opportunities and systems which heighten the success of all learners, whatever their individual characteristics (see Paper 2). Indeed, throughout his whole career he managed to hold onto the worthy ideal of promoting educational excellence for all through improved assessment arrangements:

> Many young people are very dissatisfied when they come out of the examination hall realizing that all they were able to do was a bit of one question and a small part of another. We want to give them an opportunity to feel that they have achieved something worthwhile. (Nuttall, 1987a, p. 381)

The UK education system has often been blighted by an artificial division between policy-makers, researchers and practitioners. Career routes often tend to trap talented individuals within one of these domains, thus exacerbating communication gaps that can be such an obstacle to the successful development of educational policies and practices. Desmond Nuttall was able to move freely between such areas, both in terms of the positions that he occupied, but also even more significantly in the networks he developed as he got alongside and worked with people working in different parts of the education system. In one of many recent tributes to him Harvey Goldstein has written that 'it was amazing how Desmond seemed to know almost everybody working in education, and not merely in Britain' (Goldstein, 1993). By many different accounts he was approachable, hard working, insightful, a team player as well as an individualist, and able to communicate his ideas in a way that made a wide range of people stop, think again, and in many cases change their minds. He was not just a brilliant researcher, but he also had a particular skill in relating research to practical problems, and in particular to the harsh realities of educational practice and the messy and cut-throat political dimension of fighting for change (Murphy, 1994).

Desmond Nuttall was always interested in teaching, research, and bringing about educational change. His career involved a number of moves often between quite different types of educational organizations, and yet his work, his interests and his basic passions remained with him in whatever position he was occupying. Immediately after the end of his own schooling he returned to school to spend a year teaching in a secondary modern, and then went straight on to the University of Cambridge for his first degree.

He then began his professional career in 1967 taking up his first post as a researcher at the National Foundation for Educational Research — a body set up in the early 1950s, in part at least, so that policy-making might be informed by relevant research. The commitment by the government to involving the educational research community in the discussion of policy issues was to endure until the late 1970s. For Desmond Nuttall it became, and remained, the abiding principle of his work and hence the first and central theme in any attempt to understand and assess its significance. At the NFER he quickly moved up through a number of research grades, becoming a Principal Research Officer and Head of the Examinations and Tests Research Unit from 1971 to 1973.

Desmond Nuttall's first move to another organization was to become a Senior Educational Researcher in the Schools Council Central Examinations Research and Development Unit in 1973. This body, which was closed down in 1983, is now looked back upon as the most significant representation of the three-way partnership between teachers, local education authorities and central government which characterized educational policy-making and implementation in England throughout the post-war period until the mid 1970s. The Schools Council was above all, a body that recognized the key role that teachers inevitably play in influencing the shape and quality of the education system. In recognizing the critical importance of high quality professionalism, it gave teachers a voice in national debates. It also conducted extensive research aimed at exploring how teachers' professionalism could best be mobilized in the process of educational innovation and change (Plaskow, 1985). The fact that Desmond Nuttall chose to work in such an institution is highly significant. It both reflected and reinforced his existing commitment to the development of teachers' skills as a key ingredient in the search for improved educational quality. He emerged from his involvement with that organization with the commitment to working with, and for, teachers to make educational research practical and useful in the classroom — a commitment that became the second defining principle in his professional life. In subsequent years, when he was much in demand as a speaker on in-service courses, as a consultant to local education authorities and as a writer in the popular educational press, this was a reflection of Desmond Nuttall's ability to engage with teachers in a way that was relevant to them and of his enthusiasm for linking research with practice.

Desmond Nuttall's early professional experience in these two very different organizations also resulted in a commitment to the third defining principle of his work — the importance of assessment as an instrument of educational reform. He became convinced both that it was assessment that held the key to promoting equal opportunities and hence social justice in education and that many aspects of current practice resulted in quite the opposite effect. Initially, Desmond Nuttall's concerns in this respect focused on the role of examinations and on the technical ways in which these might be improved to achieve greater equity and utility. His move to the Middlesex Regional Examining Board for the CSE in 1976 testified to his belief at that time that the kind of novel examining techniques which had become the hallmark of so much CSE work — especially school-based syllabus development and continuous assessment — were the key to success in this respect (see Paper 3). Although later developments were significantly to broaden and moderate this commitment, Desmond Nuttall never lost his early commitment to examination reform as a critical element in the search for both higher levels of quality and a greater realization of equality in the education system and this constitutes the third informing principle of his work.

In 1979, Desmond Nuttall moved to The Open University (OU) to take up a Chair in Educational Psychology. His heaviest involvement in using the distance learning apparatus of the Open University was to disseminate training for the new GCSE examination to teachers. Desmond Nuttall's commitment to linking research to both policy and practice and his enthusiasm for achieving changes through examination reform provided clear testimony to the three principles which were already characterizing his professional work.

But the period Desmond Nuttall spent at the Open University was also one of enormous ferment in English education (see Papers 4–7). It was a time when the old consensus between teachers, LEAs and central government was beginning to break down in the light of a growing realization both that the education system was failing significant numbers of students and that it was very hard to know how and why — or even to what extent — this was the case, given that so little was known about what was taught, to whom, when, and to what standard in the system as a whole. The establishment of the Assessment of Performance Unit in 1974 (Paper 6), which was designed to monitor national standards and, in particular, to identify instances of underachievement, is now seen, with hindsight, as a clear reflection of this concern. Equally symptomatic were the somewhat desultory attempts to find out what was actually being taught in schools via Circular 14/79 and the rash of documents issued by various statutory bodies at the same time (for example, HMI, Schools Council) concerning what a proper curriculum entitlement might be. Youth unemployment, the oil-crisis, the 'winter of discontent' of 1973 were all straws in a wind of change that was to challenge the easy consensus of the past and would result in radically new demands being made on the education system. Chief among these demands would be the need to raise the overall level of educational achievement nationally by raising the level of achievement of the young school-leaver and by encouraging more and more pupils to remain in education beyond the statutory leaving age. Other related demands which were to grow steadily in significance during the 1980s were rooted in the experience of national financial stringency and the consequent awakening on the part of both politicians and public that the education system must be accountable for the investment of national resources that it represented. Concerns for demonstrable efficiency and value for money gradually evolved during the 1980s into the more general preoccupation with the promotion and demonstration of quality which has become the hallmark of educational policy at all levels in the 1990s.

It was this policy context that provided the background for Desmond Nuttall's work during his time at the Open University and subsequently it was the canvas that united a number of more specific studies concerned with assessment at every level of the system — of pupils, of teachers, of institutions, of national systems and internationally — studies which in every case were informed in differing proportions by the same abiding three themes of Desmond Nuttall's work — making research relevant for policy-making and informing teachers' practice through new ways of conceptualizing and using assessment.

Desmond Nuttall's move to the Open University coincided with the period when assessment research issues ceased to be largely the preserve of examination boards and government research bodies. It was the time when the potential power of assessment as an instrument for exacting accountability came to be recognized. It was no longer primarily a selection device with attempts at reform being focused on the efficacy of examinations in this respect. The language of grades and marks, results and standards became the language of accountability, a policy tool which could be used to represent institutional and system quality. The covert practice of using assessment to manipulate and control the curriculum which had long been characteristic of English education became increasingly overt as the government came to realize the coercive power of 'high-stakes' assessment. The increasing prominence which was not confined to England but was typical of most of the Anglophone countries — had the associated consequence of opening up many new research opportunities in this field and of catapulting key researchers in this area — of which Desmond Nuttall was already one — into a potentially very influential role. In short, it was a time when the combination of new requirements which were being made on the education system, a new political ideology and a new conceptualization of the potential significance of assessment in that system, combined to produce a whole range of novel challenges in the field of assessment research.

The first of these for Desmond Nuttall was his exploration of the potential of other approaches to student assessment. His edited book *Assessing Educational Achievement* (Nuttall, 1986b), brought together a host of new thinking on this topic. Some of this thinking concerned the technical matters of assessment quality which had been so much a hallmark of Desmond Nuttall's work from the beginning (see Paper 12). More traditional concerns with validity and comparability became blended with issues relating to utility and how far different approaches to examining fulfilled the goals for which they were being used (see Papers 8 and 9). The work on the GCSE and the very different context of the vocational qualifications both attracted sustained scrutiny from Desmond Nuttall as he wrestled with issues of moderation, comparability and practicability. In particular, his seminal 1987 paper 'The

validity of assessments' (Paper 14) both reflected a growing international concern with this issue at the time and significantly raised the
quality of scholarly debate in this respect.

In 1984, however, Desmond Nuttall had bid for and won, joint
responsibility for the national evaluation of government-funded pilot
record of achievement schemes. His involvement with this project,
spurred as it was by his interest in social justice and assessment reform,
was the beginning of a new stage in Desmond Nuttall's work, an
involvement which reflected the sea change which was to take place in
the field of assessment as a whole.

The Pilot Records of Achievement in Schools Evaluation (PRAISE)
project was to last five years. Desmond Nuttall's involvement in the
detailed study of schools grappling with changes in their assessment
policies and procedures and his contribution to the two influential reports which resulted from the project led him to explore the more
fundamental implications of such reforms both technically (see Paper
10) and in terms of general, but profound questions concerning the
relationship between assessment policy and the promotion of school
quality (see Paper 13).

Early in the decade, Desmond Nuttall had begun to work in the
area of school self-evaluation (Nuttall, 1981b), a field in which the
research group he led at the OU was to subsequently publish extensively and prove very influential as the later collection '*Studies in
School Self-Evaluation*' (Nuttall, Clift and McCormick, 1987) was to
demonstrate.

Another related strand in Desmond Nuttall's work at this time
concerned the developing government interest in introducing teacher
appraisal. Once again it was Desmond Nuttall who so typically sought
to inform the debate from a research perspective (see Paper 11) and to
integrate that debate within the larger discussion of the relative merits
of formative and summative evaluation. The issues, as always for
Desmond Nuttall, were practical ones — to generate research insights
and understanding so that policy, and the goal that policy is ultimately
intended to serve, of making education more effective, would be guided
in the right direction.

Desmond Nuttall's time at the OU was a time of ferment for him
just as it was for everyone interested in assessment. It was a time when
new horizons were opening up when the government was actively
seeking research input to guide their understanding of new developments such as records of achievement, teacher appraisal and school
self-evaluation. When the old certainties concerning the role, purpose
and potential of assessment were being fundamentally challenged,

Desmond Nuttall was strategically placed to take full advantage of these opportunities in leading teams that carried out a programme of research that contributed significantly to the conceptualization and implementation of such developments.

Desmond Nuttall's move to the ILEA in 1986 again coincided with a significant change in the policy climate, a change that was to be marked above all by the 1988 Education Reform Act. Although the Act confirmed the status of assessment as a policy issue, it also represented a quite novel commitment to using assessment as the currency of an educational market as the driving force of the system on an unprecedented scale. Desmond Nuttall found much that was challenging in this new climate. He wrote extensively on the assumptions underpinning national assessment arrangements drawing on his extensive technical knowledge to critique both the conception and the practicability of the arrangements (see Paper 16) just has he had done many years before in relation to the APU (see Papers 4, 6 and 12). So significant were Desmond Nuttall's contributions perceived to be in this respect that he rapidly became regarded as an authority internationally on issues of national assessment, sharing his insights in the United States and Australia in particular and playing a significant role in influencing assessment policy formulation in those countries (see Paper 18).

Desmond Nuttall also found much to interest him in the much higher profile than before of international comparisons. His work over a period of years on the OECD indicators project resulted in a series of publications (for example, Paper 19) which include some of his most perceptive and novel contributions to assessment thinking. Yet despite his notable national and international success at this time, Desmond Nuttall was fundamentally at odds with the new development in establishment thinking. He was at odds with the crude use of performance indicators in league tables of school and local authority performance. His championship of the 'value-added' approach as a more just and meaningful representation of institutional achievement was a reflection both of his enduring concern for technical quality in assessment and of his equally long-standing concern with using assessment to improve education. Desmond Nuttall saw nothing in the punitive and misleading use of assessment information to inform a spurious educational market which was likely to lead to such an outcome. He became an outspoken critic of government policy, a spokesman for a profession overwhelmed by the impositions of an alien political philosophy but unable, often to articulate a response. Right up to the time of his death in October 1993, Desmond Nuttall was using his speaking and writing to articulate clear and realistic alternatives (see Paper 20).

At the same time, Desmond Nuttall's disillusion with government thinking spurred him to continue working on quite a different research front. Social justice is not a topic currently in evidence on the policy agenda. It remained, however a major theme within Desmond Nuttall's work as part of his overall vision of a more equitable society and of the key role of assessment in creating this. The research he instituted whilst at ILEA reflected both his own goals and those of that Authority. Both were equally unfashionable projects concerned to identify the relative achievements of boys and girls, different ethnic groups and different parts of the Authority revealed striking new insights and significant instances of underachievement. Research, which in other circumstances would have had important implications for national as well as local educational policy, but which with the abolition of ILEA, had little impact. By contrast, the well-developed tradition of school effectiveness research within ILEA (see Paper 15) also found a willing and expert champion in Desmond Nuttall. The question of how schools could be made more effective enabled him to draw on several decades spent refining his technical skills in research design and analysis, the capacity to integrate a range of different elements which was rooted in a rich variety of research experience.

Desmond Nuttall's interest in school effectiveness research reflected in a profound way what was perhaps the most abiding characteristic of his work namely the desire to make a difference. For him the academic kudos gained by publishing in prestigious journals and being a pillar of the scholarly community was not an end in itself — although this he certainly achieved. Above all, his commitment was to using research to change policy and hence, practice. His was an engaged scholarship. Desmond Nuttall never sought to be far removed from the issues of the policy arena yet the quality of his work was never corrupted by its pressures for quick solutions and easy answers. The sustained contribution to national assessment policy issues over more than twenty years that this volume illustrates is not just an intellectual achievement. It is a testimony to the character and moral quality of a person who, in his commitment to service and social reform, embodied the best of the English public school tradition by which he was so deeply influenced in his own education. A descendant of George Henry Lewis — the consort of George Eliot and a great nephew of Octavia Hill, one of the founders of the National Trust, Desmond Nuttall's own contribution to improving the individual and collective life of his fellow citizens cannot be in doubt.

Section 2

The Papers

Nuttall, D.L. (1973) 'Convergent and divergent thinking' in Butcher, H.J. and Pont, H.B. (Eds) *Educational Research in Britain*, London, ULP.

Introduction

This first paper in our collection, which was published in 1973, drew substantially upon Desmond Nuttall's recently completed PhD (Nuttall, 1971a). It has an important place in this collection in terms of the way in which it foreshadows some of the major concerns that were going to be fundamental to his work in the next twenty years. It presents a review of an area of psychometric research, which had been hugely significant in debates about intellectual development, innate abilities, and the provision of educational opportunity. Whether or not there was a case for regarding human intelligence as a single human ability, or whether there were other discrete attributes, such as 'divergent thinking' was a question that had a critical place to play in such debates. Also the whole question of whether such things could be adequately captured in psychometric tests in a way that had wider validity was also controversial and critical. Lastly but no-less crucial was the question of how much such attributes, if it was reasonable to regard them as separate attributes, were determined innately or as a result of experience.

What is particularly interesting about this article is not only the way in which it engaged with, and contributed to, those debates, but also the way in which, in doing so, it raised, out of a psychometric context, some of the concerns that were to become central to Desmond Nuttall's work in educational assessment in the years to come. First and foremost the article demonstrates a high level of scholarship as over sixty, mostly very recent, publications are dissected, rigorously analysed and compared. All of this brings to mind some comments in Michael Barber's contribution to an obituary which appeared in *Education* on 29 October 1993, commenting upon Desmond Nuttall's performance at the last conference he attended at the Centre for Policy Studies in September 1993 (see Paper 18),

> He was prepared to speak up only in favour of ideas for which there was firm evidence in the research. The significance of his contribution at the conference was thus not a matter of the strength with which he expressed his own opinion, it was its foundation in research. None of the other speakers could match him. Lord Skidelsky made a formidable intellectual case for a market-style curriculum; Anthony O'Hear argued that the classics needed to be restored to the curriculum; John Marenbon argued for a minimal curriculum; Sir Ron Dearing defended his report; only Desmond cited the evidence. He quoted the British research in depth. He demonstrated a remarkable grasp of research in the Netherlands, Australia, the United States and Scotland. He knew he would not change the minds of the committed ideologies on either side; his expressed aim was to convince the pragmatists, including, he hoped, Sir Ron Dearing.
>
> His performance was brilliant, the highlight of the conference. It was his finest hour. You might disagree with any or all of it; but to do so effectively you would have to be able to cite a comparable body of evidence.
>
> This would be very difficult, for Desmond Nuttall had an unrivalled knowledge of the research. He had a powerful, investigative mind and an entirely balanced approach to research. Unlike so many, he was always open to the persuasion of the evidence. (Barber, 1993, p. 327)

Apart from commitment to pushing forward knowledge, understanding, and educational policy through empirical research, Desmond Nuttall also in this article covers some of the core concerns of his later work. These included the measurement concerns related to the reliability or validity of test scores, the nature of human mental abilities and the extent to which they could be adequately represented by global or disaggregated sub-test scores, the effects of context, test format and other variables on performance, the ability of teachers to assess pupil abilities as an alternative to the use of standardized tests, and the dangers of reading too much into test results, which taken at face value may be quite misleading.

All of this sets in place a framework for Desmond Nuttall's later work on educational assessment. Examinations like psychometric tests can mislead their users, and are prone to all of the interference that can severely limit the reliability and validity of their results. A detailed scrutiny of the characteristics of any assessment situation will almost always reveal factors that will advantage some of those being assessed and disadvantage others. If one really wants to know about the ability and achievements of a particular learner then the assessment procedures need to be very sensitive to that learner's other unique characteristics which are liable to influence the outcome of a standard assessment procedure. It is instructive to contrast one phrase from the conclusion to this paper,

> There is therefore an urgent need for more reliable tests whose content is more relevant to the interests and abilities of the groups for whom the tests are designed . . . (Nuttall, 1973a, p. 129)

with passages in a recent volume by Gipps and Murphy (1994) on equity in educational assessment. Their emphasis upon the need to relate assessments to the relevant experiences and culture, of the individual being assessed, echoes some of the concerns voiced so strongly in Desmond Nuttall's early work, concerns which were to continue to influence much of his work in subsequent years.

Educational tests and assessments can at one level be viewed as simple and straightforward means of generating data about the abilities and achievements of individual learners. However Desmond Nuttall's work, along with that of other researchers working in this area in the period since the early 1970s, has shown that there is an acute need to attend to the broader characteristics of individual learners: to recognize the context bias that is so frequently built into assessments and so to seek for that those optimize the chances of individual learners revealing their real capabilities.

> In an assessment which looks for best rather than typical performance, the context of the item should be the one which allows the pupil to perform well; this would suggest different contexts for different pupils or groups, an awesome development task. (*ibid.*, p. 274)

CONVERGENT AND DIVERGENT THINKING

While the analysis of thinking processes has a long tradition in British philosophy, stemming from the work of Hobbes in the seventeenth century (see

Shouksmith, 1970), it is only relatively recently that processes other than logical reasoning have had any experimental or psychometric investigation. Despite isolated attempts to test imaginative thinking (for example, Hargreaves, 1927), it was not until the early 1960s that the 'creativity' testing movement established a major foothold. The work of Torrance (1962) and Getzels and Jackson (1962) were mainly responsible for stimulating work in this country, and they themselves owe a major debt to Guilford's formulation of his Structure-of-Intellect model (Guilford, 1956 and 1967).

In his now famous presidential address to the American Psychological Association, Guilford (1950) criticized existing tests of ability as being too limited in their scope and suggested that, in the study of creativity, tests to measure the fluency, flexibility and originality of thinking would be required. He and his colleagues proceeded to develop tests of these abilities and in later formulations of his model, they were classified in the Operations category of Divergent-Production. In general, each test presents a problem situation in which there are many, if not an infinity of, appropriate responses, requiring the individual to 'diverge' in his thinking. Divergent-Production thus stands in stark contrast to the remainder of the five Operations categories (Cognition, Memory, Convergent-Production and Evaluation) where there is usually a unique correct answer to the test problem to be chosen from among five alternatives. In tests in the category of Convergent-Production, the candidate has to produce the answer in his own words rather than to choose an answer as in a multiple-choice item, but the term 'convergent thinking' is most commonly used now to cover all those situations where the problem has a unique correct solution, whether the candidate has to generate his own response or merely to select it.

In the following review, convergent thinking is used in this broad sense. The review concentrates on five major areas: whether divergent thinking can be considered a unitary trait, the relationship of divergent and convergent thinking abilities, the validity of divergent thinking tests, the influence of environmental and educational conditions on performance in divergent thinking tests, and factors affecting the reliability of such tests. A number of studies, of course, produce evidence relating to several of these issues.

Is Divergent Thinking a Unitary Trait?

The majority of divergent thinking tests give rise to more than one score. Almost invariably, one score is simply the total number of responses produced, disallowing any responses that clearly do not meet the requirements of the problem (the fluency score); another very common score is for originality, which, in an attempt to avoid subjective judgment, is usually based on the statistical infrequency of the responses. A flexibility score is sometimes used: it consists of the number of different categories of response that a candidate uses and often gives rise to problems in defining the categories.

Nuttall (1971) found very high correlations between fluency, flexibility and originality scores within any one test, the median intercorrelation for four tests being 0.74. Ward (1967) and Fee (1968) in their reanalyses of the data of Wallach and Kogan (1965) found that uniqueness (originality) scores loaded on the same factor as fluency scores, although Ward's analysis also gave rise to a factor, accounting for only 6 per cent of the variance, on which fluency scores loaded but uniqueness scores did not. The factor analysis of Child and Smithers (1971) revealed that fluency and originality scores from the same tests always loaded on the same factor and the same is true, with minor exceptions, in the factor analysis of Richards and Bolton (1971) who also used flexibility scores with two of their tests. In both cases, the flexibility score loaded with the fluency score.

The method used to score divergent thinking tests thus seems to be largely irrelevant and Dacey, Madaus and Allen (1969) concluded from their own results that 'the task-specific measures are highly related, almost to the point of being redundant' (p. 263). No British study has produced results that in any way support the idea of separate factors of fluency, flexibility and originality that cut across tests, although this is implied by Guilford's model.

Although the correlations within a test may be high, the same is not necessarily true of correlations between tests. Many researchers write of divergent thinking as though it were a single dimension and have tended to add scores from different divergent thinking tests to produce a single score, even though the correlations among the tests have sometimes been quite low. For example, Getzels and Jackson (1962) formed a composite score from scores on five divergent thinking tests, all predominantly verbal in nature, and contrasted this score with IQ even though the correlations among the divergent thinking tests were of the same order as those between the divergent thinking tests and IQ. Hudson (1966), too, formed a composite score from scores from the Uses of Objects Test and the Meaning of Words Test even though these tests had a correlation of 0.30, little higher than their correlations with convergent thinking measures.

The most important single piece of evidence in favour of a single factor of divergent thinking stems from the work of Wallach and Kogan (1965). Their composite score based on fluency and uniqueness scores from each of five tests had internal consistencies of up to 0.93, but all their tests, administered individually under game-like conditions, required verbal responses even though some of the stimulus material was visual. Fee's reanalysis (1968) did suggest some slight differentiation between 'verbal' and 'visual' divergent thinking, but Ward's (1967) did not.

When tests sampling a wider range of content are used, there is a growing body of evidence to suggest that divergent thinking is far from being a unitary dimension. Lovell and Shields (1967), working with a group of fifty 8–10-year olds all with IQs greater than 140 on the WISC verbal scale, found that their divergent thinking tests (those used by Getzels and Jackson) defined a reasonable factor but that many of the tests showed substantial loadings on other factors identifiable as academic attainment factors. They concluded: '. . . while the remaining dimensions (factors) suggest that divergent thinking cannot be accounted for by one dimension; rather the able pupil is "creative" in different degrees according to the task that is set him' (p. 207). Child and Smithers (1971) found that the Circles Test loaded on a different factor from the Uses and Consequences tests, although there was a correlation of 0.30 between the two factors, and earlier Child (1968) found that his divergent thinking tests spread themselves across a number of different factors. Richards and Bolton (1971) found that their various divergent thinking tests all loaded on the same factor, but the loadings from the Circles, Consequences and Make-Up Problems tests were all low and there was another factor on which the Circles and Consequences tests had high loadings and the other divergent thinking tests low loadings. Nuttall (1971) found very low correlations between the Squares Test (an alternative form of the Circles Test), the Uses Test, the TH Test (five letter words beginning with TH) and a Number Routes Test (ways of reaching 12 starting with 6, e.g. $6 + 3 + 3 = 12$, $6 + 17 - 11 = 12$). The median correlation among a sample of secondary school fourth-formers broadly representative of the whole ability range was only 0.14 and among a sample of fifth-formers, 0.10.

Divergent thinking therefore appears to be far from a unitary trait and is better considered as a number of distinct abilities. These abilities seem to depend largely upon the stimulus material; that is, there is evidence for a verbal divergent thinking factor, a diagrammatic factor, a numerical factor and so on. Much more research is needed to demonstrate this conclusively and there is an added complication in that low correlations between divergent thinking tests may in large part be due to their unreliability (see below). There has been considerable looseness in applying the title 'divergent thinking' to open-ended tests and a clearer picture may emerge when divergent thinking tests are classified more carefully. Butcher (1968) has suggested that the possible number of responses to such tests may be an important consideration: many tests such as the Uses Test and the Circles Test have a seemingly infinite number of possible responses, whereas the Meaning of Words Test and the TH Test have a strictly limited number of possible responses and would also seem to be highly dependent upon the candidate's breadth of vocabulary. The mode of response is also likely to be important, as are the conditions of testing.

The Relationship Between Divergent and Convergent Thinking Abilities

Getzels and Jackson (1962) claimed to have differentiated between intelligence and 'creativity'. Reviewing their work, Burt (1962) suggested that they had adopted an oversimplified view of both concepts and Marsh's reanalysis (1964) of their data provided no evidence for separate dimensions of 'creativity' and intelligence. Both Burt (1962) and Vernon (1964) suggested that divergent thinking is better seen as a facet of general ability and, indeed, divergent thinking tests have been included as an integral part of early versions of the new British Intelligence Scale (Warburton, 1970).

The view is borne out by the results of Hasan and Butcher (1966). Using Getzels and Jackson's divergent thinking tests among others, they found positive and significant correlations between the Verbal Reasoning Quotient (VRQ) and all the divergent thinking tests, these correlations being higher than those among the divergent thinking tests. The correlation between VRQ and the Fables test was no less than 0.726, in contrast to a value of 0.131 in Getzels and Jackson's study. The mean VRQ of the 175 Scottish schoolchildren (aged 12) in Hasan and Butcher's study was 102, while in Getzels and Jackson's sample of over 500 adolescents the mean IQ was 132; the standard deviations of the quotients in the two samples were comparable, so that restriction of range cannot explain the differing results.

Guilford's Structure-of-Intellect model and the results of his factor analytic studies suggest that the relationships between divergent and convergent thinking abilities are negligible. Guilford tends to employ samples which are highly homogeneous in ability and factor analytic techniques which maximize the chances of obtaining uncorrelated factors. Vernon (1969a) has argued that the British favour the hierarchical model of abilities, which implies substantial correlations between abilities, largely because their samples tend to be more heterogeneous in ability and because they prefer the group factor analysis technique. This latter point is demonstrated in a study by Sultan (1962) who used a wide variety of Guilford's Divergent-Production tests together with a number of conventional convergent thinking tests with a sample of 170 13–14-year-old grammar school pupils. Using Varimax rotation on his Principal Components, he found evidence for distinct Ideational Fluency and Originality factors (as postulated by Guilford, 1959), but no evidence for any of Guilford's three Flexibility factors, the marker tests for these factors tending to load with the convergent thinking tests. A group factor analysis of the same data led to the usual British hierarchical model of abilities with no evidence for any separate divergent thinking factors.

Hudson (1966), working with samples of very clever schoolboys all destined for university, found very little relationship between divergent thinking and intelligence, as measured by the AH 5 test. Cameron (1968), using the same tests with a similar group of pupils in Scotland, also found negligible relationships, the median correlation between the two divergent and two convergent thinking measures being 0.08. With university students, Christie (1970) obtained a correlation of exactly zero between the Miller Analogies tests and a composite divergent thinking score based on the Circles, Problems and Impossibilities tests, and Child and Smithers (1971) found a median correlation of 0.075 between six measures of divergent thinking and the two parts of the AH 5 test.

In samples more representative of the whole ability range, Vernon (1967) and Nuttall (1971) also found a distinct separation between divergent and convergent thinking measures. Haddon and Lytton (1968), however, found a correlation of 0.48 between VRQ and a composite divergent thinking test score among a sample of children aged 11–12 representative of the whole ability range. On retesting most of the same children with the same divergent thinking tests some four years later, Haddon and Lytton (1971) found a correlation between VRQ at age 11 and divergent thinking at age 15 of 0.615. In contrast, Lytton and Cotton (1969) found a correlation of only 0.17 between VRQ and the divergent thinking tests used by Haddon and Lytton among a sample of 14-year-olds whose mean VRQ at 112 was some ten points greater than the mean VRQ of the children in Haddon and Lytton's study.

While there is a tendency for correlations between divergent and convergent thinking measures to be higher among samples representative of the whole ability range than they are among highly selected groups, as would be expected on the grounds of restriction of range, the general picture is far from clearcut. An alternative explanation stems from the threshold hypothesis, which postulates that a minimum level of general ability is required for a high level of performance on divergent thinking tests, but that above that level there is little relationship between general ability and divergent thinking ability. This hypothesis is sufficient to explain the conflicting results of Getzels and Jackson (1962) and Hasan and Butcher (1966).

Haddon and Lytton (1968) also tested the threshold hypothesis. They found that the correlation between VRQ and divergent thinking was 0.076 among the group with VRQ of 115 or higher, 0.164 among the group with VRQ of 100 or higher (which included the first group) and 0.512 in the group with VRQ below 100, thus lending support to the hypothesis. The evidence of Nuttall (1971) also supports the hypothesis: among 100 fourth-year children attending grammar schools the median correlation between four divergent thinking test scores and two scores from a general ability test was 0.01, while among 524 fourth-year children attending secondary modern schools the median correlation was 0.16.

Barker Lunn (1970) isolated a group of pupils scoring in the top 5 per cent on her tests of divergent thinking (based on those of Torrance and scored for fluency in ideas, flexibility in ideas and associations and statistical originality of response) and found that approximately two-thirds of these pupils were above average in ability (as measured by both verbal reasoning and English attainment tests) and that one-third were of average ability. A number of American studies (for example, Yamamoto, 1965) also tend to support the threshold hypothesis, but there is one exception in the results of Lytton and Cotton (1969): while the correlation between VRQ and divergent thinking was lower (0.037) in the group with VRQ of 116 or more than it was in the group with VRQ of 101 or more (r = 0.141; the second group included all members of the first), the correlation in the group with VRQ below 101 was unexpectedly even lower and slightly negative (r = −0.058).

In summary, it appears that divergent thinking abilities can fairly readily be distinguished from convergent thinking abilities among high ability individuals, but that among individuals of lesser ability, the distinction is far less marked. As was the case when examining relationships among tests of divergent thinking, there is always the danger that the correlations between convergent and divergent thinking tests are considerably attenuated because of the unreliability of the latter tests.

The Validity of Divergent Thinking Tests

Ten years ago, divergent thinking tests were usually described as tests of 'creativity'. For every ten studies using such tests and accepting the validity of this title, only one attempted an empirical validation of the tests against criteria of creativity and few of these met with any great success. For this reason, the title 'divergent thinking' has come to be increasingly preferred, but whatever title is used, few researchers would dispute Cronbach's statement that 'most of the tests have been announced to the world prior to any solid validity studies' (Cronbach, 1970, p. 395).

Two British studies have attempted to validate divergent thinking tests against teachers' ratings of the creativeness of their pupils. Lovell and Shields (1967) found that the teachers' ratings loaded on a factor orthogonal to that on which the divergent thinking tests loaded, but Haddon and Lytton (1971) met with slightly greater success. They obtained a significant correlation of 0.286 between the divergent thinking test composite scores and ratings of the pupils' creativeness by teachers of English, but found no relationships between either the test scores or the rating and a pupil's Interest Blank 'Things Done on Your Own' devised by Torrance (1962) as a possible criterion measure of creativity. In studies of this type, the criterion measures may legitimately be criticized as being of dubious validity and Shapiro (1968) presents a stimulating discussion of the criterion problem in creativity research. Ratings by teachers are particularly prone to 'halo' effect, and Lovell and Shields (1967) found a much higher relationship between ratings of originality and tests of logical thinking than between the ratings and divergent thinking tests, which suggests the presence of 'halo' in the ratings.

Convincing validation of the tests as measures of creativity thus appears to be lacking, but interesting relationships between the tests and other variables have been found. Hudson (1966 and 1968) has based most of his work on a comparison of divergers and convergers. A diverger is not necessarily someone who scores highly on a divergent thinking test; divergence is a matter of bias: a diverger is someone whose standing relative to his peers is much higher on the dimension of divergent thinking than on the dimension of convergent thinking, while the reverse bias defines a converger. 'All-rounders', a group to which Hudson pays scant attention, demonstrate no bias, scoring equally well (or equally badly) on both types of test.

Hudson (1966) showed that male divergers were much more likely to specialize in arts subjects than in science subjects in the sixth form, and male convergers in science subjects rather than in arts subjects. There were exceptions (for example, more convergers than divergers specialized in classics, and there was an even split in biology) and, among girls, Hudson (1968) found that the association between specialization and convergence/divergence was far less clearcut: 'as with boys, divergent girls tend to avoid science subjects, but convergent girls are equally likely to go into arts or physical sciences' (p. 23). Haddon and Lytton (1971) also found a considerable difference between the sexes in this respect. Pont's review (1970) shows, however, that the majority of studies attempting to replicate Hudson's work have met with a fair degree of success (for example, Child, 1968; and Mackay and Cameron, 1968). Christie's study (1970) is a recent exception; he found no association between cognitive bias and faculty (arts, social science, medicine, technology and science) among third-year university students, the testing having been done some years earlier while the students were in the grammar school sixth form.

Child and Smithers (1971) used a slightly different approach. Instead of classifying their sample of first year undergraduates studying science, social science and languages as convergers or divergers on the basis of test scores, they asked the undergraduates to complete the convergent/divergent self-rating questionnaire devised by Joyce and Hudson (1968). This questionnaire consists of twenty items (for example, 'I seem to do rather well on intelligence tests'; 'I dislike the idea that science will one day explain every aspect of human experience') to which the respondent has to agree or disagree. The pattern of responses purports to provide an estimate of the individual's degree of convergence or divergence. Subsequent work (Child and Smithers, 1973) has shown that an individual's degree of convergence or divergence as assessed by the questionnaire is only marginally related to his degree of convergence or divergence as assessed by the use of convergent and divergent thinking tests. They found, in fact, that the results of the questionnaire were much more closely related to arts or science bias. The validity of the questionnaire as a measure of convergence or divergence is thus extremely suspect. The results obtained by Child and Smithers (1971) using this questionnaire are therefore not discussed further here.

Another of their findings was that science bias was associated with a high level of performance in the verbal divergent thinking tests. This illustrates the falsity of the conclusion that many have drawn on the basis of Hudson's results, namely that arts specialists (being divergers) score more highly on divergent thinking tests than science specialists.

Further evidence on the falsity of this conclusion comes from two studies. Haddon and Lytton (1971) found no significant differences between a group of arts specialists and a group of science specialists (as far as these were discernible at the age of 15) on their battery of divergent thinking tests and Mills (1970) found no significant differences on either the Uses of Objects Test or the Meaning of Words Test between five groups of ten upper sixth form boys classified by their intended university specialization (physics/engineering, natural sciences, medicine, languages/law and English/history). The group with the highest mean score on both tests was composed of natural scientists. On the other hand, one study among undergraduates at the University of Keele (Hartley and Beasley, 1969) showed a tendency for arts specialists to do better than science specialists on the same two tests that were used by Mills, but no significant differences in test scores were found between a group of less extreme science specialists who were also taking at least one social science option and a group of arts specialists likewise taking a social science option.

These studies suggest that the *level* of divergent thinking test scores is not very different for arts and science groups. Since the association of the *bias* score between divergent and convergent thinking and arts/science choice is fairly well established, it may simply be differences in *level* of convergent thinking scores that are giving rise to this relationship. Child (1969) showed that science and technology students obtained significantly higher IQ scores than social scientists and Child and Smithers (1971) found that science and language students scored significantly more highly than social scientists on both parts of the AH 5 test. While the differences were not significant, language students tended to score more highly than scientists on the verbal and numerical section, while the opposite occurred on the diagrammatic section. Mills (1970), using the AH 6 test (AG version) with sixth formers, found no differences between the five specialist groups on total score but did find significant differences between the groups on the verbal and the numerical sections, but not on the diagrammatic section.

Hudson (1968) has also looked at this problem. With a sample of 139 15-year-old boys from three schools, he found a much sharper discrimination between arts and physical science specialists on convergent thinking alone than on divergent thinking alone; using both measures to provide a bias score, the discrimination was sharper still. It thus seems reasonable to conclude that divergent thinking tests are not just 'passengers' in this matter of arts/science differences, but that bias within the domain of convergent thinking abilities may be just as fruitful an area of study.

The divergent thinking tests used to establish cognitive bias have been almost exclusively verbal in nature. If there are indeed independent dimensions of divergent thinking, it follows that an individual classified as a diverger with tests of verbal divergent thinking (and, of course, a suitable convergent thinking test) may well be classified differently with tests of, say, mathematical divergent thinking. The present writer feels, however, that it is more profitable to enquire further into differences between arts and science specialists, rather than simply to pursue differences between convergers and divergers, however so classified. In this respect, it seems a pity that Hudson (*ibid.*) oscillates between comparisons of divergers and convergers and comparisons of arts and science specialists, apparently equating convergers with science specialists and divergers with arts specialists.

The relationship of academic attainment and divergent thinking has often been investigated since Getzels and Jackson (1962) concluded that divergent thinking was a more important determinant of attainment than IQ, among adolescents of high ability. McNemar (1964) has neatly demonstrated that exactly the opposite conclusion may equally validly be drawn from their results, and Hasan and Butcher's study (1966) failed to replicate Getzels and Jackson's results. Hasan and Butcher found very high correlations between divergent thinking and attainment in English and arithmetic (0.76 and 0.62 respectively) but the correlations between VRQ and attainment were even higher.

Richards and Bolton (1971) also investigated, indirectly, the relationship between divergent thinking and mathematical attainment. On their first factor, identified as general ability, the attainment tests and verbal reasoning tests had high loadings and the divergent thinking tests low loadings. On their second factor, the majority of the divergent thinking tests had high loadings and about half the mathematical attainment scores had low loadings, the other half having negligible ones. They therefore concluded 'that the most important determinant of the performance in mathematics is general ability and that divergent thinking plays only a minor role' (p. 34).

Nuttall (1971) correlated performance on divergent thinking tests with performance in a wide range of CSE and GSE 'O' level examinations. Unlike the attainment tests used in other studies which tend to be in multiple-choice or short-answer format, these examinations usually require longer answers and the aims of the examinations in art and English language, as set out in the syllabuses of a number of boards, place some emphasis on the assessment of creative ability. Two of the divergent thinking tests (the Squares Test and the Uses Test) showed no significant relationships with attainment, but the TH Test and the Number Routes Test showed positive and significant correlations with about half the examinations studied. However, on the application of multiple regression techniques, it was found that the variance in attainment attributable to divergent thinking was negligible once the variance attributable to convergent thinking had been accounted for. Cronbach (1968) makes a strong case for the use of multiple regression techniques in this field, since it enables the burden of proof to be placed on the newer psychological variable of divergent thinking.

Freeman, M'Comisky and Buttle (1969) investigated the relationship of the A–C (Performance) Test to academic performance among architecture and economics students. They found that the ten best architecture students, as assessed by examination results, had achieved significantly better total accuracy scores on the divergent thinking section of the A–C test than the ten poorest architecture students. The test, described in some detail in Freeman, Butcher and Christie (1971), involves the classification of sixteen blocks varying in size, shape and colour into two groups of eight in each of four different ways, and then into four groups of four in three different ways, the principles of classification being left up to the candidate in the 'divergent' section. The facts that the test is scored for accuracy and that the number of classifications requested is limited suggest that this test is not, perhaps, a typical divergent thinking test, but this is not to deny its potential value. No significant difference in total accuracy scores ('divergent' thinking) appeared between the ten best and ten poorest economics students.

The studies reviewed above treat divergent thinking in the main as a cognitive variable. Just as many writers (for example, Cattell and Butcher, 1968) consider that, above a certain minimum level of general ability, affective factors are of greater importance than cognitive abilities in the study of creative ability, so a number of writers feel that divergent thinking may better be considered as an affective dimension or, at the least, as bridging the artificial gap between cognitive and non-cognitive dimensions. For example, McHenry and Shouksmith (1970) obtained highly significant correlations between both the Uses and the Meaning of Words tests and a test of suggestibility, a factor which is hypothesized to be of importance in the study of creativity. They also found non-significant but positive correlations between the two divergent thinking tests and a test of visual imagination.

Shouksmith (1970) tested ninety-eight first year university students with a battery of measures including divergent and convergent tests and new tests of cognitive style and problem-solving style. Among men, he found that high performance on divergent thinking tests was associated with inconsistency, as assessed by responses to a number of insoluble problems, but the same relationship did not obtain among women. Among both men and women, Shouksmith identified a dimension of 'divergent flexibility of style' which was not associated with performance in divergent thinking tests but which he hypothesized to be of importance in creativity.

There thus seem to be good grounds for extending the investigation of the validity of divergent thinking tests further into the realms of cognitive style and personality. Meanwhile, in the realm of cognitive abilities, it seems that we know much more about what divergent thinking tests are *not* measuring than about what they are measuring. This again may be a criticism of existing tests of divergent thinking more than it is a criticism of the concept of divergent thinking itself.

The Influence of Environmental and Educational Conditions

Critics of progressive education have suggested that progressive methods lead to lower attainment in the basic skills than do more traditional methods. Research (for example, Barker Lunn, 1970) has shown that this is not necessarily so, but researchers have striven to find tests that might reveal a clear superiority of progressive methods and divergent thinking tests have been an obvious choice.

Haddon and Lytton (1968) tested 211 children, aged 11 to 12, half coming from 'formal' and half from 'informal' primary schools who were matched for mean VRQ and socioeconomic background. As hypothesized, the pupils from the 'informal' schools showed significantly higher performance on the verbal and non-verbal tests of divergent thinking than their peers from 'formal' schools. They also found that the correlation between VRQ and the divergent thinking scores were consistently higher in the 'informal' schools than in the 'formal' schools. Haddon and Lytton (1971), following up the majority of these children some four years later and retesting them with the same tests, found that children who had attended the 'informal' primary schools continued to perform significantly more highly on the divergent thinking tests than the children who had attended the 'formal' schools, irrespective of the type of secondary school attended. Their use of the technique of multiple regression again illustrates its elegance and power. Lytton and Cotton (1969) compared 14-year-old pupils from 'formal' and 'informal' secondary schools, again matched for mean VRQ and socioeconomic background. There were no significant differences on four of the divergent thinking tests; on the Imaginative Stories Test, there was a significant difference in favour of pupils from the 'informal' schools, but on the last test (Incomplete Circles) the difference was significantly in favour of the pupils from the 'formal' schools. Lytton and Cotton attribute these essentially negative findings to the inappropriateness of the simple labels 'formal' and 'informal' for secondary schools, whose organization is much more complex than that of primary schools. Cabot (1969), however, did find significant differences on the Uses and Meaning of Words tests in favour of sixth form pupils from two progressive boarding schools, comparing them with pupils from a traditional boys' public school and a mixed comprehensive school, while on IQ, the difference was significant in the other direction.

As part of a major study on the effects of streaming, Barker Lunn (1970) tested a group of 1800 children at the end of their third and fourth years in the primary school with two parallel tests of divergent thinking scored for fluency, flexibility and originality. Within unstreamed schools, she distinguished two types of teacher: the type 1 teacher was in favour of progressive methods but the type 2 teacher was less in favour of progressive methods and her attitudes resembled those of the typical teacher in a streamed school. The most startling finding was that boys in streamed schools showed a significant drop on all three aspects of divergent thinking between the third and fourth years; in the case of girls in streamed schools, the differences were in the same direction but were not significant. Pupils with type 2 teachers in unstreamed schools also showed the same tendency towards deterioration, but only in the case of girls' originality scores was the drop significant. In contrast, pupils with the type 1 teachers tended to show an improvement in fluency and flexibility scores, although the differences were not significant, but no consistent differences emerged for originality scores. Barker Lunn also showed that, on the basis of scores in the fourth year, type 1 teachers had the highest percentage of pupils among those scoring in the top 20 per cent on a composite divergent thinking test score, while type 2 teachers had the lowest (teachers from streamed schools being intermediate). Conversely, among pupils in the bottom 20 per cent, type 1 teachers had the lowest percentage and type 2 the highest.

Two recent studies have concentrated on differences between 'traditional' and 'modern' methods of mathematics teaching. Gopal Rao, Penfold and Penfold (1970) found that the performance of third and fourth year secondary school pupils following 'modern' courses was significantly superior to that of a group of pupils (comparable in ability) following 'traditional' courses on three divergent thinking tests (Hidden Words, Uses of Objects and Concept Formation); the differences on the other two tests (First and Last Letters and Make-Up Problems) were in the same direction but not significant. Richards and Bolton (1971) compared final year pupils from three primary schools: in school C, mathematics was taught by a discovery approach, in school B by traditional methods and in school A, by an amalgam of both methods. The three schools were matched for IQ and socioeconomic status. The performance of school C on the mathematics attainment tests, which ranged from a test of mechanical and problem arithmetic to the recent NFER Intermediate Mathematics Test which stresses understanding of concepts rather than routine calculation, was consistently lower than that of the other two schools, though not always significantly so. Schools A and C tended to score consistently more highly than school B on the divergent thinking tests (Circles, Uses of Objects, Consequences, Pattern Meanings and Make-Up Problems), but only in the case of the Circles tests was the performance of pupils in school C significantly higher than that of the pupils in the other two schools.

These studies have produced fairly consistent findings suggesting that pupils studying under progressive regimes score more highly on tests of divergent thinking than their peers in 'traditional' schools. While this evidence is important in helping to establish the construct validity of the tests, there is a danger that it is educationally meaningless when the concurrent and predictive validity of the test has proved so hard to establish. Similarly, caution must be exercised in interpreting the results of Vernon's cross-cultural research (Vernon, 1967 and 1969b), in which he included a battery of divergent thinking tests. In particular, he found that the median fluency score of a small group of maladjusted English boys was 106 and their median originality score 108, compared with a figure of 100 for normal schoolchildren of the same age. Only on two other tests (Incomplete Drawings, separately scored but considered as a test of divergent thinking, and Kohs Blocks) did the maladjusted boys score more than 100 and on all the conventional paper and pencil attainment and general ability tests, their scores were around ninety. A group of delinquent boys also showed their highest median scores on the divergent thinking tests, but these did not exceed 100.

Barker Lunn's results suggest that the pupil's interaction with his teacher is of great importance. Among medical students, Joyce and Hudson (1968) also found such an interaction. Four tutors were rated for their convergence/divergence by each other, by themselves, by their students and by an independent observer and a remarkable degree of agreement between these different ratings emerged. It was found that, while the four groups of students each taught by one of the four tutors did not differ in their attainment on the final statistics examination, certain types of student gained better examination results if they were taught by particular teachers. It was not consistently the case, however, that divergent students learned best from divergent teachers nor that convergent students learned best from convergent teachers.

Again in the realm of medicine, Byrne, Freeman and M'Comisky (1970) compared the behaviour of five discussion groups composed of general practitioners and structured according to the divergence or convergence of their members (as assessed by tests) and various of their personality attributes. It was found that the two groups containing divergent individuals produced more new ideas than the convergent and 'all-rounder' groups but that these ideas were not of significantly higher quality (as rated by three independent judges). These groups were also rated higher on 'group interaction' but they showed a greater tendency to splinter. A number of other differences between the groups was also reported. More studies such as this which consider personality attributes alongside divergence and convergence are obviously required.

Factors Affecting the Reliability of Divergent Thinking Tests

As already indicated, many of the inconclusive findings that emerge from studies using divergent thinking tests may be attributable, at least in part, to deficiencies in the tests themselves. Lack of reliability is one obvious deficiency. Nuttall (1971) obtained test-retest reliability coefficients of between 0.54 and 0.65 for his four tests over an interval of two weeks, and Hudson (1968) obtained a parallel forms coefficient of 0.53 with the Uses Test over an interval of four months. Over four years, Haddon and Lytton (1971) obtained a test-retest coefficient of 0.62 for their battery, but the reliabilities of the two parts (verbal and non-verbal) were somewhat lower (0.55 and 0.50 respectively). Such values, which are comparable to those obtained in a number of other studies, fail to inspire confidence and make the interpretation of low correlations between divergent thinking tests and other measures difficult.

Lack of reliability is not the only problem and, as Hudson (1968) points out, need not worry us unduly if we can establish and replicate valid relationships with criteria external to the tests. Of more concern are the results of a series of small studies in which Hudson (1968) showed that the number of responses elicited on tests of divergent thinking was dependent upon the instructions given, the number and type of examples provided and on the 'target' figure set. The most striking demonstration of these effects emerged when a group of boys were tested with the Uses Test on two occasions. On the second occasion they were asked to impersonate a typical scientist and a typical artist. There was a tendency for those boys originally classified as convergers to be relatively more fluent than divergers in impersonating the scientist, and the reverse occurred for the impersonation of the artist. There was also only a very marginal tendency for those who had been the most fluent under the normal conditions to be the most fluent when impersonating the two characters. Hudson concluded: 'Between them these two studies make it clear that an individual's fluency is not a fixed feature of his mental life' (*ibid.*, p. 70).

Corroborative evidence comes from a number of studies elsewhere in the world. For example, Nicholls (1972) found significant relationship between intelligence and verbal and 'non-verbal' divergent thinking (using the tests of Wallach and Kogan, 1965) when the divergent thinking tests were administered under test-like conditions, but non-significant relationships when the tests were administered under game-like conditions. This finding held for both boys and girls. Vernon (1971), who provides a comprehensive review of the literature in this area, found similar but not quite so marked differences between testing conditions. Elkind, Deblinger and Adler (1970), using Wallach and Kogan's tests, and employing a balanced experimental design, found that the scores of children taken to be tested from an 'uninteresting' task were nearly twice as great as the scores of children taken from an 'interesting' task.

Getzels and Madaus (1969) have suggested that there are so many conflicting findings in the whole field of divergent thinking research largely because 'methods' factors (such as testing conditions and scoring procedures) are playing such a large part. They advocate fullscale multitrait-multimethod investigations (Campbell and Fiske, 1959) to clarify the situation, and the studies discussed in this section would certainly seem to imply that such investigations are overdue. But if Hudson is right that fluency is not a stable ability, no amount of sophisticated research methodology can produce harmony out of conflict.

Some Conclusions

To suggest that there are many deficiencies in existing tests of divergent thinking may be rather harsh: an ability, or abilities, that are so unstable are worthy of psychological study in their own right and this very fact may cause us to look again at the extent to which such effects are present in more conventional ability tests (see also Heim, 1970). But in terms of studies of the validity of divergent tests along traditional lines, such deficiencies are of major significance. Hudson's studies suggest that there is no uniform 'practice effect' on such tests and as more and more children come to take divergent thinking tests, greater rather than less conflict in results is likely to emerge. There is therefore an urgent need for more reliable tests whose content is more relevant to the interests and abilities of the groups for whom the tests are designed — the A–C Performance Test of Freeman, M'Comisky and Buttle (1969) would seem to be a step in the right direction. With existing tests, we are forced to accept that the generalizability of conclusions from individual studies is very limited.

The value of divergent thinking tests in fields such as educational and vocational guidance has yet to be demonstrated and past work gives rise to little confidence that it eventually will. The promise of divergent thinking tests seems rather to lie in that uncharted area where cognitive and non-cognitive aspects of the mind overlap — in areas such as cognitive style, problem-solving and motivation.

References

BARKER LUNN, J.C. (1970) *Streaming in the Primary School*, Slough, National Foundation for Educational Research.

BURT, C. (1962) 'Critical notice — "Creativity and Intelligence"', British Journal of Educational Psychology, 32, pp. 292–8.

BUTCHER, H.J. (1968) *Human Intelligence*, London, Methuen.

BYRNE, P.S., FREEMAN, J. and M'COMISKY, J.G. (1970) 'General practitioners observed: A study of personality, intellectual factors and group behaviour', *British Journal of Medical Education*, 4, pp. 176–84.

CABOT, I.B. (1969) 'Creativity as a function of type of education' in ASH, M. (Ed) *Who Are the Progressives Now?*, London, Routledge & Kegan Paul.

CAMERON, L. (1968) 'Intelligence, creativity and the English examination', *Scottish Educational Studies*, 1, pp. 55–60.

CAMPBELL, D.T. and FISKE, D.W. (1959) 'Convergent and discriminant validation by the multitrait-multimethod matrix', *Psychology Bulletin*, 56, pp. 81–105.

CATTELL, R.B. and BUTCHER, H.J. (1968) *The Prediction of Achievement and Creativity*, Indianapolis, in Bobbs-Merrill.

CHILD, D. (1968) 'Convergent and divergent thinking and arts/science', *Abstracts of the British Psychological Society, Education Section Annual Conference, 1968*.

CHILD, D. (1969) 'A comparative study of personality, intelligence and social class in a technological university', *British Journal of Educational Psychology*, 39, pp. 40–6.

CHILD, D. and SMITHERS, A. (1971) 'Some cognitive and affective factors in subject choice', *Research in Education*, 5, pp. 1–9.

CHILD, D. and SMITHERS, A. (1973) 'A validation of the Joyce-Hudson scale of convergence and divergence', *British Journal of Educational Psychology*, 43, pp. 57–61.

CHRISTIE, T. (1970) 'Cognitive bias, university faculty and degree of success', *Abstracts of the British Psychological Society, Education Section Annual Conference, 1970*.

CRONBACH, L.J. (1968) 'Intelligence? Creativity? A parsimonious reinterpretation of the Wallach-Kogan data', *American Educational Research Journal*, 5, pp. 491–512.

CRONBACH, L.J. (1970) *Essentials of Psychological Testing* (3rd ed.), New York, Harper and Row (Harper International Edition).

DACEY, J., MADAUS, G.F. and ALLEN, A. (1969) 'The relationship of creativity and intelligence in Irish adolescents', *British Journal of Educational Psychology*, 39, pp. 261–6.

ELKIND, D., DEBLINGER, J. and ADLER, D. (1970) 'Motivation and creativity: The context effect', *American Educational Research Journal*, 7, pp. 351–7.

FEE, F. (1968) 'An alternative to Ward's factor analysis of Wallach and Kogan's "creativity" correlations', *British Journal of Educational Psychology*, 28, pp. 319–21.

FREEMAN, J., BUTCHER, H.J. and CHRISTIE, T. (1971) *Creativity* (2nd edition), London, Society for Research into Higher Education.

FREEMAN, J., M'COMISKY, J.G. and BUTTLE, D. (1969) 'Student selection: A comparative study of student entrants to architecture and economics', *International Journal of Educational Science*, 3, pp. 189–97.

GETZELS, J.W. and JACKSON, P.W. (1962) *Creativity and Intelligence*, New York, John Wiley.

GETZELS, J.W. and MADAUS, G.F. (1969) 'Creativity' in EBEL, R.L. (Ed) *Encyclopedia of Educational Research* (4th ed.), New York, Macmillan.

GOPAL RAO, G.S., PENFOLD, D.M. and PENFOLD, A.P. (1970) 'Modern and traditional mathematics teaching', *Educational Research*, 13, pp. 61–5.

GUILFORD, J.P. (1950) 'Creativity', *American Psychology*, 5, pp. 444–54.

GUILFORD, J.P. (1956) 'The structure of intellect', *Psychology Bulletin*, 53, pp. 267–93.

GUILFORD, J.P. (1959) 'The three faces of intellect', *American Psychology*, 14, pp. 469–79.

GUILFORD, J.P. (1967) *The Nature of Human Intelligence*, New York, McGraw-Hill.

HADDON, F.A. and LYTTON, H. (1968) 'Teaching approach and the development of divergent thinking abilities in primary schools', *British Journal of Educational Psychology*, 38, pp. 171–80.

HADDON, F.A. and LYTTON, H. (1971) 'Primary education and divergent thinking abilities — four years on', *British Journal of Educational Psychology*, 41, pp. 136–47.

HARGREAVES, H.L. (1927) 'The "faculty" of imagination', *British Journal of Psychological Monograph*, 3.

HARTLEY, J. and BEASLEY, N. (1969) 'Contrary imaginations at Keele', *University Quarterly*, 23, pp. 467–71.

HASAN, P. and BUTCHER, H.J. (1966) 'Creativity and intelligence: A partial replication with Scottish children of Getzels and Jackson's study', *British Journal of Educational Psychology*, 57, pp. 129–35.

HEIM, A.W. (1970) *Intelligence and Personality*, Harmondsworth, Penguin Books.

HUDSON, L. (1966) *Contrary Imaginations*, London, Methuen.

HUDSON, L. (1968) *Frames of Mind*, London, Methuen.

JOYCE, C.R.B. and HUDSON, L. (1968) 'Student style and teacher style: An experimental study', *British Journal of Medical Education*, 2, pp. 28–32.

LOVELL, K. and SHIELDS, J.B. (1967) 'Some aspects of a study of the gifted child', *British Journal of Educational Psychology*, 37, pp. 201–8.

LYTTON, H. and COTTON, A.C. (1969) 'Divergent thinking abilities in secondary schools', *British Journal of Educational Psychology*, 39, pp. 188–90.

MACKAY, C.K. and CAMERON, M.B. (1968) 'Cognitive bias in Scottish first-year science and arts undergraduates', *British Journal of Educational Psychology*, 38, pp. 315–8.

McHENRY, R.E. and SHOUKSMITH, G.A. (1970) 'Creativity, visual imagination and suggestibility: Their relationship in a group of ten-year-old children', *British Journal of Educational Psychology*, 40, pp. 154–60.

McNEMAR, Q. (1964) 'Lost: Our intelligence? Why?', *American Psychology*, 19, pp. 871–82.

MARSH, R.W. (1964) 'A statistical re-analysis of Getzels and Jackson's data', *British Journal of Educational Psychology*, 34, pp. 91–3.

MILLS, J. (1970) 'Convergent/divergent skills and sixth form courses', *Abstracts of the British Psychological Society, Education Section Annual Conference, 1970.*

NICHOLLS, J.G. (1972) 'Some effects of testing procedure on divergent thinking', *Child Development*, 42, pp. 1647–51.

NUTTALL, D.L. (1971) 'Modes of thinking and their measurement', unpublished PhD thesis, University of Cambridge.

PONT, H.B. (1970) 'The arts — science dichotomy' in BUTCHER, H.J. and PONT, H.B. (Eds) *Educational Research in Britain 2*, London, University of London Press.

RICHARDS, P.N. and BOLTON, N. (1971) 'Type of mathematics teaching, mathematical ability and divergent thinking in junior school children', *British Journal of Educational Psychology*, 41, pp. 32–7.

SHAPIRO, R.J. (1968) 'Creative research scientists', *Psychologia Africana Monogr.*, 4.

SHOUKSMITH, G.A. (1970) *Intelligence, Creativity and Cognitive Style*, London, Batsford.

SULTAN, E.E. (1962) 'A factorial study in the domain of creative thinking', *British Journal of Educational Psychology*, 32, pp. 78–82.

TORRANCE, E.P. (1962) *Guiding Creative Talent*, Englewood Cliffs, NJ, Prentice-Hall.

VERNON, P.E. (1964) 'Creativity and intelligence', *Educational Research*, 6, pp. 163–9.

VERNON, P.E. (1967) 'A cross-cultural study of "creativity tests" with 11-year boys', *Research in Education*, 1, pp. 135–46.

VERNON, P.E. (1969a) 'Ability factors and environmental influences' in WOLFLE, D. (Ed) *The Discovery of Talent*, Cambridge, MA, Harvard University Press.

VERNON, P.E. (1969b) *Intelligence and Cultural Environment*, London, Methuen.

VERNON, P.E. (1971) 'Effects of administration and scoring on divergent thinking tests', *British Journal of Educational Psychology*, 41, pp. 245–57.

WALLACH, M.A. and KOGAN, N. (1965) *Modes of Thinking in Young Children*, New York, Holt, Rinehart & Winston.

WARBURTON, F.W. (1970) 'The British intelligence scale' in DOCKRELL, W.B. (Ed) *On Intelligence*, London, Methuen.

WARD, J. (1967) 'An oblique factorisation of Wallach and Kogan's "creativity" correlations', *British Journal of Educational Psychology*, 37, pp. 380–2.

YAMAMOTO, K. (1965) 'Effect of restriction of range and test unreliability on correlation between measures of intelligence and creative thinking', *British Journal of Educational Psychology*, 35, pp. 300–5.

Nuttall, D.L. (1975) 'Examinations in education' in Cox, P.R., Miles, H.B. and Peel, J. (Eds) *Equalities and Inequalities in Education*, London, Academic Press.

Introduction

This article focuses on examinations and their key role in the education system in the UK. This aspect of educational assessment was also a central focus of Desmond Nuttall's early work at the NFER in the early 1970s, and at the Schools Council, where he was when he wrote this article. It was a concern that later led him in 1976 to apply for and become the Executive Secretary of the Middlesex CSE Examination Board. Even when he moved out of direct involvement in the world of examinations, three years later, Desmond Nuttall retained his interest in this research topic. He believed passionately that producing effective examinations was a key part of improving the effectiveness of the educational experiences of pupils and students. Producing effective examinations was never easy, and it was a task that Desmond Nuttall devoted himself to for over twenty years.

An interesting feature of this paper is that it is taken from a volume with the title *Equalities and Inequalities in Education*. This title mirrors his concern that examinations can, at their worst, contribute to inequality and disadvantage, and at their best make a vital contribution to the process of attempting to provide equal opportunities in education. Their institution in China over 2000 years ago was reputed to have been as a counter to nepotism and other unfair practices. However, in the ensuing period they have resulted, sometimes inadvertently, in the introduction of other forms of unfairness, bias and disadvantage (Gipps and Murphy, 1994).

The article is also significant for the way that it puts down markers for some of the topics that were to become the heart of Desmond

Nuttall's later research work on examinations. The gradual move toward greater teacher involvement in the assessment of coursework and the associated moderation and standardization procedures, and the move towards a more criterion-referenced approach to reporting achievement. Above all the paper points to 'curriculum control' as being the most profound issue at the heart of most so-called assessment debates. Desmond Nuttall's now infamous quote in this article that 'my reading of the political entrails is that this issue is going to emerge further from the shadows in the next few years' pointed a prophetic finger at the assessment-led curriculum changes that were to occur in the 1980s first through the introduction of GCSE and then later through the even more influential National Curriculum with its associated assessment arrangements.

EXAMINATIONS IN EDUCATION

I must at the outset make it clear that I am going to confine most of my discussion to public examinations taken by secondary school children, namely the Certificate of Secondary Education (CSE) and the Ordinary Level of the General Certificate of Education (GCE), which are usually taken at the age of 16, and the Advanced Level of the GCE, normally taken at 18. In British education, there is of course a multiplicity of other examinations, from the 11+ at one end of the spectrum to university finals and professional examinations at the other, but my experience only qualifies me to talk with any real knowledge about CSE and GCE. More importantly, the Schools Council has responsibilities for only these public examinations; specifically these responsibilities fall under two headings:

(i) the co-ordination of secondary school examinations in England and Wales;
(ii) the tendering of advice to the Secretary of State for Education and Science on matters of examinations policy.

Secondary school examinations have never been as much in demand as they are today. In summer 1972 (the last year for which official figures are available) no less than 844,847 individuals were candidates for GCE 'O' and 'A' level and for CSE — a small proportion of these were adults taking evening classes or studying by correspondence, but it would be safe to say that 750,000 of this group were between the ages of 15 and 19. Between them, these students entered for 1.35 million CSE subject examinations, 2.30 million GCE 'O' level subject examinations and 470,000 GCE 'A' level subject examinations (Department of Education and Science, 1974). These figures pre-date the effect of the raising of the school-leaving age, and all the signs are that the numbers of candidates and subject entries in summer 1974 will be substantially larger, particularly in the case of the CSE.

Why this massive volume of examining, that might almost be termed an industry? Why are schools, teachers, parents and pupils prepared to see virtually the whole of every summer term devoted to examinations, which disrupt the normal activities of the school? To attempt to answer these questions, I would like first to take a brief look at the history of examinations. Historians of examinations (for example, Morris, 1961) invariably trace their origins to the Chinese Empire in the days of the first millenium BC. Competition for the Imperial Service was intense and nepotism was rife; in an attempt to stamp out nepotism and bribery, a system of practical examinations was instituted, involving horse-riding, archery and other such skills. Over the years, the system evolved placing more emphasis on academic skills, through the medium of written papers, and less on practical skills. The final result was, then, a system of highly competitive examinations not unlike the current scholarship examinations set by colleges at Cambridge and Oxford. There then is a Dark Age for examinations, and apart from the *viva voce* examinations at degree level, examinations only began to be instituted in this country in the early nineteenth century. It is interesting to note that the major reason for their introduction was identical to that which led the Chinese to establish them, namely to eliminate nepotism and other unfair practices. Later in the nineteenth century, the old-established universities, worried about selection and academic standards, instituted their own mechanisms for examining schools and school children. The first of these examination boards was the Oxford Delegacy of Local Examinations which was established in 1858, but other universities were not slow to follow suit. Coordination among these boards only came, however, after the great upheavals, both in education and in society, in the early twentieth century. In 1918, the boards were asked to bring in a uniform system known as the School Certificate and Higher School Certificate. The School Certificate examination system remained virtually unchanged, until following the Norwood Report (Board of Education, 1943) and the Butler 1944 Education Act, the School Certificate was replaced by the General Certificate of Education in which the first examinations were set in 1951. Apart from the fact that the GCE was to be a single-subject examination in contrast to the grouping of subjects in the School Certificate, the changes were relatively small and so this system persists to this day. Of course, relatively minor changes to grading schemes have been made over the years and major changes have taken place in the techniques of examining and assessing pupils, but the essential philosophy of the system remains, in my view, virtually unaltered. The GCE examination, like the School Certificate before it, was primarily designed to be an examination in academic subjects aimed at pupils in grammar and public schools, in other words, the 'elite' 20 to 30 per cent of children in the age group. It was not long before many other schools were entering candidates, in many cases inappropriately, for the GCE, and other examination bodies (such as the Royal Society of Arts and the London Chamber of Commerce) were setting examinations for the secondary modern child. Local examinations also began to proliferate, and to bring order into increasing chaos, the Minister of Education set up a committee, under the chairmanship of Beloe, to see if the system could be rationalized. The Beloe Report (Ministry of Education, 1960) recommended the establishment of the Certificate of Secondary Education. The essential features of the CSE system were:

(i) that it was designed for pupils between the fortieth and eightieth percentiles of ability; i.e. essentially for school children who would not be continuing in full-time education; and

(ii) that it was to be an examination controlled by school teachers, and hence organized on a regional basis.

The first CSE examinations were set in 1965 (the year after the Schools Council was established to take over the responsibilities, in relation to public examinations, of the Secondary Schools Examinations Council) and since 1965, the CSE has expanded dramatically; in the case of some boards, the number of subject entries in summer 1974 show increases of more than 70 per cent over the number in 1973. In the last decade, the expansion has been of the order of some 400 per cent. If CSE and GCE 'O' level are considered together, it is almost certainly true to say that 80 per cent of 16-year-olds in England and Wales took one or more public examinations in summer 1974.

This brief historical review has illustrated some of the main reasons why the proponents of public examinations believe that these examinations are an essential feature of the educational system. I now wish to consider the reasons in more detail before I turn to look briefly at some of the possible alternatives to public examinations.

The prime function of public examinations is undoubtedly to assess the attainment of an individual at the end of a course of study. Chief Examiners and Chief Moderators direct virtually all their attention to ensuring that the examination is a fair and comprehensive test of what has been taught and learned, and that the results it yields are as precise and reliable as possible. Linked with this function is that of the maintenance of educational standards; by having a nationally-validated system of public examinations, justice can be seen to be done and society may judge for itself one very important aspect of the efficiency of the educational system. Also linked to these functions is the licensing function of examinations. Most professional qualifications serve this function: many of those who defend external examinations take great delight in asking whether you would be prepared to subject yourself to the surgeon's knife if you were not certain that his peers and teachers had judged him competent to wield it. The sort of examinations that I am discussing do not really have this licensing function to any great degree, but perhaps employers, further and higher education look for passes in English language and mathematics, in particular, as indicators of general competence.

These three interlinked functions — the assessment of attainment, the maintenance of standards, and licensing — raise what, to many, is the crucial issue in any discussion of public examinations, namely central control of the curriculum. To my mind, this is a political issue and a professional issue, a matter for teachers and politicians to debate, and I do not therefore propose to discuss it at length. Nevertheless one must accept that much of the discussion and debate that centres around public examinations in the teaching profession, and in the Schools Council itself, is primarily concerned with the issue of who should be responsible for what is taught in schools. This issue is not, of course, unique to this country, but my reading of the political entrails is that this issue is going to emerge further from the shadows in the next few years; indeed, I believe one has only to look across the Atlantic to see the twin spectres of 'educational accountability' and 'teacher-proof curriculum packages' to realize the directions in which the debate might move.

A further function of examinations, clearly seen from the days of the Chinese Empire, is as instruments of selection. I am neither a politician nor a sociologist and I therefore trust that I am not being naive in suggesting that some form of selection will always be with us. We may see the day when we have universal comprehensive secondary education, and perhaps we might see the day when we have a comprehensive system of further and higher education, but I cannot foresee the day when all jobs and professions are going to be equally attractive and the forces of supply and demand will be in balance. While we still have selection in secondary and tertiary education, we are obliged to consider whether examinations are either a desirable or necessary part of the selection process. Recent research at the National Foundation for Educational Research has shown that 'A' levels are, by and large, rather poor predictors of success at university, where success is measured in terms of the class of one's final degree (NFER, 1973). The same research showed that a Test of Academic Aptitude, modelled on the American Scholastic Aptitude Test, was, generally speaking, a rather worse predictor of university success than 'A' levels and, indeed, added virtually nothing to the efficiency of prediction of 'A' level in multiple regression analyses. Other educational researchers are investigating the potential of non-cognitive measures as predictors; there is some evidence that such measures, for example of achievement motivation and study habits as well as of dimensions of personality, can enhance the predictive efficiency of 'A' levels, but on their own do not match the predictive efficiency of 'A' levels (for example, Entwistle, 1974). No selector is, of course, ever likely to use 'A' levels or psychometric measures (or both) without recourse to other evidence obtained from interviews and references; even so, examination results currently play a key role both as screening devices and as selection devices.

Before passing on to look at the way in which employers use examination results, I would like to refer to the perennial problem that faces the psychometrician, the criterion problem. In the research that I have been discussing, the criterion of success was the class of one's final degree. This has the merit of being quantifiable — though there are scaling problems — but does it really describe comprehensively what success at university comprises? Even if it is a valid measure of success, which Einstein and Darwin would have doubted (Hudson, 1964), is it reliable and comparable from university to university? Could we devise a measure of success that was more valid, more reliable and more comparable? I doubt it. If I am right, then it might be fair to say that the relative lack of predictive efficiency of 'A' levels lies partly on the side of the criterion measure of success. In practice, the blame (if such it may be described) probably lies equally on both sides of the walls of the ivory towers of our universities. Two further points need to be made: first, 'A' levels are designed primarily as measures of attainment, not as measures of future potential, and, secondly, there is an important technical factor which will always make a high level of predictive efficiency difficult to obtain; that is, the marked homogeneity of the population of university applicants.

No discussion of the criterion problem can be complete without a mention of the phenomenon described by Professors Wall and Simon earlier today. This is the phenomenon of the self-fulfilling prophecy (Pidgeon, 1970), described more graphically by Rosenthal and Jacobson (1968) as 'Pygmalion in the classroom'. Such writers tell us, in effect, that the predictive efficiency of examinations such as the 11+ is as good as it proved to be (for example, Yates and Pidgeon, 1957) because of the effect that the knowledge of results had on the attitudes and behaviour of the pupils, their teachers and their parents. It would be interesting to know if such writers would feel that part of the predictive efficiency of 'A' levels is due to this same effect. If they feel so and are correct in their feeling, the burden of the admissions tutor can be somewhat lifted — from now on, all he really needs is a pin!

Employers, particularly of young school leavers, appear to be ambivalent in their attitudes towards examinations. No large-scale survey of their selection policies has been carried out and I agree with Jennings (1974) that such a survey is long overdue. National bodies of employers and many professions have for years stipulated minimum requirements in terms of performance in public examinations and these minimum requirements are becoming stiffer and stiffer; ten years ago, a professional body might have demanded five passes at GCE 'O' level: today, they would be more likely to demand two passes at 'A' level and a further three at 'O' level. To what extent they discriminate among those applicants who have achieved the minimum requirements on the basis of their examination results is not clear, and practices obviously vary. Nevertheless, it is quite apparent that employers set considerable store by the results of public examinations and a leader writer in *The Guardian* on 17 January 1974 had this to say on the subject:

> When some teachers say that public examinations can be bad indicators of a student's ultimate ability they are probably right. But even if 'O' and 'A' levels and CSEs do not necessarily reveal much about an individual's real ability it does not follow that they are worthless.

Even if some teachers dismiss them as false prophets of ability, employers do not. Rightly or wrongly a CSE, an 'O' level, or an 'A' level is a passport. Employers and universities recognize them as such. A school-leaver without one has left school at a disadvantage in a world which has begun to ask shoe-shop assistants for 'O' levels in English and mathematics.

There are, of course, still plenty of jobs which do not demand 'O' levels. But most of them are deadends. Some of them are jobs which will soon be done by a machine that is about to be invented. Moreover the people in the deadend jobs soon notice where they are heading and resent it. A student who for one reason or another has been inadequate at school feels inadequate again — not necessarily to the extent of throwing bricks through windows but certainly to the extent of feeling that his school has let him down. And perhaps it has.

The impact of public examinations on the individual pupil and on the teacher must then be of central concern. It is perhaps a condemnation of myself and other research workers in the field of public examinations that I can do no better than to quote from the 1911 Report of the Consultative Committee on Examinations in Secondary Schools, but I have the comfort of knowing that this passage has also been quoted by Wiseman (1961), who called it a 'forgotten classic', and in the Beloe Report (Ministry of Education, 1960). The passage reads as follows:

It will be convenient if we summarize what we believe to be the more important effects of examinations (1) on the pupil, (2) on the teacher:
1   The good effects of examinations on the pupil are
  (a)   that they make him work up to time by requiring him to reach a stated degree of knowledge by a fixed date;
  (b)   that they incite him to get his knowledge into reproducible form and to lessen the risk of vagueness;
  (c)   that they make him work at parts of a study which, though important, may be uninteresting or repugnant to him personally;
  (d)   that they train the power of getting up a subject for a definite purpose, even though it may not appear necessary to remember it afterwards — a training which is useful for parts of the professional duty of the lawyer, the administrator, the journalist, and the man of business, and secretary;
  (e)   that in some cases they encourage a certain steadiness of work over a long period of time; and
  (f)   that they enable the pupil to measure his real attainment:
    (i)   by the standard required by outside examiners;
    (ii)   by comparison with the attainment of his fellow-pupils; and

39

(iii) by comparison with the attainments of his contemporaries in other schools.

On the other hand, examinations may have a bad effect upon the pupil's mind

(a) by setting a premium on the power of merely reproducing other people's ideas and other people's methods of presentment, thus diverting energy from the creative process;

(b) by rewarding evanescent forms of knowledge;

(c) by favouring a somewhat passive type of mind;

(d) by giving an unfair advantage to those who, in answering questions on paper, can cleverly make the best use of, perhaps, slender attainments;

(e) by inducing the pupil, in his preparation for an examination, to aim rather at absorbing information imparted to him by the teacher than at forming an independent judgment upon the subjects in which he received instruction; and

(f) by stimulating the competitive (and, at its worst, a mercenary) spirit in the acquisition of knowledge.

2 The good effects of well-conducted examinations upon the teacher are

(a) that they induce him to treat his subject thoroughly;

(b) that they make him so arrange his lessons as to cover with intellectual thoroughness a prescribed course of study within appointed limits of time;

(c) that they impel him to pay attention not only to his best pupils, but also to the backward and the slower amongst those who are being prepared for the examination; and

(d) that they make him acquainted with the standard which other teachers and their pupils are able to reach in the same subject in other places of education.

On the other hand, the effects of examination on the teacher are bad:

(a) in so far as they constrain him to watch the examiner's foibles and to note his idiosyncrasies (or the tradition of the examination) in order that he may arm his pupils with the kind of knowledge required for dealing successfully with the questions that will probably be put to them;

(b) in so far as they limit the freedom of the teacher in choosing the way in which he shall treat his subject;

(c) in so far as they encourage him to take upon himself work which had better be left to the largely unaided efforts of his pupils, causing him to impart information to them in too digested a form or to select for them groups of facts or aspects of the subject which each pupil should properly be left to collect or envisage for himself;

(d)　in so far as they predispose the teacher to overvalue among his pupils that type of mental development which secures success in examinations;

(e)　in so far as they make it the teacher's interest to excel in the purely examinable side of his professional work and divert his attention from those parts of education which cannot be tested by the process of examination.

I have attempted to show that examinations serve a useful function in education and society, and are likely to do so for some time to come. If public examinations were to be abolished, it is difficult to see what would take their place. The danger is that each employer, professional body, institute of higher and further education would establish their own selection procedures. Young people would perhaps go from employer to employer, taking battery after battery of aptitude and attainment tests — in many cases, probably the same battery of tests — and the end result might well be anarchical. Interestingly enough, it was the existence of a very similar kind of anarchy that led to the establishment of the CSE, within which control of the syllabuses and assessment techniques rested, and still rests, with the teaching profession.

Is there a middle course to steer between the elaborate machinery of a public examination system and no public examinations at all? I believe there is. I have been careful not to define too closely what is meant by the term 'public examination'. Most of us remember the system as it was some years ago when a public examination tended to mean two three-hour written papers often taken on the same day at the height of summer. The public examinations of today are often very different, particularly in the CSE. Internal assessment by the candidate's own teacher of oral work, project work and general coursework very often counts for up to 50 per cent of the candidate's mark. No longer is it a case of teacher and pupil trying to defeat the 'outsiders', the external examiners. Assessment becomes part and parcel of the teaching process. This internal assessment need not necessarily be on work derived from a syllabus laid down by an examination board. The syllabus may be devised by the teacher in part or in whole. In the latter case, an internal syllabus examined by internal assessment, an option available in both GCE and CSE, where it is known as Mode 3, we reach a position where, in my view, we have nearly all the advantages of examinations as expounded in the 1911 Report and few of the disadvantages. But such a system requires a validating stage, the process of moderation, so that these internal examinations can yield results which are nationally valid. The Schools Council is currently conducting an evaluation of moderation techniques; all I can say at the present time is that, to be successful, such techniques demand money and, above all, the time of experienced teachers.

Other countries are moving towards much more internal assessment which is then externally moderated to yield nationwide, or at least regional, comparability of standards. Two examples are New Zealand and some

Australian states. This system permits great flexibility in the curriculum from school to school. This same freedom is not apparent in countries such as France and Germany which appear on the surface to have no examination at the age when compulsory schooling ends; and the often-quoted example of Sweden (Henrysson, 1964), where moderation is done by way of a nationally-set common core reference test (rather than by visiting moderators) and where the test consequently tends to define a National Curriculum, is unlikely to be of much help to us in England.

Externally-moderated internal assessment is then an option which is already open to most secondary school teachers in England and Wales, at least in public examinations at 16+, but it does require a profession knowledgeable in assessment techniques. At the moment, the profession acknowledges its relative lack of knowledge (see, for example, Schools Council, 1971) and, indeed, many teachers still prefer a totally external system of public examinations. This means that the examining boards and the Schools Council are, and will remain, constantly on the search for improved techniques of assessment that will minimize the backwash effect on the curriculum and teaching methods and that will enhance the technical efficiency of the examinations, without prejudicing the validity of the examination and the principle that the examining system should put the curriculum first (*ibid.*). The place of criterion-referenced testing, as opposed to the current essentially norm-referenced testing, is also under debate as is the possibility of reporting attainment in terms of profiles rather than as a global grade (see, for example, Eggleston, 1974; White, 1974). White tells a cautionary tale in connection with profiles:

> I always remember the delightful cartoon of many many years ago which showed a victim of the earlier part of the century with a sandwich board in Piccadilly, a man who had served both in the Boer War and the First World War. His sandwich board read, 'two wars, three wounds, four medals, one wife, six children — total 16'. There are some personal evaluations which can operate in very much the same way.

Reforms to the system of public examinations have invariably followed reforms in the structure of secondary education, as the Schools Council's paper, *Arguments for a Common System of Examining at 16+* (Schools Council, 1973a), demonstrates. As Professor Simon indicated, the move towards comprehensive education has led in turn to a consideration of the replacement of our present dual system by a common system of examining at 16+. Other possible reforms to the system of public examinations at both 17+ and 18+ are also in the air, but unfortunately there is no time to discuss them. However, many of the possible improvements to the system that I have been discussing have been carefully considered in Council publications (Schools Council, 1971, 1973b and 1973c) and, whether or not the structure is changed, public examinations will continue to evolve for the benefit of both pupils and teachers.

In conclusion, I therefore feel that, first, public examinations will continue for many years to come and, secondly, particularly if the trend is indeed towards improved techniques and more internal assessment, public examination will continue to have both a necessary and a valuable part to play in education.

References

BOARD OF EDUCATION (1943) *Curriculum and Examinations in Secondary Schools* (The Norwood Report), London, HMSO.

DEPARTMENT OF EDUCATION AND SCIENCE (1974) *1972 School Leavers, CSE and GCE. Statistics of Education Vol. 2*, London, HMSO.

EGGLESTON, J.F. (1974) 'Prediction, selection, description and choice', *Forum*, 16, p. 61.

ENTWISTLE, N.J. (1974) 'Personality and academic attainment', in BUTCHER, H.J. and PONT, H.B. (Eds) *Educational Research in Britain 3*, London, University of London Press.

HENRYSSON, S. (1964) 'The Swedish system of equalising marks', *Educational Research*, 6, p. 156.

HUDSON, L. (1964) 'Academic sheep and research goats', *New Society*, 108, p. 9.

JENNINGS, A.H. (1974) 'Examining at 16+', *Report of a Conference on Examinations and Assessment*, London, Chelsea College, mimeo.

MINISTRY OF EDUCATION (1960) *Secondary School Examinations other than the GCE* (The Beloe Report), London, HMSO.

MORRIS, N. (1961) 'An historian's view of examinations' in WISEMAN, S. (Ed) *Examinations and English Education*, Manchester, Manchester University Press.

NFER SCHOOL TO UNIVERSITY RESEARCH UNIT (1973) *The Prediction of Academic Success*, Slough, NFER.

PIDGEON, D.A. (1970) *Expectation and Pupil Performance*, Slough, NFER.

ROSENTHAL, R. and JACOBSON, L. (1968) *Pygmalion in the Classroom*, New York, Holt, Rinehart and Winston.

SCHOOLS COUNCIL (1971) *A Common System of Examining at 16+, Schools Council Examinations Bulletin 23*, London, Evans/Methuen Educational.

SCHOOLS COUNCIL (1973a) *Arguments for a Common System of Examining at 16+*, London, Schools Council Publications.

Schools Council (1973b) *16–19: Growth and Response. 2. Examination Structure, Schools Council Working Paper 46*, London, Evans/Methuen Educational.

SCHOOLS COUNCIL (1973c) *Preparation for Degree Courses, Schools Council Working Paper 47*, London, Evans/Methuen Educational.

WHITE, W.M. (1974) 'Examinations in relation to the curriculum', *Report of a Conference on Examinations and Assessment*, London, Chelsea College, mimeo.

WISEMAN, S. (1961) 'The efficiency of examinations' in WISEMAN, S. (Ed) *Examinations and English Education*, Manchester, Manchester University Press.

YATES, A. and PIDGEON, D.A. (1957) *Admission to Grammar Schools*, London, Newnes for NFER.

Nuttall, D.L. (1978) 'The case against examinations', Supplement to *Education*, 152, 2, pp. v–vi.

Introduction

By the time this next article was written Desmond Nuttall had moved to become the Secretary of the Middlesex Regional Examining Board for the CSE. It was characteristic of his commitment to educational research that even as an Examination Board Secretary he was prepared to put 'the case against examinations'. This short piece, the first of four in this volume taken from *Education*, a weekly publication, which is produced largely for educational managers and policy makers, fore-shadows many of the debates that were to figure prominently in the years to come. It points to the shortcomings of examinations, and the dangers of over-stretching the validity of their results by for example using them in their raw form for league-table comparisons of schools.

Among other things this article demonstrates Desmond Nuttall's ability to lay out important policy issues clearly and succinctly, drawing as ever upon his close knowledge of the available research evidence.

THE CASE AGAINST EXAMINATIONS

Desmond Nuttall argues that tests and other forms of assessment cannot give all the answers

Examination results are one of the very few quantitative measures of the success of education, both for the individual and for the system as a whole. Comments on standards in the great debate were usually critical and at the anecdotal level, but the professionals were quick to answer by pointing out the increasing proportion of school leavers passing public examinations: in 1970, 56 per cent left with one CSE grade 5 or better while, in 1976, no less than 83 per cent left with one CSE grade 5 or better. Of course, the raising of the school leaving age boosted the figures dramatically since, prior to 1974, children leaving at the minimum age were not eligible to sit the CSE; but throughout the early 1970s, the percentage of leavers with at least one examination grade was on a rising trend.

Others have purported to show that the examination results from comprehensive schools are not as good as those from grammar, technical and secondary modern schools taken together. At first sight the argument looks convincing but, when one delves deeper to look at the effects of creaming (very noticeable in some nominally comprehensive areas like the ILEA, at least until recently), the social composition of unrecognized areas and other more detailed points, one realizes that examination results blur rather than clarify the issues.

Examination results have thus been made to carry a load that they were never designed to bear. All they are designed to do is to report how well an individual student has fared at the end of a course of study prescribed in a syllabus. The reporting is done on a nationally valid grading scale, but the problems of comparability of standards between examining boards and from year to year are very great. The courses of study differ from board to board, and change over the years, so that comparisons are hard to make and even harder to interpret. Both sets of examination boards, GCE and CSE, have major programmes of research into comparability of standards but the results of such studies are seldom clearcut. In one study, over a ten year period, the syllabus and approach to one subject had changed so much that the examiners had to confess that they were unable to make any judgment about a change in standards at all — judging two pieces of chalk when one piece was, in fact, made of cheese. Aggregating results from different boards and different years, therefore, inevitably blurs the picture.

Perhaps the most serious criticism of examination results as a measure of standards is their lack of comprehensiveness. The typical candidate takes only four subjects at CSE and fewer at GCE 'O' level, so that one does not obtain a complete picture of attainment across the whole curriculum. Most candidates take English and some form of mathematics, but less than half take any other subject in any public examination though all will have studied subjects such as history, geography, science, art and religious education for most of their school lives. And in any case academic attainment is not all that schools seek to foster and develop in children. Most examinations do not attempt to assess social or moral development, physical education or the whole range of extracurricular activities (such as school plays, bands, orchestras, clubs and societies) that play such an important part in the life of the school.

The limitations of examination results for the measurement of standards at the national level are minor compared with the problems when it comes to 'league tables' of schools. Here the publication of examination results can do more harm than good. First, schools differ markedly, for valid educational reasons, in their policies over entering candidates for public examinations.

Some enter nearly all their pupils, even though a few of them will have little chance of obtaining more than CSE grade 5 at best; others will choose to run special courses for the less able that do not lead to public examinations.

Secondly, there is the problem of subject comparability. Although the findings are hotly contested, there is a growing body of research that suggests that it is substantially more difficult to obtain a given grade in subjects like physics, chemistry, modern languages and classical languages than it is in English, geography, biology and most craft subjects. If schools enter candidates for different mixes of subjects, as they undoubtedly do, some may appear to obtain better examination results than others simply by virtue of the lack of comparability of standards between subjects.

But the most telling argument against the publication of examination results school by school is the variation in the calibre of each school's intake. Suppose that, in one school, 40 per cent of the fifth year achieve three or more GCE grades A, B or C or CSE grade 1, while in another school 30 per cent achieve similar results. Which is the better school? That is the question that parents, and even perhaps education committee members, might be tempted to ask, but it should be obvious that the worth of any school cannot possibly be judged solely by examination results. But what of the more precise question: which school achieves better examination results at this level? (There are, of course, many other indices of examination results, for example, proportion achieving one or more 'A' level passes, proportion achieving one or more CSE grade 4 or better, and so on.)

The answer clearly depends upon the quality of the intake. If the first school, with the 40 per cent rate, admits a higher proportion of able children than the second school, its better results rate is to be expected and tells us little about the comparative success with which it prepared candidates for public examinations. Indeed, the second school, given a rather poor intake, might be doing a better job in preparing candidates for examinations than the first school. In short, the figures from different schools cannot be fairly compared.

Some LEAs are known to be investigating ways of adjusting a school's examination results in the light of the quality of its intake, as measured for example by the Verbal Reasoning Quotients assessed at 11+. The statistical techniques for making such adjustments are, however, open to criticism; indeed, similar techniques used by the NFER in Schools Council-sponsored studies of comparability between examination boards over the past ten years have been so heavily criticized that studies of that kind have now been discontinued.

If, as I have argued, examination results are an unsatisfactory measure of standards in our schools, is there a better measure? At the national level, the work of the APU, designed, unlike examinations, specifically to measure standards, is likely to be more satisfactory, since the testing programme is designed to be more comprehensive than public examinations. The APU is investigating six lines of development, the first three of which, mathematical, language (including a foreign language) and scientific development, are well advanced. Investigation of the other three lines of development, aesthetic, physical, social and moral, are more contentious and only at the exploratory stage. The problems of comparability between different examining boards do not arise, and only a very small proportion of each age group (less than 2 per cent) will be tested. Nevertheless, the APU is breaking new ground in its testing strategy by requiring each pupil tested to take only a small sample of the questions from the bank of questions that together constitute the measure of standards, and new, and relatively untried, statistical techniques are needed to build up the national picture of standards. Moreover, since the bank of questions for the mathematical line of development is designed to cover the whole range of mathematical activities in schools across the country, it is inevitable that some of the topics will not have been studied by some of the children tested. Interpretation of the results will, therefore, be difficult: poor performance on one topic may mean that teaching and learning has been poor, or that many schools do not teach that topic. This problem is likely to be particularly acute in the testing of scientific development especially among the older age groups.

It is, in fact, a problem that bedevils the testing of standards at any level. Examinations can be related to prescribed courses of study, while monitoring tests have either to be limited to what is common to the curriculum of all schools, hence losing to the rich diversity that is the hallmark of English and Welsh education and many of the qualities that are really important in education, or broad enough to encompass all that goes on in schools, hence losing a stable base of comparison. Few LEAs seem to have resolved this dilemma in their own testing programmes, though the wiser ones have chosen to move slowly so that they can capitalize upon the experience of the APU and involve the teaching profession in the design of the tests and other assessments — other assessments because modern examinations and the APU do not rely solely upon conventional paper-and-pencil tests.

LEA testing programmes seem to have a variety of purposes. Screening tests given to all pupils at certain ages, typically 7 and 10 or 11, are common and desirable, to identify pupils at risk; both the Bullock Committee and now the Warnock Committee have recommended such programmes. But tests designed to identify accurately the handicapped or retarded minority of about 20 per cent are generally not suitable to assess across the whole ability range. Blanket testing is not necessary if testing is wanted solely to assess standards within an LEA, as the APU work demonstrates, and American experience points to the serious educational dangers of blanket testing.

But no testing programme is likely to be satisfactory if the aim is to compare school with school. Although well constructed monitoring tests might be an improvement on examination results in a number of respects for this purpose, there is no solution to the problems of comparison created by differences in school intakes. To my mind, the attempt to compare different schools against common, and, therefore, often inappropriate, criteria is doomed to failure and might be harmful to teachers, parents and LEA alike. A more constructive and enlightened model of accountability requires each school to specify its own aims and objectives and to evaluate the degree to which it has achieved them. Tests and other forms of assessment will almost always play a part in such an evaluation, but many other quantitative indices, such as absence rate and take-up of extra-curricular activities, coupled with qualitative judgments on the more intangible but vitally important outcomes of education made by teachers, advisers and HM Inspectorate, will paint a much more rounded and relevant picture of the quality of education. This strategy has the added advantage that is much more likely to identify appropriate means of improving the quality of education. The APU will paint a clearer picture of national standards of attainment that examination results, but neither will tell us why the picture comes out as it does.

Nuttall, D.L. (1979a) 'A rash attempt to measure standards', Supplement to *Education*, 154, 12, pp. ii–iii.

Introduction

By the time this next article was written in 1979 Desmond Nuttall had taken up the post of Professor of Educational Psychology at the Open University and the Government had set up the Assessment of Performance Unit (APU), which although it was originally intended to identify children with learning difficulties, soon took on a broader role, attempting to monitor changes in educational standards in schools over time. The technical challenges of assessing change over time were considerable, and the use of the Rasch model to attempt to overcome them was beginning to attract quite a degree of criticism.

In this next article Desmond Nuttall discloses some of the assumptions that the Rasch model depends upon. On the basis of these he was highly dubious about the credibility of the Rasch model in the context of the APU testing programme. He did, however, also explore the relative merits of other approaches. Ultimately he suggests that there can be no straightforward way of measuring changes in educational standards over time. (This is a theme that is pursued in more detail in Paper 12 and which relates as well to the arguments in Paper 5.) Change is occurring all the time in the school curriculum and in society and such changes quickly influence the precise validity of any educational test. This can result in major problems if comparisons are being made in performance standards over several years using the same test or item bank as the reference point. There are, however, many important questions that can be raised by a detailed study of educational test results within any one year, and Desmond Nuttall argues for more resources to be directed to that end.

A RASH ATTEMPT TO MEASURE CHANGING STANDARDS

Desmond Nuttall questions some assumptions behind the APU's testing procedure

How many 15-year-olds in 1979 know the meaning of the word 'mannequin'? How many 15-year-olds knew its meaning in 1954? If the number has dropped over the past twenty-five years, have educational standards fallen? The word 'mannequin' appears in one of the reading tests used in the four-yearly surveys of reading standards that ended with the 1970 survey, whose results were the main stimulus to the establishment of the Bullock Committee. The same test was used in the recent HMI Primary Survey, so the questions above are not merely academic.

In measuring standards over time, we would like an unchanging yardstick of attainment against which to measure children, akin to the device in doctor's surgeries for measuring height that allows us with great confidence to chart the increasing average height of 10-year-olds over the past thirty years, an increase attributable to better nutrition (and free school milk?) and a general improvement in living conditions. But attainment is not as easily defined and measured as height. As language changes, words like 'mannequin', 'haberdashers' and 'wheelwright' (two other words in the reading tests) fall into disuse, so that a decline in scores on a test using such words may not be telling us about a fall in reading standards but about a change in the difficulty of the test over time. In short, the measuring instrument has itself changed and no longer yields measurements comparable to those of the past.

Of course, changes in language are only one of the influences on attainment. Curricular changes, reflecting in part the values of society, and changes in teaching method, to say nothing of technological change, mean that a test constructed in the early 1950s is almost certainly not fully appropriate today in any subject. This point was brought home in a study designed to compare standards in 'A' level chemistry between 1963 and 1973. The content of the syllabus and the approach to teaching the subject had changed so much in those ten years that the examiners were obliged to conclude that they could make no comparison of standards.

The Government's Assessment of Performance Unit has, therefore, had to seek strategies to overcome this problem so that fair comparisons can be made over time, but in my opinion none of the strategies so far suggested are completely satisfactory. In the remainder of this article I look at some of the strengths and weaknesses of each, and conclude by looking at two rather different approaches to the problem.

The most favoured solution uses banks of questions. The bank can be replenished with new questions as the original ones become out of date or unusable because, for example, they have been published in the APU reports, or to reflect changes in the curriculum. The tests used in any year can, therefore, be drawn from a bank that is entirely appropriate for that year (provided, of course, that there is general agreement on the specification of the bank in terms of curricular coverage and balance, an issue that would require a separate article). But we can only compare standards between two different tests used in, say, 1980 and 1985 if we can find some way of calibrating all the questions in the bank, new and old, so that the measurement scale remains the same.

It is at this point that the debate hots up. While it is generally accepted that conventional methods of analyzing tests scores are not appropriate, there is no agreement yet about a method that can cope. One possible candidate is the Rasch model of item analysis which in recent years has generated much enthusiasm and been applied to testing programmes all over the world.

The Rasch model was devised by the Danish mathematician, Georg Rasch, in 1960 to overcome the limitations of existing models, though work on similar lines had started in the USA a few years earlier. 'Model' is used in the scientific sense, that is, a mathematical representation attempting to describe the real world. Newton's law of gravitation, about the magnitude of the force attracting two objects, is a better-known example of a scientific model. It provides a very good approximation to the behaviour of everyday objects, and even of more exotic objects like communications satellites, and can be used by the scientist and the engineer to predict the future behaviour of those objects. But in the past century it was observed that the precession of the orbit of Mercury could not be explained by Newton's law, and it took the genius of Albert Einstein to develop a model that could do all that Newton's law could do and that could successfully explain the observation about Mercury. So a mathematical model can be adequate for most practical purposes, but still fail to explain precisely all the relevant observations.

The Rasch model is very simple in essence: all it says is that the outcome of a person's attempt at a question (i.e. whether he gets it right or wrong) depends upon only two things, the difficulty of the question and the ability (or attainment according to context) of the person. This simple formulation has a number of corollaries. First, it means that the difficulty of the question must be independent of its context, that is, it must be the same whichever questions precede or follow it. There is evidence to show that this assumption is not always met: an easy question following a hard question often appears harder than when it follows another easy question. Secondly, the model implies that the difficulty of a question will remain constant for different groups of pupils, such as minority groups for whom English may not be the first language, or groups following different curricula. If some of the pupils have never studied one of the topics in the test (calculus, say, in a mathematics test), then it is highly likely that they will find the calculus questions more difficult than another group of pupils (of the same level of attainment as measured on other parts of the test) who have studied calculus. Given the broad curricular coverage of the APU item banks, this sort of occurrence is likely to be common, and even more frequent as the curriculum changes over time.

One of the merits of the Rasch model is that these (and other more technical) corollaries can be put to the test, though there is not complete agreement on the criteria by which their validity can be proved or disproved, and professional judgment will, therefore, be needed in the last analysis. If, as I suspect, their validity will not be upheld for the reasons outlined above, then the Rasch model must be deemed not to be an adequate model for the purpose for which it is required. The only way out for Rasch is to use Procrustes' bed: only items (and people) that fit the model are retained in the bank, thus distorting the educational coverage and balance of the bank, a prospect that should be unacceptable even to Rasch's most fervent disciples.

If the Rasch model does not prove to be adequate, other more complicated models of the same basis type might be tried but there is a general feeling that they are unsuitable for use with an item bank. Another rather different approach that is being investigated by the teams responsible for the science testing programme depends upon another mathematical model which makes different and somewhat more plausible assumptions. Unfortunately, some of these assumptions cannot be readily put to the test, so it will again be a matter for debate as to whether this model is adequate and more suitable than the Rasch model.

While not denying that these methods ought to be investigated further, I take the view that attainment is far too rich and varied, and the behaviour of human beings far too complex, to be satisfactorily reduced to such simple mathematical models, certainly given the very primitive state of our knowledge about education and psychology. Instead, I would offer two possible approaches, one that takes a more subjective approach to the measurement of changes in standards and the other that goes as far as suggesting that direct comparison of standards over time is fruitless.

The first approach draws upon the experience of the examination boards, who every year are obliged to do their best to maintain the standard of each grade even though the questions are completely different. Though informed by statistical information, the final judgment about standards is made subjectively by experienced examiners and teachers scrutinizing samples of the candidates' work. Perhaps the APU should develop a similar system using panels of teachers and others from within and outside education. The procedure would have its imperfections, but at least it could take some account of the changing curriculum and language.

The second approach effectively acknowledges that, anyway over a fairly long time span, even subjective judgment cannot make sensible comparisons (cf. the example of standards in 'A' level chemistry quoted above). If we accept this, we could then concentrate our energies on constructing a test wholly appropriate to the year in question, and on investigating differences in performance between groups of particular interest (girls and boys, for example, or large schools and small) in that year to see if the pattern of such differences had changed over the years. This would probably yield as many, if not more, valuable insights into attainment, teaching and learning than any other approach.

The APU is saddled with its terms of reference that require it to attempt to measure changes in standard, even though many have pointed out that it is not whether standards are rising or falling that matters but whether, at any given time, they are adequate for the needs of society. Freed from chasing the chimera of measuring change, the APU could devote its energies to answering more relevant questions.

Acknowledgments

Desmond Nuttall wishes to thank Professor Harvey Goldstein and Dr. Robert Wood for the many discussions that have helped to shape his thinking.

Nuttall, D.L. (1979b) 'The myth of comparability', *Journal of the National Association of Inspectors and Advisers*, 11, pp. 16–18.

Introduction

Desmond Nuttall once referred to 'comparability' as 'the English disease'. There has certainly been a fascination with comparing standards both between years, and between examination boards, and between different subjects. Furthermore a great deal of examination research in the 1960s and 1970s was devoted to this topic. Much of this was done by the boards' own research staff, but Desmond Nuttall and his colleagues at the NFER and the Schools Council were also involved, along with a few University-based researchers.

In this article Desmond Nuttall explores the different types of comparability and exposes the very shaky philosophical basis for considering comparability between different subjects as anything other than a very approximate and ultimately untestable, comparison. As with so many arguments about assessment the question of how important this concern is hinges very much upon the use to which assessment results are to be put. If the users of examination grades realize that grade B in chemistry is a very different thing than a grade B in French then there is no problem. However if someone else tries to use them as direct equivalents then they are placing an emphasis on the meaning of subject grades that is impossible to defend.

Desmond Nuttall's ultimate position on comparability is set out in this article. He clearly identified himself with other researchers who had decided that between subject comparability studies were largely a waste of time. Bob Wood (1976), another key figure in the world of examinations research, at that time had written an earlier piece in the *Times Educational Supplement* in July 1976, provocatively entitled 'Your chemistry equals my French'. That article conveyed a similar message:

With such vexatious problems surrounding comparability in the same subject, even within the same board, one might be forgiven for raising one's eyebrows at the suggestion that standards in different subjects ought also to be comparable. Just the thought of French and chemistry examiners sitting at the same table to discuss standards is enough to dispose of this lunatic idea.

THE MYTH OF COMPARABILITY[1]

Comparability of standards in public examinations is viewed as the supreme virtue; far more research effort is lavished upon it than on any other aspect of examinations; the constitution of each CSE Board makes it one of the duties of the Board to secure a reasonable degree of comparability between the standards of its examinations and those of other boards. But what does comparability of standards mean?

Clearly it does not mean that two students, one with an 'O' level grade C in history from the University of London Board, for example, and the other with the same grade in history from the Joint Matriculation Board, will know exactly the same facts and have mastered exactly the same skills (for example, historical reasoning or empathy). The syllabuses followed will have been different — possibly covering completely different historical periods — and, though the skills may have more in common than the facts, the emphasis may be different. Indeed, the opportunity for choice among syllabuses is considered by many to be the great strength of the GCE system of examining. Even within one board (GCE or CSE), there can be several different syllabuses in the same subject, so that two candidates with the same grade in the same subject from the same board will not necessarily have acquired the same knowledge and skills. But even if there were only one syllabus, it is important to realize that candidates who had achieved the same grade, or even the same mark, would not necessarily have achieved this grade or mark in the same manner: to take a simple example, where there is no choice of questions, one candidate might have got all the odd-numbered questions right and all the even-numbered ones wrong, while the other might have done the reverse.

So comparability of standards does not mean identity of performance. No one seems to have offered a satisfactory definition of exactly what comparability does mean, but perhaps the best encapsulation of the concept appears in the definition of CSE grade 1, which is to be awarded to a pupil who, had he followed a course leading to the GCE 'O' level examination, might reasonably have expected to secure an 'O' level grade A, B or C. Now this sort of definition, which could readily be generalized to other contexts, makes it clear that comparability is a matter of probability rather than certainty ('reasonably have expected to secure' rather than 'would have secured'). At best it is also a matter of human judgment rather than rigorous statistical analysis, and examination boards generally attempt to see that this definition is met by bringing together teachers with experience of CSE and 'O' level to make this very difficult judgment as best they can. In practice, these teachers rely more on their knowledge of the skills and content mastered by a typical CSE grade 1 candidate from their experience of previous years' examinations than on hypothetical definitions. This inevitably means that standards are determined primarily with reference to subject-based, or more specifically syllabus-based, criteria of attainment. These criteria are only very crudely transferable to different syllabuses (particularly under Mode 3), and moderators and examiners can only 'trade off' criteria displayable on one scheme (for example, knowledge of the date of the Battle of Hastings) against criteria displayable on another scheme (ditto knowledge of the date of the Battle of Waterloo). In reality, of course, the criteria are much more complex than these two examples suggest, and the task of judging appropriate 'trade off' that much more difficult.

Given the present definition of comparability, this paper is therefore arguing that there is no way of investigating or attempting to achieve comparability other than relying on trained, but fallible, human judgment. The user should be made aware of the vagueness of the concept of comparability, and the inevitable imprecision in our attempts to achieve it.[2]

Does Comparability Matter Anyway?

There are four forms of comparability that are usually identified:

(i)   between boards in a given subject;
(ii) between years in a given subject in a given board;
(iii) between subjects in a given board;
(iv) between alternative syllabuses (including those under Mode 3) in the same subject in a given board.

Form (a) is normally considered the most important and is certainly the most researched. At higher levels, for example, for entrance to university, clearly students with the same grades in the same subject from different boards are competing (though, as noted above, these grades will not mean the same thing in terms of attainment), so one can understand the desire for board comparability. At lower levels (below CSE grade 1, say), school leavers are generally not competing against others who have taken the examinations of different boards; they want local jobs and compete against others with certificates from the same board. Board comparability is therefore not nearly so important.

Between years the arguments are similar: students from widely different years are generally not in competition so it does not matter from their view if standards steadily drift (upwards or downwards) over the years. Employers might, however, legitimately complain if they have done detailed analyses which show that without a grade 1, say, in mathematics apprentices will not be successful; few have done such analyses, and in any case the content and approach to mathematics is continuously changing. Year comparability is also important if examination results are to be used as measures of educational standards in general, as they often have been; with the growth of the work of the APU, this source of pressure may be lifted.

Subject comparability is the thorniest issue of the lot. Clearly many users ask for five 'O' level grade Cs or better (or more typically grade C in English and mathematics plus any three others), and assume therefore that a grade C in history is in some way exchangeable for a grade C in geography. If one accepts that standards are subject-specific, this is clearly a nonsense; there is no reason to suppose that the intellectual demands as expressed in the syllabuses and assessments of the two subjects are the same (though some boards do try to make them as similar as possible to the best of their ability; but if it is difficult to compare two history syllabuses how much more difficult is it to compare two syllabuses in disparate subjects). Even if one takes a different view of what comparability is meant to mean (for example, a wholly norm-referenced definition giving grade A to the best 10 per cent and so on), there are many who feel that the investigation of subject comparability is intractable (for a host of technical reasons).

Comparability between alternative syllabuses is perhaps the most important but its problems and limitations have been discussed in the first part of the paper. In the world of 'O' level and CSE candidates, a student is much more likely to compete with another with the same grade in a different syllabus in the same year than any of the other possible combinations from (i)–(iv).

Even where comparability does matter, there is a much more important factor that sets a limit to the extent to which comparability can be achieved. Examinations — indeed, any assessment of one human being by another — are not perfectly accurate in the grades they yield. A candidate, faced on a different day with a different but equally valid question paper marked by a different examiner, could easily achieve a different grade; research evidence suggests that the margins of error in a candidate's grade at 'O' level or CSE is about one grade in each direction (i.e. all that can be confidently said about a candidate awarded grade C is that he deserved a B, C or D grade).[3] For an individual candidate, lack of comparability pales into insignificance beside the inevitable inconsistency of the assessment process.

The Consequences

Comparability can only be rough and ready, and is seldom as important as it is made out to be. More should be done to expose this situation, but one should be alive to the danger that if one rocks the boat too much there will be pressure for standardizing syllabuses, and prescribing the criteria that should be tested in any English (or mathematics etc.) examination. There are already pressures for this from the Standing Conference on University Entrance at 'A' level; and the Waddell Report, reinforced by the previous Government's White Paper and subsequent discussions about the establishment of a National Co-ordinating Body, moves in this direction for a common system at 16+.

For a school-leaving certificate as a replacement for or supplement to public examinations, one faces a dilemma: should one pander to the genuine, if somewhat (but only somewhat) misguided, desire for comparability by setting up inevitably elaborate procedures for moderation, validation and accreditation and give labels, either in words or in grades, that are designed to have some common currency between schools (but warning of the limitations of the commonness of the currency) or should one allow each school to develop its own reporting procedures? The latter invites employers, universities and colleges to take much more initiative in devising their own selection procedures: in many senses this would be thoroughly constructive, but it does invite 'league tabling' of schools, nepotism and all those bad effects that public examinations were originally devised (first in China 3000 years ago, and in the nineteenth century in this country) to overcome. It also implies a boom in (often inappropriate) psychological and educational testing by employers with possible unfortunate backwash into the schools, let alone the creation of problems for children on the milkround of job seeking. How can one avoid leaping from the frying pan into the fire?

Notes

1   This paper was originally written in the summer of 1978 and delivered at a PRISE Conference on Assessment held on 31 March 1979 at Oxford. It has been slightly amended for publication.
2   For a development of these arguments and more technical detail about the problems of investigating comparability, see *Comparability in GCE* published by the JMB on behalf of the GCE Boards (May 1978) and *Comparability of Standards in Public Examinations: Problems and Possibilities* prepared by the Schools Council Forum on Comparability and to be published shortly by the Schools Council.
3   See, for example Willmott, A.S. and Nuttall, D.L. (1975) *The Reliability of Examinations at 16+*, London, Macmillan.

Nuttall, D.L. (1980a) 'Will the APU rule the curriculum?', Supplement to *Education*, 155, 21, pp. ix–x.

Introduction

The powerful influence that assessment systems have on the curriculum is a recurring theme in Desmond Nuttall's work. In the late 1970s the prominent new arrival on the assessment scene had been the Assessment of Performance Unit (see also Paper 4). In the next article Desmond Nuttall explores the possible influence the APU tests were likely to have upon the curriculum experienced by pupils in the nation's schools. Alongside that consideration he also explores once again the extent to which changes in standards over time can be assessed, and also the equally contentious subject of the use of APU results in determining the allocation of resources to schools, through for example the identification of underachievement in local authority areas.

The APU has been seen by many as a significant forerunner for the National Curriculum, and it is interesting to see highlighted in this article some of the key arguments that were to come to the fore in the late 1980s, in relation to the implementation of the National Curriculum in England and Wales, some ten years later.

WILL THE APU RULE THE CURRICULUM?

Some three months ago, the DES published *Mathematical Development*, the APU's first report, covering the survey of mathematical attainments among 11-year-olds carried out in May 1978. Press coverage was extensive but, as always, short-lived, and if anything at all is now remembered it will probably be the small proportion of children who could calculate Boycott's batting average, a question that has since been accused of being both sex-biased and culturally biased. My own conversations with some fifty heads of primary schools and mathematics teachers in secondary schools suggest not only ignorance of the report's findings but also a strong feeling that the results are in any case an irrelevance, since what matters to them is what *their* pupils can do mathematically, not what the nation's children can do. Their one fear is that the APU's testing programme will ultimately be used to define what should be taught in every school.

The motives of those who established the APU are shrouded in mystery, particularly because its foundation was announced, seemingly almost as an afterthought, in a White Paper on educational disadvantage. Its terms of reference have a clear link with disadvantages: 'to promote the development of methods of assessing and monitoring the achievement of children at school, and to seek to identify the incidence of underachievement'. Associated with these terms of reference are these tasks:

1   To identify and appraise existing instruments and methods of assessment which may be relevant for these purposes.
2   To sponsor the creation of new instruments and techniques for assessment, having due regard to statistical and sampling methods.
3   To promote the conduct of assessment in cooperation with local education authorities and teachers.
4   To identify significant differences of achievement related to the circumstances in which children learn, including the incidence of underachievement and to make the findings available to those concerned with resource allocation within government departments, local education authorities and schools.

Although it is true that neither the terms of reference nor the tasks make explicit mention of investigating changes of standard over time, the APU's publicity leaflets make it quite clear that such investigations are planned: 'We need such information (facts and figures about standards) not only to describe the current position but also to record changes as they occur.' A further use for the results is also seen: 'Such information would help teachers in planning the balance of pupils' work in schools, without an attempt at national level to define detailed syllabus content.'

Can the APU achieve any of its major aims? I want to look at them under the following headings: planning the balance of pupils' work, measuring change in standards, resource allocation and the incidence of underachievement. An issue common to all of them is that facts and figures about performance are not enough: the prime interest of teachers and policy-makers is in *reasons* why the facts and figures are as they are; only then will they be in a position to seek remedies (or to congratulate themselves).

Curricular Planning

The APU's summary report on the first survey concluded that the results 'indicate that while most 11-year-olds can do mathematics involving the more fundamental concepts and skills to which they have been introduced, and cope with simple applications of them, there is a fairly sharp decline in performance as their understanding of the concepts is probed more deeply and their basic knowledge has to be applied in more complex settings'. What implications does this have for curriculum planning? That more time should be spent on other than routine applications of skills (as HMI reports have been urging for some time)? If so, at the expense of what? Does more depth have to be at the expense of breadth? How do individual teachers decide whether they should change the emphasis in their mathematics teaching when they cannot be sure that the APU's findings are applicable to their pupils, since only a small sample of the questions (and, by design, not a representative sample) has been published? What difference in performance between routine and non-routine applications is acceptable?

Perhaps the APU's reports will stimulate discussion of these questions, but we should beware of the limitations of the APU's testing strategy. First, apart from the small-scale testing of practical mathematics (which itself showed that children often tackled the tasks differently from the way they tackled similar paper-and-pencil tasks), the questions were almost all marked either right or wrong with no investigation of how the children attempted to solve the questions. More open-ended questions are planned for use in future surveys, but at present little information of diagnostic value is yielded. Second, no information about the frequency with which particular topics or concepts are *taught* in schools is being collected, so that we do not know, for instance, whether poor performance in unusual applications is due to lack of opportunity to practise such applications or to a failure on the part of pupils to master such applications despite intensive teaching (or, of course, to some combination of these across the nation). Before APU results are used for curricular planning, we need more information.

Measuring Changes in Standards

Measuring changes in standards is fraught with difficulty, partly for technical reasons and partly because one has to assume that the questions that are used to measure standards do not themselves change in difficulty despite changes in teaching method, syllabuses and broader cultural changes. This assumption was certainly not met in the four-yearly surveys of reading standards over the period of 1946 to 1970 when the test included words such as 'mannequin' and 'wheelwright'. While the APU hopes to avoid such obvious dating in its tests, similar but more subtle influences are always present and the method by which it is suggested that these influences might be detected (the Rasch model of item analysis) is under severe scrutiny at the moment.

But, assuming that we could measure changes in standards, we are no closer to understanding why they have arisen unless we relate the changes to possible causes, or concomitant changes. In particular, we need information about the curriculum and the way it changes (or, more precisely, about the curricula in each school where APU tests are given), noting that the APU results themselves may stimulate such changes. However, other possible causes are legion: changes in teacher competence, pupil interest or motivation, growth in the use of calculators and microprocessors, changes in the amount and type of in-service education, increases or decreases in the resources allocated to mathematics.

Resource Allocation

Very similar considerations apply to the possible use of APU results to help with resource allocation. Clearly all sorts of factors explain why levels of performance are what they are, or why they change. In its regular light-sampling surveys the APU cannot possibly hope to measure all these factors, and such few that they can measure are powerless to elucidate causes. This is graphically illustrated by one of the results in the first survey: performance across virtually the whole range of mathematics was *better* in those schools with 27.5 or more pupils per teacher than it was in those schools with a PTR of less than twenty. The report is quick to point out possible reasons, for example that the PTR is often better in schools in deprived areas and that PTR is not a measure of class size as taught. But even class size as taught is probably not a very relevant measure in the primary school where the types of organization (group work, individual work, class teaching) are variable within a single class; in any case, class size as taught in the year of testing may not necessarily be much more important than class size over the previous years.

Incidence of Underachievement

Despite many years of warnings by psychologists, the term 'under-achievement' is as much in vogue as it ever was. For instance, the Welsh Office continues to use it throughout their reports investigating the disparity in examination results between Wales and England. The concept is enshrined in that commonplace of school reports: 'Could do better.' No doubt, we would all do better, so in one sense we are all underachievers; some presumably are worse underachievers than others. But in the context of national surveys, some objective yardstick of underachievement is needed but none has yet been devised. (The old concept of comparing attainment with IQ has been well and truly scotched by the realization that statistically for every underachiever there is an overachiever, whatever that strange creature may be.) So it looks as though the APU has no alternative but to look not at the incidence of underachievement but at the incidence of relatively low achievement, and at the characteristics of those pupils who score well below the average for 11-year-olds. Again, though, we should remember that the APU has virtually no information about such pupils except sex and age.

'Ours Not to Reason Why. . . .'

The preface to the first report, by the former Head of the APU, states: 'It was not part of the Unit's job to draw conclusions from the survey, but merely to assess what children had learned.' I do not think that the APU can afford to take that view; if its results are to be of any value, it must provide much more information as a background against which the results may be interpreted. (In fairness I must add that I believe that many within Elizabeth House and on APU committees would agree with me.) But I also believe that, while further analyses of existing APU results will be useful, the light-sampling monitoring surveys *cannot* adequately investigate cause-and-effect relationships, or even collect the sort of information about changes in teacher competence and so on that I listed above. Research in a variety of different styles, sometimes intensively in a few schools, sometimes action research, occasionally the large-scale survey, will be needed if we are to begin to answer the question 'Why?'. And that means that the budgets for APU work, already sizeable in the world of educational research, will have to be increased dramatically. Perhaps the value for money question that lies behind the pressures for accountability and monitoring will then come home to roost.

References

DES ASSESSMENT OF PERFORMANCE UNIT (1980) *Mathematical Development: Primary Survey Report No. 1*, London, HMSO.

APU *Summary Report No. 1: First Primary Mathematics Survey*, London, DES.

APU *Assessment — Why, What and How?* (leaflet available free from room 2/11 Elizabeth House — as are four other leaflets and three consultative documents).

Paper 7

Nuttall, D.L. (1980b) 'Did the secondary schools get a fair trial?', *Education*, 155, 2, pp. 46–51.

Introduction

Desmond Nuttall had a long standing interest in the work of Her Majesty's Inspectors of Schools (HMI). They, like himself, were centrally interested in evaluating the effectiveness of the provision of education in schools. He was often, however, critical of their methods and felt at times that they broke some fairly basic rules of systematic, impartial evidence gathering. In this next paper he discusses the results of the recently (in January 1980) completed HMI Secondary Survey of 384 secondary schools.

As he carefully scrutinizes the quality of the evidence collected by the HMIs in the course of this investigation Desmond Nuttall applies all of the normal criteria for judging educational assessments familiar to his own context. Judgments are made very frequently in education, as in life, and the attention that is paid to their validity and reliability from one context to another is remarkably variable. Researchers like Desmond Nuttall are used to subjecting their evidence to rigorous scrutiny to determine its worth. This is less common in inspections, where the judgments of inspectors are often given a special status that depends more on trust than any real evidence of their dependability. Desmond Nuttall thus argues that if HMI's judgments are to be given greater credibility then HMI need to reveal the way in which they collect their evidence, so that its credibility can be tried and tested, along with everything else in education.

DID THE SECONDARY SCHOOLS GET A FAIR TRIAL?

The aim of the Secondary Survey — 'to offer some account of how well schools provide and their pupils respond in the fourth and fifth years of secondary education' — sounds modest. Its scale — 384 schools each visited by a team of typically five inspectors for a full week and each completing very detailed questionnaires about school characteristics, staffing and curriculum, supplemented by data on special problems, gifted children and external examinations — places it among the world's largest educational inquiries. The 150,000-word report, though often cautious in tone — 'it is at least worth asking what might be the effect . . . if fewer subjects disappeared from pupils' programmes' — in the main does not pull its punches and contains more recommendations than do the reports of most committees of inquiry.

It is, therefore, both important and legitimate to examine the quality of the evidence upon which the conclusions and recommendations are based. The evidence came from three main sources: the detailed questionnaires yielding largely factual data, gradings of provision by the school and gradings of response by the pupils to that provision. and written reports amplifying the judgments underlying the gradings and picking out features of note. The sample consisted of 10 per cent of secondary schools in England; an appendix demonstrates that, within the constraints of the constantly changing nature of the population over the period of the survey, the sample adequately represented the population in respect of school type and sex, but contained a slightly disproportionate number of larger schools that was unlikely, however, to cause bias.

The questionnaires are reproduced in full in the report and appear unexceptionable; the parts of the report based on their analysis are sound and informative. Far less information is given about the gradings and the reports. The six points of the grading scale are defined, and, for each aspect of the investigation (language, mathematics, science, and personal and social development), the criteria used in forming the final grading judgments are made explicit. We are told that these criteria were amplified by guideline papers, which are not directly reproduced, and that the gradings were agreed by the team of visiting HMI. Since, however, for each grading there were multiple criteria, the scope for different teams to disagree in the weighting and interpretation of the criteria seems great; this potential unreliability is acknowledged to be at its most acute in the gradings of personal and social development. Elaborate analysis of the gradings themselves, therefore, does not play a prominent part in the report, and the comparisons of gradings between, say, large and small schools are relegated to an appendix and interpreted with the utmost caution. It does seem to me, though, that the report errs too much on the side of caution in suppressing virtually all the quantitative data from the gradings, denying others the chance to look for patterns and inconsistencies.

Despite the report's and my own reservations about the validity and reliability of the gradings, many of the principal results of the survey are expressed in terms of them. This reinforces the need to make explicit not only the criteria themselves but also the way in which the criteria were interpreted and combined to form a single grading judgment whereby a school's provision in mathematics, for example, was deemed 'unsatisfactory' (15 per cent of schools received this assessment for their provision for their more able pupils, 26 per cent for their average pupils and 47 per cent for their less able). Indeed, the report itself suggests that 'it could be helpful to schools to have some criteria whereby to assess their curricular provision and the resources they may need to sustain it' and, implying the use of some criteria, that LEAs 'will want to consider whether there are unjustifiable inequalities between schools in the resources allocated to them or in the use schools make of their resources, or in the performance of schools seemingly in comparable circumstances.'

There is one rather curious feature about the gradings for provision and response. There are about eighteen direct comparisons between the two sets of gradings and in sixteen of these cases the response is graded significantly better than the provision. Yet the definition of response is response to the provision, so that grading response more highly than provision would seem to be logically inconsistent. These findings are discussed only briefly and, to me, not convincingly, since judgments seem to have been made about what the pupils might have achieved had adequate provision been made, a procedure which is both highly speculative and seemingly inconsistent with HMI's own specified criteria. These findings must cast doubt upon the validity of the gradings.

The gradings and the criteria were also very important in the construction and interpretation of the written reports. Two short paragraphs describe the nature of these reports, and it is difficult to judge from these paragraphs and the infrequent quotations from, and references to, reports how similar they were in their underlying structure to the HMI reports issued after routine inspections. It is clear that their surface structure could be different, in that the reports were not issued to schools nor LEAs (though 'full discussion took place with the head and members of staff at the end of each visit'). The quotations and illustrations from the reports, themselves incorporating some occasionally delightful and some often disturbing quotations from children's work, provide the occasional glimpse of the inspectorial mind: 'The project was frequently allowed to develop into "scissors-and-paste" compilations of cuttings; in one such, a unit in a "French background" project on the wines of Anjou was illustrated with pictures of Sandeman's port, seemingly unnoticed.'

It is clear that the reports formed the main body of evidence. It was from them that hypotheses arising from comparisons of the gradings were explored, and tentative explanations of cause and effect put forward. Underlying the reports, then, there must be theories or models of how schools function as institutions and of the nature of teaching, learning and the curriculum. For example, the criteria for provision and response in science imply a view of what scientific concepts and processes should be taught and how they should be taught that rests upon particular psychological and pedagogical models. The report has virtually nothing to say about this 'hidden' theory; moreover, among the grand total of six references to other published works (five of which are HMSO publications) in the whole report, only two have a theoretical framework, and then both in the field of language.

For all these reasons, it is very difficult to judge from the report where evidence stops and speculation and opinion begin. Most of the evidence consists of a collation of subjective impressions. That is not an objection in itself; indeed, much of the best research in the social sciences uses similar evidence. But what is not lacking in the best research is a clear exposition of the theoretical and methodological assumptions, which provides a framework for the reader to assess the quality of the evidence and to recognize the point at which interpretation of the evidence takes over from its presentation. Nor, incidentally, can HMI duck these problems by denying that the survey is research; systematic observation and fact-gathering, using techniques designed to minimize subjectivity by standardizing observers and employing quantitative and qualitative data analysis, cannot be described as other than research.

The report has many admirable qualities: it is easy to read and undoubtedly achieves its major aim of painting a richly diverse picture of the fourth and fifth years of secondary education. Most of its recommendations will be warmly received in one quarter or another for one reason or another (more money should be spent, more can be done with existing resources, more school-based INSET and so on) and both the educational hawks and doves will have plenty to feed upon. It lifts the great debate on to a higher plateau of informed discussion and for all its weaknesses it will be of more value at all levels from the Secretary of State to the classroom teacher than all the activities of the APU and local authority testing programmes.

But, in the final analysis, the only criterion for judging the adequacy of the report's findings is one's faith in HM Inspectorate. Though commendably more willing to expose their values and criteria than in years gone by, HMI would have served us better if they had been prepared to go much further, according to established research principles and procedures, in telling us what they did, and; even if one doesn't accept that research criteria are appropriate, one's faith could be enhanced by greater explicitness.

Nuttall, D.L. (1983) 'Unnatural selection?', *The Times Educational Supplement*, 18 November.

Introduction

There are many professional people who develop and use their professional abilities to a high degree, but never appear to question the social implications of the work in which they are involved. Not so Desmond Nuttall, who always had a keen eye for the social and political arguments pertaining to his research. This next article illustrates this exceptionally well as it unpacks some of the issues relating to the use and abuse of educational assessment in performing selection functions in our society.

Another notable characteristic of this article is the fact that it was written for the *Times Educational Supplement*, and as such reveals Desmond Nuttall's considerable ability to disseminate technical educational research findings in such a way that they could be easily understood by a wide audience of interested parties. Desmond Nuttall's career brought him into regular contact with policy-makers and practitioners and he knew how to speak in a language that they would not only understand, but would want to act upon.

All educational assessments have shortcomings. They rarely provide a completely adequate picture of individual learners' aptitudes and achievements, and their ability to predict future achievements is even less dependable. Nevertheless assessment results are frequently used as a major factor in decision making about entry to higher education, employment and professional training.

Such simplistic systems for determining important life choices lie at the root of social injustice. Those failing to gain access to higher education or employment may have just as much potential for success as those who gain entry. The demise of the 11+ removed one obvious source of unfair, and socially divisive selection. However, assessments continue to play a vital selection function at 16 and 18 in England and

Wales. In this article Desmond Nuttall draws upon some Open University data to demonstrate how successful some people who have been labelled as educational failures may ultimately be. In the midst of the 1990s debates about extending the provision of higher education even further to those who would have in the past been denied this opportunity, this article is highly pertinent.

Desmond Nuttall's close association with the CSE examination, the Open University and, in later years, the Inner London Education Authority allowed him a variety of chances to do something about enhancing the educational opportunities of those who might otherwise have been disadvantaged in an elitist education system and much of his research work was devoted to this end.

UNNATURAL SELECTION?[1]

Desmond Nuttall criticizes the continued reliance on exams which are known to be unreliable predictors of future success.

Exams have a multiplicity of purposes, both educational and social. They function as agents of curriculum control — more explicitly than ever before in the development of criteria for the common system at 16+.

Historically they have been regarded as the setters and guardians of standards. Though at one stage, it looked as though the establishment of the Assessment of Performance Unit might take the heat off public examinations, the legal requirement for secondary schools to publish their exam results and the long-running controversy surrounding the exam results of different types of schools have meant that exams and standards continue to be inseparable.

Within the school, exams are often defended as an important device for motivating students — and teachers — and, for society, professional exams that license practitioners (doctors, lawyers and plumbers alike) offer an important safeguard.

But pre-eminent among the purposes of exams is selection. Since the days of imperial China, nearly 3000 years ago, exams have been used to pick out the most promising applicants for jobs or for particular forms of education. Sometimes, as in scholarships, the best 10, or whatever, are chosen regardless of the absolute standard of their performance. On other occasions, the exam is used to set the minimum acceptable performance level (for example, a B and two Cs at 'A' level), more akin to a process of attesting minimum competency.

In reality, though, this minimum level is not set after a careful analysis of the basic requirements of knowledge and skills necessary for satisfactory performance on the course or in the job, but simply as a response to market forces. A popular university department demands high 'A' level grades largely to ease the task of selection among the many who apply; an unfashionable one asks for two Es in the hope of attracting enough students to fill the places available.

Of course, no selector relies solely upon examination results: other information, from interviews, references, heads' reports and application forms, is always used. But it is clear from research into university selection and into employers' use of exam results that the results are crucial, not least in the process of short-listing. So how good are exam results at predicting future success?

At a recent seminar, organized jointly by the Banking Information Service and the Centre for the Study of Comprehensive Schools and attended by many representatives from business and commerce, I asked if anyone could refer me to studies of the predictive efficiency of examinations in employment, but no one could. My experience is borne out by that of Janet Jones, until recently BP School Teacher Fellow at the University of Reading, who has just completed a major study of employers' use of examination results. During her enquiries, no one produced any evidence about the validity of examinations as selection devices.

So, despite the widespread use of examinations in selection for employment, evidence about whether they do really help the employer pick out the best applicants is hard to come by. In the field of education, though, there is more evidence. Despite the fact that there is considerable similarity between the predictor (exam results) and the criterion of subsequent success (another exam result), the general conclusion has to be that exams are very modest predictors of subsequent educational success.

For example, a study some years ago of the predictive value of CSE grades for further education concluded:

> While showing that CSE can provide additional information for allocating students to further education courses, the findings of this project confirm the prescience of the Beloe Report in thinking it important that 'ways should be left open for those who are not able to show their quality in terms of school examination results'. Students with low CSE grades possessed a high chance of success on a number of the further education courses investigated. Sixty-five per cent of the students ungraded or awarded grade 5 in mathematics, for instance, subsequently passed the craft studies courses with credit. It cannot be said that the opportunities of further education are closed to those who perform badly in CSE.

The same is true of 'O' level grades as predictors of 'A' level grades in the same subject. Many of the correlations are fairly small, ranging from about 0.6 in physics or French down to 0.3 in history or English literature. There is no universally accepted way of expressing the meaning of such

correlation coefficients. The most stringent is the index of forecasting efficiency: a correlation of 0.6 means that the efficiency is 20 per cent better than
selection completely at random, while a correlation of 0.3 implies an efficiency
only 5 per cent better than chance. Other measures give a slightly more
favourable future, but all imply that there are plenty of students whose good
'O' level performance is not reflected at 'A' level and many others with poor
'O' level performance and impressive 'A' level grades.

As might be expected, the relationship between 'A' level grades and class
of degree some three or four years later is even weaker. Correlations range
from 0.4 for the sciences down to below 0.2 for arts subjects (an improvement over chance of 8 per cent at best and a derisory 2 per cent at worst).
Detailed work by the NFER in the 1970s led to the broad conclusion that 'A
levels correlate only poorly with subsequent examinations', but admitted that
'although A level results fall a long way short of perfection, they do provide
the best single predictor of university success'. (Later work showed that the
number of 'O' levels passed was virtually as good — or as bad.)

We can conclude, therefore, that exams are by and large poor predictors
of future educational success. There are plenty of understandable reasons for
this: people mature at different rates, their interests and enthusiasms change
and the subjects themselves make different intellectual demands at different
levels. But if we recognize such eminently sensible explanations, why do we
persist in placing so much reliance on exam results in selection?

One exam that is, or was, a rather good predictor — at least *ten times* as
efficient as 'A' level is at predicting university success — deserves a mention.
Indeed, information from around the world suggests that it is probably the
most efficient selection exam ever devised. It is, of course, the 11+. Despite
its relative efficiency, it still fell so far short of perfection that tens of thousands of young people were inappropriately placed in different kinds of secondary school, with disastrous social, educational and personal consequences.

In large measure, its lack of perfection as a selection device rightly led to
its demise (in most parts of the country, at least). The fact that the 11+ is
relatively so much better than 'A' level as a predictor is, naturally, no argument for its reinstatement, but its fate certainly has implications for 'A' level.

The key to abolishing the 11+ was the existence of an appropriate alternative: the open access comprehensive school. What would happen if we were
to have open access higher education? As in Europe, quotas would no doubt
be necessary in some universities and polytechnics and most departments of
medicine and other popular subjects, but quotas could be based not on previous attainment (as in effect they are at present) but on many other principles, some of which are being tried in Europe. Quotas can readily be
manipulated to create greater social justice by favouring disadvantaged groups.

The guiding principle at the Open University is 'first come, first served'.
Previous qualifications are not used for selecting applicants, but information
about them is collected so that we can look at the success rates of different
groups. The chart (figure 1) shows the percentage of students who passed at

Figure 1: The performance of Open University students with different entry qualifications

Highest educational level on entry	Percentage gaining some credit in 1982
No formal qualification	56.1
CSE	58.0
'O' level	66.9
Average for all students	71.0
'A' level	73.0
HNC/HND	74.9
Teaching certificate	77.1
First degree	72.3

least one of the courses they studied, though rarely more than two, in 1982. The remainder of the students were more likely to have dropped out during the course for personal or domestic reasons than to have failed the course.

In line with all our experience and the evidence quoted above, there is a tendency for those with higher educational qualifications to be more successful but the relationship is far from perfect. Over 50 per cent of those with no qualification higher than CSE passed, while nearly a quarter of those in the most successful group did not pass the course. To have restricted entry to those with 'A' levels or higher qualifications would not have been a particularly efficient way of selecting the students most likely to be successful.

So the experience of the Open University and comparable institutions throughout the world confirms that exams are poor selection devices within education. How much poorer are they likely to be in job selection where the criteria of success are so much more diverse and less like exam-taking? Anyone using exams as selection devices should be obliged to supply evidence that they *are* relevant and appropriate in that particular application, and should have the sense to be looking at alternatives which provide more information about the qualities needed for success on the job.

Note

1   This article is based on a talk given at the BIS/CSCS Seminar referred to.

Nuttall, D.L. (1984) 'Doomsday or a new dawn? The prospects for a common system of examining at 16+' in Broadfoot, P. (Ed) *Selection, Certification and Control*, Lewes, Falmer Press.

Introduction

This next paper analyzes in some detail the events in the 1960s, 1970s and 1980s that led up to the launch of the GCSE examination. Written in 1983 it pre-dates the final decision to go ahead with the GCSE in 1987, but the long awaited move away from the dual CSE and GCE 'O' level system had been under debate since 1966, the year after the launch of the CSE.

The force of this paper is the way in which it disentangles the politics of curriculum control from what might appear superficially to have been a debate about examination reform. The paper reveals insights, based upon Desmond Nuttall's relatively recent involvement in the management and conduct of CSE public examinations. These insights are brought to bear on the intricacies of the long sustained and tortuous saga of the search for a common system of examining at 16+. By 1983 the grassroots clamour for a comprehensive examination to serve the recently instituted comprehensive school system had been hijacked by the politicians, and the DES, as a means of gaining greater central control over the school curriculum. This followed years of considerable teacher autonomy and a succession of frustrated attempts by the DES, and by HMI, to steer the school curriculum in ways that those at the centre desired (Lawton, 1992). This was a scenario described some years later by Ted Wragg as being the secret garden of the curriculum invaded by a Secretary of State, who not only got in but who started to wreak havoc by trampling all over the flower beds.

The debate surrounding the attempt to introduce a common

system of examining at 16+ set the scene for the National Curriculum that was to follow, with the passing of the 1988 Education Reform Act, where to an even greater extent the assessment tail has been used to wag the curriculum dog (Murphy, 1987 and 1989). This article reveals how clearly Desmond Nuttall saw the issue as one of a battle between teacher autonomy and politicians who wanted to gain greater control over the school curriculum. Technical debates about the pros and cons of different assessment formats obscured the much more profound debates about the rights and wrongs of politicians prescribing a core curriculum and using assessment as a means of policing whether that curriculum was being implemented successfully by teachers.

In the event some of Desmond Nuttall's worst fears about GCSE were on this occasion to prove unfounded and in a later article (Nuttall, 1990b) he reviewed progress after the first year of GCSE and was able to point to some very positive curriculum influences:

> Nevertheless, I must make it clear that there is increasing evid-
> ence that the GCSE courses have stimulated more imaginative
> teaching and learning, including a move away from teaching
> that relies on dictating notes, and examination papers that re-
> quire the regurgitation of those notes. The requirement that
> there should be more practical and oral work has certainly begun
> to affect classroom practice, as is made clear in the preliminary
> evaluation by Her Majesty's Inspectorate (HMI, 1988). There
> can be positive effects of an assessment led curriculum. (p. 146)

Of course, by the time that GCSE was examined for the first time in 1987 the National Curriculum debate was already well underway, and Desmond Nuttall saw that the plans for a 5–16 curriculum, with national assessments at 7, 11, 14 and 16 years, would put some doubt on the long term future of GCSE:

> I do not think that we shall have national assessments at 16+
> until 1995 or 1996. With that in mind, unprecedented as it is for
> an English examination to last for less than twenty years, I
> would predict that the last GCSE examination will be in 1998.
> (*ibid.*, p. 148)

Whether the 1994 Dearing Report changes in the National Curriculum, including the decision to focus the National Curriculum and its asso-
ciated assessment arrangements on a more restricted curriculum from 5–14 years of age, would have caused Desmond Nuttall to revise that particular prediction in an issue to which we will return in Section 3.

DOOMSDAY OR A NEW DAWN? THE PROSPECTS FOR A COMMON
SYSTEM OF EXAMINING AT **16+**

For over fifteen years there has been pressure to merge the Ordinary level of
the General Certificate of Education (GCE 'O' level) and the Certificate of
Secondary Education (CSE) into a common system of examining at 16+ (DES/
Welsh Office, 1982). The aim of this paper is to examine the aims and motives
of those seeking the reform, and of the Department of Education and Science
(DES) in reacting to their proposals. The principal thesis that I seek to establish is that the DES has seized upon the occasion of examination reform to
make changes to the structure and control of examinations that have no special link to the notion of a common system. The background to the actions
of the DES is not discussed in detail since the principal issues of teacher
autonomy, standards and curricular relevance affecting those actions are fully
covered by Bowe and Whitty in their paper in this volume. Against that
background and the aims of the reformers and the DES, this paper evaluates
the prospects for a common system of examining at 16+ as they appear in
early 1983.

The Roots of the 16+ Proposals

The first set of CSE examinations had barely been taken nationwide before
the problems of having two separate examination systems began to emerge.
The Joint GCE/CSE Committee of the Schools Council, for example, recommended in 1966 that 'the problem and the nature of the existing situation
point towards the development of a common system of grades . . .'[1].

The potentially divisive effect of having more than one system of examinations was recognized much earlier by the far-sighted Norwood Committee
who feared that the School Certificate (established in 1917), being taken in
only one type of school, might 'mark off the secondary grammar school from
other forms of secondary education. A system will then become established
under which parity in secondary education will become impossible . . .'[2]. Reporting in 1943, they recommended the replacement of the grouped School
Certificate by a single-subject examination but only for a transitional period
of seven years; after that 'in the interest of the individual child and of the
increased freedom and responsibility of the teaching profession, change
. . . should be in the direction of making the examination entirely internal,
that is to say, conducted by the teachers at the school on syllabuses and papers
framed by themselves . . .'[3].

The single-subject examination duly came into being in 1951 in the form
of GCE 'O' level, but the next stage of a wholly internal examination envisaged by the Norwood Committee has yet to come. Moreover, the examination was designed for, and remained the preserve of, the grammar schools.
Predictably there was very soon pressure from the secondary modern schools

to be included in the public examination system. In 1955 the then Minister of Education rejected the suggestion that the standard of an 'O' level pass should be lowered so as to bring the examination within the reach of more pupils.[4] He also stated that he did not favour the establishment of any new general examinations of national standing for secondary schools, but encouraged groups of schools to experiment in organizing their own examinations. Many did so, while others entered fourth-year pupils for examinations organized by national or regional bodies like the Royal Society of Arts or the Union of Lancashire and Cheshire Institutes; the increasing number of those who stayed on into the fifth year beyond the statutory school-leaving age tended to be entered for 'O' level.[5]

Growth in the demand for external examinations during the 1950s could not be stemmed, and by 1960 the Crowther Committee and the Beloe Committee had both recommended the establishment of an examination for pupils of lower ability than those who would be entered for GCE.[6] The final shape of the new CSE examination proposed by the Secondary School Examinations Council (SSEC) and approved by the DES in 1962 was somewhat different from that proposed by the Beloe Committee in 1960; in particular, the top grade was linked to the standard for an 'O' level pass in an attempt to help the new examination gain national currency and respect.

The Development of the Proposals

While national bodies were creating two separate examinations with an eye on the two principal kinds of secondary school — grammar and modern — a much more important movement was gathering momentum: comprehensive schools were slowly being established. There is irony in the fact that it was the same year — 1965 — that saw both the first CSE examinations in some parts of the country and the issue of DES Circular 10/65 which encouraged the move towards comprehensive reorganization. It is not surprising, then, that it was only a short time before the Schools Council (which had inherited the examination responsibilities of the SSEC in 1964) began to point out the problems created by the dual system. At this early stage, most concern was expressed about the confusion created in the minds of the public by the existence of a pass/fail classification at 'O' level and a graded system in CSE that were linked through CSE grade 1, but the organizational, curricular and administrative problems (all of which are considered in more detail below) did not pass unnoticed.

Nevertheless, the CSE introduced many positive features into English public examination practice. CSE examinations employed a much wider range of techniques of examining and assessing than had been the norm in GCE and hence brought a wider range of skills and abilities into the net of assessment; in particular, the participation of the candidate's own teacher in the process of assessment became common along the lines of the Norwood Committee's recommendation. This participation was at its greatest in Mode 3 examinations, where the department or even the individual teacher devised the syllabus and scheme of examination and carried out the assessment, subject only to moderation by the CSE board. The criteria which a Mode 3 proposal was obliged to meet were straightforward and liberal: the subject had to be capable of being examined and moderated, and the title had to provide a correct description of the content.[7] Few proposals failed to meet the first criterion of being capable of being examined and moderated (even in landlocked Middlesex one could find a moderator for navigation and seamanship); but for many years most boards took the view that physical education could not be examined, moderated and graded in a manner comparable to other subjects and this criterion was therefore used to reject Mode 3 PE proposals. The second criterion — precise titling — was designed to help users and to stop their being misled; for example, a syllabus consisting exclusively of arithmetic could be titled 'arithmetic' but not 'mathematics'. But what of a syllabus that was mainly arithmetic with a sprinkling of other kinds of mathematics? Titles such as 'Arithmetic with basic mathematics' had to be invented. Each subject area created similar problems. The result was a proliferation of different titles, a proliferation that was later to be attacked (see below). The only other major control available to a CSE board in respect of Mode 3 was the right to impose a grade ceiling, to rule, say, that no grade higher than 3 could be awarded, if a syllabus did not seem to make comparable demands to similar syllabuses in the same subject.

Until the establishment of the CSE, the GCE system had been subject to some central control. The SSEC had had to approve new syllabuses at both 'O' level and 'A' level before a board could introduce them. The Schools Council recognized that the potential number of CSE syllabuses meant that it could not approve each one individually, and it consequently also gave up the practice of approving new 'O' level syllabuses. For CSE examinations, the Schools Council acted as a court of appeal in the few cases where a board and a school could not reach agreement; for GCE 'O' level, its powers were negligible though the GCE boards informed the Schools Council if new subjects were to be examined, and the Council sometimes asked to see and comment upon these new syllabuses. At 16+, then, central control or even monitoring of examination syllabuses was relaxed in the 1960s to such an extent that it was virtually non-existent. (At 'A' level, though, the Schools Council retained the right to approve all new syllabuses.)

It was, however, considerations of politics and philosophy as much as considerations of practicality that led the teacher-controlled Schools Council to allow the CSE boards, also teacher-controlled, more autonomy in the sphere of syllabus approval than the GCE boards had had under the reign of the SSEC. In retrospect, one can see this era of the mid-1960s as the zenith of the period of autonomy of schools and teachers. One of the principal bastions of defence against the further spread of teacher autonomy was the GCE boards, most of which were controlled by the universities in the final analysis, though teachers played a large and increasing part in the determination of policy. One of the motives of some of those arguing for a merging of CSE and 'O' level, especially the teacher-politicians in the Schools Council, was the desire to remove this obstacle to increased teacher autonomy by importing the typically more democratic methods of the CSE into the realm of the GCE. Others simply wanted to see the wider range of examining methods and opportunities of CSE available in GCE as well.

But these were arguments that seldom reached the surface of the debate within the Schools Council.[8] There, and later more widely, stimulated by Schools Council publications and leaflets,[9] the principal arguments were about the divisiveness of a dual system (as forecast by the Norwood Committee) and about the organizational, curricular and administrative problems that it created. The divisiveness came about from the lack of status accorded by parents and employers to the CSE in comparison to the well-established GCE. The failure of the CSE to gain parity of esteem with the GCE mirrored the failure of the secondary modern to gain parity of esteem with the grammar school. In the eyes of its supporters, comprehensive education required a comprehensive examination system; the effect of a dual system within the comprehensive school was to create grammar and secondary modern streams. Children had to be categorized into GCE and CSE groups, often at the beginning of the fourth year; not only did this categorization fail to match any natural division between the aspirations or abilities of the children, but it also created organizational and timetabling problems. To provide a safety net, many schools entered borderline candidates for both GCE and CSE, putting a severe burden on just those pupils who were having difficulty with the GCE course. And a severe burden, as well as a considerable increase in costs, was placed on the schools who had to cope with at least two different boards, with their different entry dates, stationery and examination timetables.

Aware of all these problems created by the dual system, in July 1970 the Governing Council of the Schools Council resolved, by sixty-four votes to one, 'that there should be a single examination system at the age of 16+ and that this should be under the Schools Council'. A working party was quickly established; it reported in 1971, making a number of firm recommendations about the proposed system (notably that the percentile range 40–100 should be adopted initially as the range of ability to be covered) and indicating areas needing further study, such as the technical problem of examining over a wide range of ability.[10]

Then began one of the largest programmes of feasibility and development studies of a proposed educational innovation ever mounted in England and Wales. Some fifty studies were mounted by consortia of GCE and CSE boards, most involving examinations leading to the award of both GCE and CSE certificates (rather than simply trial papers leading to no qualification).

In 1974 these examinations spanned seventeen major areas of the curriculum and about 68,000 subject entries were made. Ironically enough, many of these experimental examinations, albeit slightly modified in the light of experience, continue to this day, most notably in Wales and the north of England, and have recruited hundreds of thousands of entries. At the same time, research into related topics such as the moderation of coursework and into Mode 3 was being undertaken by the staff of the Schools Council.[11]

The task of evaluating this programme of work and hence the feasibility of the common system of examining at 16+ fell upon the Joint Examinations Sub-Committee of the Schools Council who delivered their report in the summer of 1975.[12] Their principal conclusions were that the common system was feasible and that the research programme indicated ways in which the outstanding problems could be solved. Given the power of the common system to eliminate the problems of the dual system, they had no hesitation in recommending that a common system should be established as soon as possible. After nearly a year of consultation and public debate about the report, the Governing Council of the Schools Council decided in July 1976 to endorse the recommendations of their sub-committee and forwarded them to the DES, where the decision whether or not to implement them constitutionally rests.

Proposals for a teacher-controlled and fairly liberal new examining system, linked to the ideal of comprehensive education, could not have been sent to the DES at a less auspicious time than the middle of 1976. In the wake of what Halsey dubbed 'the rotting of public confidence in public institutions'[13] and precipitated by the economic effects of the oil crisis of 1973/74, there was growing concern about the responsiveness of the educational system to national needs and the standards of education being provided, especially by comprehensive schools. Elsewhere in this volume Bowe and Whitty analyze the forces at work and show how concern about the relevance of the curriculum was later overtaken by concern about the broader issue of standards: in both cases, however, a large part of the blame for the inadequacies of the system was placed upon the teaching profession, whose autonomy should, it was felt, therefore be curbed. The principal issues were the curriculum and teaching methods, and the DES, with the help of HM Inspectorate, were eager to have more influence over these, as the Yellow Book (a confidential memorandum prepared in the DES) made clear. The Yellow Book was part of the briefing for the famous speech made in October 1976 by the then Prime Minister, James Callaghan.[14] He made it clear that the public, as well as the teaching profession, had a right to a say in what goes on in schools, and launched the so-called Great Debate about education. A formal part of this debate was a series of regional conferences early in 1977 at which the agenda covered four main topics: the curriculum; the assessment of standards; the education and training of teachers; school and working life. It is the debate on the curriculum and its consequences that are of particular significance for the proposals for a common system of 16+.

The Curriculum Debate

After the regional conferences, the Government published a Green Paper (DES, 1977). It identified four points of concern about the curriculum in secondary schools, two of which concerned the problems caused by variations in the curriculum between schools, and the third the lack of match between the curriculum of many schools and life in a modern industrial society. The proposed remedy was some form of core curriculum common to all secondary schools, but the difficulty of creating a suitable core curriculum was acknowledged.

Subsequent events showed how right the Government was to acknowledge the difficulty. Four years of information-gathering and consultation later, the proposals in *The School Curriculum* (issued by the DES in 1981) were bland in the extreme. A leader in *The Times Educational Supplement* of 27 March 1981 had this to say:

> *The School Curriculum* represents the liquidation of commitments to a core curriculum and a defined framework, which Ministers entered into without understanding what was involved. It is not a very glorious retreat, but at least it gets this tiresome business out of the DES's hair and leaves it to the professionals. (p. 2)

The Examination Debate

Variation in the curriculum from school to school was mirrored in — some might say, fuelled by — the variation in examination syllabuses. The Expenditure Committee (Home Office, Education and the Arts) of the House of Commons stressed the importance of comparability of standards in public examinations and argued for a reduction in the diversity of the content of syllabuses in the same subject.[15] Similar points about unnecessary and harmful diversity were made at many of the regional conferences during the Great Debate; at one, the Secretary to the University of London University Entrance and School Examinations Council (the London GCE Board) proposed that all 'A' level syllabuses in the same subject should share some common core of content, a proposal that was hailed by the press as one of the more sensible suggestions to emerge from the Great Debate.[16]

Partly as a result of these pressures and partly as a result of the continuing process of syllabus revision at 'A' level, the GCE boards began to see merit in delineating material that might be common to all syllabuses in a given subject, starting with mathematics. The Standing Conference on University Entrance enthusiastically latched on to this idea, on the grounds that it would ease the task of teaching in the first year of a university course if all students had experienced much the same course in the sixth form, and just beat the GCE boards to the production of a suggested common core for mathematics.

Many other subjects have since been covered, and new syllabuses embodying some of the common cores are now in use.

Diversity in syllabus content was not the only charge levelled at public examinations. Burgess and Adams (1980) summarized many others: their lack of comprehensiveness in covering all the aims of education, their exclusion of a large minority, their cost and their obtrusiveness into the organization and administration of schools, to name but four. HM Inspectorate, in their survey of secondary schools, roundly criticized the way in which concentration upon examination requirements narrowed learning opportunities in the fourth and fifth years (HMI, 1979). They felt that the curriculum and examinations had to be brought more closely together, to make examinations a force for good rather than a force for harm. To do this, they argued,

> . . . there is a case for the participation of more teachers both in devising syllabuses and in assessing their pupils, particularly in those aspects of work which cannot easily be tested within a timed written examination. The benefits of a balance of board-based and school assessment would apply to all pupils and not merely to the average and less able. The introduction of a new system of examining would afford opportunity as well as reason for the development of more broadly based methods of assessment which match changes in the curriculum. (p. 244)

Consideration of the 16+ Proposals by the DES

The DES have reacted slowly and cautiously to the proposals for a common system of examining at 16+, ever since the Schools Council sent them in mid-1976. Their slowness has no doubt been due in part to the changes of government and of ministers, but both their slowness and caution have been influenced by the public debate about the curriculum, examinations and standards. At the same time, there seems to have been a growing realization that, as the Inspectorate point out in the quotation above, the occasion of examination reform provides the ideal opportunity to put right a number of defects in the existing examination system that

> are quite independent of the existence of a dual system of grading. There are too many awarding bodies and too many syllabuses, including an unnecessary number with the same title: and different titles which sometimes conceal only marginal differences in the scope of syllabuses. Moreover, the relationship between overlapping grades needs to be properly established. Since examination requirements in many subjects are not clear, schools can interpret them in a way which is harmful to good education. The performance expected of candidates needs to be clearly described and the standards for each grade need to be made more explicit.[17]

As the Government now see it, the way to remedy these defects is through the development of national criteria; the history of these national criteria in the development of the 16+ proposals *shows how they have emerged from almost nowhere in 1976 to be the key factor in determining the future of the 16+ proposals.*

The National Criteria

The criteria governing the acceptance or rejection of a Mode 3 submission have been described above and are considered by Bowe and Whitty in their paper. Bowe and Whitty also point to the very much more stringent criteria applied to Mode 3 submissions by the GCE boards. This difference in practice led the Schools Council to note that 'consideration would have to be given, in the development stage of a new examination, to the criteria by which (Mode 2, and Mode 3 and mixed-mode) schemes might be accepted.'[18] This was the only reference to criteria in the 16+ proposals, though the criteria to be applied by boards to Mode 3 submissions in the proposed Certificate of Extended Education were debated fully in the Schools Council and spelt out in some detail in the proposals that also went to the DES in 1976.

The response of Shirley Williams, at that time Secretary of State for Education and Science, to the Schools Council's 16+ proposals came within a week of Callaghan's famous speech at Ruskin College, and was cautious in the extreme. Ignoring the defects of the existing examinations seized upon by her successors in office, she wrote: 'I believe that the public has confidence in the standards of the existing examinations and their consistency across the country. This confidence is too valuable to be put at risk.'[19] She announced that she felt it necessary to institute a further 'intensive and systematic study' of the proposals and the evidence that supported them.

This study was carried out by a committee composed of nominated persons from inside and outside the world of education, including HMIs and civil servants, under the chairmanship of Sir James Waddell (himself a retired civil servant). Inevitably, it went over exactly the same ground as the Schools Council had, but could draw on two more years' experience of the experimental 16+ examinations and had more staff and resources at its disposal. Nevertheless, the Committee reached essentially the same conclusions as the Schools Council, in particular that a common system of examining was feasible. But it was critical of the trial examinations in many subjects, because they had employed examination papers (or other assessment devices) taken by all candidates in common. These, the Committee (and many others) felt, could not do justice to candidates at the extremes of the ability range. The Committee therefore recommended much more extensive use of alternative papers at different levels of difficulty (what they termed 'differentiated papers') so that more able candidates could follow a harder route and less able candidates an easier one but without access to the award of the top grades. They also recommended much stronger central coordination of the examination system than had been seen in the past, with nationally agreed criteria as the key ingredient.[20]

The Government accepted the conclusions and recommendations of the Waddell Committee. In a White Paper published in October 1978, they announced that

> . . . publicly known general criteria should be established to ensure that syllabuses in subjects important for subsequent stages of education or of vocational relevance have sufficient in common, and are relevant to the needs of subsequent courses of education and employment, to enable the grades awarded to be accepted with confidence by those concerned. (DES, 1978, p. 10)

They also required criteria specific to each major subject, and expected the national criteria 'to ensure that alternative papers are used wherever this is necessary to maintain standards' (*ibid.*, p. 11).

The change in government in May 1979 caused a pause in the consideration and refinement of the 16+ proposals. The new Conservative Government was more receptive to the lobbying of the GCE boards, whose initiative in establishing common cores at 'A' level had surely not gone unnoticed and whose role in maintaining standards and in resisting teacher control was widely recognized (as Bowe and Whitty demonstrate). So, in February 1980 when Mark Carlisle, the new Secretary of State for Education and Science, announced that the Government would continue with the plans to establish a common system, it was no surprise that, in addition to reaffirming support for national criteria and differentiated papers, he gave the GCE boards a special accolade. In a DES Press Notice Carlisle observed:

> Any reforms must ensure that the high standards associated with GCE 'O' level are maintained. This must be our first priority. We intend to make the GCE boards responsible for the higher grades in the new scale. (DES, 1980)

He also indicated that schools would still be free to choose among the examinations offered by the various groups of collaborating GCE and CSE boards. This principle of freedom of choice of board reflects existing practice in the GCE system (in contrast to the practice in the CSE system where the freedom of choice is between modes of examination within a board, and not between the syllabuses of different boards); the principle is also held very dear by the GCE boards.

The GCE and CSE boards then jointly embarked upon the preparation of criteria at the invitation of the DES, though they were given relatively little guidance: 'The exact nature and scope of the criteria are difficult to predict at this stage. It may not be possible to be precise until a good deal of further work has been done.'[21] It was thus left to the GCE and CSE boards to clarify the nature of the criteria, which they decided should cover aims, assessment objectives, content, techniques of assessment and grade descriptions for Grade 3 (equivalent to 'O' level Grade C) and Grade 6 (CSE Grade 4). During 1982, the draft criteria for some twenty subjects were published, in many cases receiving extensive criticism, and revised draft criteria were submitted to yet another new Secretary of State, Sir Keith Joseph, early in 1983.

One of the most criticized acts of Sir Keith Joseph has been the abolition of the Schools Council, announced in summer 1982, and its replacement by a proposed School Curriculum Development Council and the Secondary Examinations Council, which started work in April 1983. The Secondary Examinations Council consists of the nominees of the Secretary of State (admittedly largely picked from names offered by a wide range of educational bodies), rather than democratically appointed representatives of different interests as in the Schools Council; more significantly, fewer than one-quarter of its members are practising teachers so that any possibility of teacher domination has been clearly eliminated from the central controlling mechanism for the public examination system. The first task of the Secondary Examinations Council is to appraise the revised draft national criteria and to advise the Secretary of State (with whom rests the final decision) as to whether these criteria provide a satisfactory basis for the implementation of a common system of examining at 16+.

The aims and nature of the national criteria are spelt out in a DES policy statement issued in November 1982. In most respects they follow the previous DES policy statements discussed above, but more detail is given and more implications are spelt out. For example, the diversity of syllabuses under Mode 3 that, as Bowe and Whitty show, has allowed important curriculum development, not least response to the calls for relevance to industry and commerce, will be drastically curtailed; although all modes of examining will be permitted under the new system, the proviso is that the syllabuses and schemes of assessment comply with the national criteria. Moreover, there will be criteria for the inclusion of a subject in the list of those available for examination, implying that any new subject (the 1980s equivalent of computer studies, perhaps) may have a long battle before it can be admitted to the ranks of the 'examinable'. More positively, the DES

> will be looking for criteria which reflect the best of current curriculum practice and reinforce an approach to the secondary school curriculum which recognizes the practical application of academic skills: and which are sufficiently flexible to allow new developments to take place.[22]

These requirements will no doubt warm the hearts of HM Inspectorate: Sheila Browne, the Senior Chief Inspector, feels that '. . . the exercise to establish criteria for the common exam system at 16-plus offers yet another chance — perhaps the last this century — to embody in the exam system aims long aspired to' (reported in *Education*, 30 October 1981, p. 340).

But can the national criteria achieve such a laudable goal? The Inspectorate (as evidenced by their collective view quoted above) feel that participation by more teachers in the processes of syllabus development and the assessment of their own pupils, coupled with the development of more broadly-based methods of assessment, are important steps towards this goal. At the present time, the draft national criteria have failed to inspire confidence on these points; in particular, they have consistently revealed a distaste for school-based assessment, which arguably provides the only real way of widening the range of assessment objectives. By giving the GCE boards a right of veto, the DES has ensured that this distaste will be perpetuated in the common system. By requiring Mode 3 proposals to meet the national criteria, the DES has closed off an important avenue of curriculum development and experimentation (and may have blocked a vital professional safety valve), and made it likely that fewer teachers rather than more will be involved in syllabus development and assessment.

Conclusions

If the opportunity for much needed reforms as perceived by HM Inspectorate has been largely lost in the very slow movement towards a common system of examining at 16+, what of the original advantages seen in the late 1960s — the elimination of divisiveness, greater curricular and organizational flexibility, and simpler administration?

Few of these advantages now seem likely to be present in a common system. By insisting on differentiated assessment in most if not all subjects, the DES have perpetuated the need to select pupils for different courses at about the age of 13 or 14 (though possibly somewhat later than under the dual system), with all that this selection implies in terms of a differentiated curriculum and class organization in the fourth and fifth years. Moreover, by limiting the target group for the design of the examination to the top 60 per cent of pupils in each subject another sort of divisiveness (between the examined and the non-examinable) would become more obvious than it is at present and further curricular complexity would be introduced into the comprehensive school.[23]

By allowing schools a choice of board and groups of boards (and exhorting LEAs not to restrict this freedom of choice[24]), the DES has failed to maximize the chances of administrative streamlining. There may be a common examination timetable nationwide, thus eliminating the possibility of a candidate entering the same subject in more than one board, but there will be different sets of entry forms, stationery requirements and regulations for schools to cope with.

Above all, the incredibly slow pace of the reform and the fact that those with the greatest vested interest — the boards themselves — have been given the task of doing all the drafting make it unlikely that the new system will adequately meet today's curricular needs in which the education and training of those over 16 has taken on a new significance and will head in new directions. Assessment as a teaching and counselling device through the medium of profiles has become the norm for 17-year-olds on vocational preparation courses in further education,[25] and both profiles and graded tests are spreading rapidly in secondary education in an effort to counter the divisive effect of the current public examination system and the feared greater divisiveness of the proposed common system (see, for example, Harrison, 1982; Balogh, 1982; and Goacher, 1983). The inevitable problems of negotiating changes to the national criteria once established make the likely pace of any future development needed to meet changing educational and societal needs so ponderously slow that an analogy between the common system and a dinosaur, and their respective evolutions, is compelling.

In short, there is every danger that the common system now being created will be divisive, bureaucratic, retrogressive and obsolescent — almost exactly the opposite of the common system as desired by its proponents of the late 1960s and early 1970s.

But some features of a common system could be very different. The DES has taken upon itself a much more overt role in steering examination reforms and giving themselves rights (unprecedented since 1945) over the approval of the detailed content of examination syllabuses and schemes of examination, since it is the DES that have the final say over the national criteria. Having failed in their attempts to control or influence markedly the curriculum through documents like *A Framework for the School Curriculum*, they can succeed by another route, at least for the curriculum of secondary schools.

In practice, this seizing back of control by the DES will have three main effects. First, the number of syllabuses and subjects for which examinations will be available will be drastically curtailed, and the professional autonomy of schools and teachers to design a secondary school curriculum to meet the needs of their pupils correspondingly reduced. Second, the autonomy of the examination boards is similarly being reduced and, as is true more broadly in the sphere of local government, local and regional powers of decision-making are fading away while the powers of central government and institutions grow. This centralization of control is designed, in part at least, to curb the autonomy of teachers in their schools and classrooms, and collectively in the examination boards. The third effect is even more obviously to limit teacher influence at the centre; by replacing the democratic Schools Council, with its responsibilities for coordinating the public examination system and advising the DES on policy, by a Secondary Examinations Council with members nominated by the Secretary of State and with teacher-members in a small minority, teacher influence on examinations policy and practice has been cut back at all levels of the educational decision-making process.

The terms on which a common system might be introduced have been made increasingly stringent by the DES ever since 1976; the judges of the criteria are the DES, acting on the advice of the Secondary Examinations

Council, with Sir Keith Joseph and Dr Rhodes Boyson as the final arbiters. The criteria for judging the national criteria were clarified in 1982:

> The national criteria will need to do justice to all pupils in the range of ability for which GCE and CSE examinations are designed, and to set standards at least equal to those of existing examinations at 16+. The syllabuses and forms of assessment adopted must be seen to promote good educational practice and give schools and pupils an incentive to demonstrate their attainments. The arrangements must be intelligible to parents and employers and demonstrably more efficient in the use of resources than the present arrangement.[26]

But the DES has also realized that its particular goals (reducing curriculum diversity and curbing teacher autonomy) could be achieved within the existing system, that is, without the need for introducing a common system of examining at 16+. If the national criteria do not 'fully satisfy' the DES, it would wish to see 'how the national criteria, as by then developed, might best be used to harmonize and improve the dual system'.[27] The threat is quite clear: if the boards do not or cannot create the system the DES want to see, the existing systems will continue with virtually none of the advantages originally hoped for in a common system and with major restrictions placed upon existing practice in syllabus design and assessment methods. A step towards a comprehensive examination for the comprehensive school, as the common system of examining was perceived by many, will be bought at a very heavy price, if indeed it can be bought at all. And the price of an abortive purchase will be even higher.

Notes

1 *Examining at 16+*, The report of the Joint GCE/CSE Committee of the Schools Council, HMSO, 1966, p. 5. (Although the first CSE examinations were held in some parts of the country in 1965, it was not until summer 1966 that all fourteen CSE boards held examinations.)
2 *Curriculum and Examinations in Secondary Schools*, Report of the SSEC appointed by the President of the Board of Education (the Norwood Report), HMSO, 1943 (reprinted, 1962), p. 46. The School Certificate was the major matriculation requirement of the universities, and to gain the Certificate or the Higher Certificate it was necessary to satisfy the examiners simultaneously in a specified number and range of subjects (an arrangement commonly called a grouped certificate). Only a very small proportion of school leavers, exclusively from grammar and independent schools, gained the Certificate.
3 *ibid.*, p. 140.
4 Circular 289, Ministry of Education, 1955.
5 This use of 'O' level in secondary modern schools exacerbated the tendency for the curriculum of the secondary modern to ape that of the grammar school, and its failure to develop a distinctive approach.

6   *15 to 18*, A Report of the Central Advisory Council for Education (England) (the Crowther Report), HMSO, 1959; *Secondary School Examinations Other than the GCE*, Report of a Committee appointed by the SSEC (the Beloe Report), HMSO, 1960. For a more detailed account of the history of examinations see Montgomery (1965).

7   Memorandum to Examining Boards No. 13 issued by the SSEC, c. 1963.

8   For details of the debate within the Schools Council, see *Examinations at 16+: Proposals for the Future*, The report of the Joint Examinations Sub-committee of the Schools Council on a common system of examining at 16+, with an evaluation, conclusions and recommendations, Schools Council, 1975.

9   *Arguments for a Common System of Examining at 16+*, Schools Council leaflet, 1973 and *ibid*.

10 *A Common System of Examining at 16+*, Schools Council Examinations Bulletin 23, Evans/Methuen Educational, 1971.

11 This research programme and its findings are summarized in *Examinations at 16+: Proposals for the Future*. The principal studies were reported in full in Schools Council Examinations Bulletins 34 and 37.

12 *Examinations at 16+: Proposals for the Future*.

13 Paper given by A.H. Halsey at an SSRC Seminar on Aspects of Accountability, 11 September 1979.

14 The speech is reported in *The Times Educational Supplement*, 22 October 1976. For a fuller account of the events leading up to and following from Mr Callaghan's Ruskin Speech see, for example, *Accountability and Evaluation*, Block 1 of Course E364, *Curriculum Evaluation and Assessment in Educational Institutions*, The Open University Press, 1982.

15 Tenth Report from the Expenditure Committee, *Attainments of the School Leaver*, HMSO, 1977.

16 A.R. Stephenson, personal communication.

17 *Examinations at 16+: A Statement of Policy*, para. 3.

18 *Examinations at 16+: Proposals for the Future*, p. 61.

19 Letter from Mrs Shirley Williams to Sir Alex Smith, Chairman of the Schools Council, 25 October 1976.

20 *School Examinations*, Report of the Steering Committee established to consider proposals for replacing the General Certificate of Education Ordinary-level and Certificate of Secondary Education examinations by a common system of examining (the Waddell Report), HMSO, 1978 (Cmnd 7281).

21 Letter from P.H. Halsey (Under-Secretary at DES) to the Secretary of the Standing Conference of Regional Examining Boards, 28 February 1980.

22 *Examinations at 16+: A Statement of Policy*, para. 22.

23 The existing CSE and 'O' level systems are jointly designed, officially at least, for the top 60 per cent of the ability range in each subject, but in practice well over 80 per cent of 16-year-olds take examinations in English and a mathematical subject and more than 90 per cent take at least one public examination. So that under a new system, with a rigidly enforced target group policed by national criteria, a substantially larger proportion of 16-year-olds could expect to be 'unexaminable'.

24 *Examinations at 16+: A Statement of Policy*, para. 14(ix).

25 For a variety of examples see *Profiles*, Further Education Unit, 1982.

26 *Examinations at 16+: A Statement of Policy*, para. 4.

27 *ibid.*, para. 32.

References

BALOGH, J. (1982) *Profile Reports for School Leavers*, London, Longman.

BURGESS, T. and ADAMS, E. (Eds) (1980) *Outcomes of Education*, London, Macmillan Education.

DES (1977) *Education in Schools: A Consultative Document* (Cmnd 6869) (the Green Paper), London, HMSO, p. 11.

DES (1978) *Secondary School Examinations: A Single System at 16 plus* (Cmnd 7368) (the White Paper), London, HMSO.

DES (1980) *Single Sixteen Plus Exam System*, DES Press Notice, 19 February.

DES/WELSH OFFICE (1982) *Examinations at 16-plus: A Statement of Policy*, London, HMSO, November.

GOACHER, B. (1983) *Recording Achievement at 16+*, London, Longman.

HARRISON, A. (1982) *A Review of Graded Tests*, Schools Council Examinational Bulletin 41, London, Methuen Educational.

HMI (1979) *Aspects of Secondary Education in England: A Survey of HM Inspectorate of Schools*, London, HMSO.

MONTGOMERY, R.J. (1965) *Examinations: An Account of Their Evolution as Administrative Devices*, London, Longmans Green.

Nuttall, D.L. and Goldstein, H. (1984) 'Profiles and graded tests: The technical issues' in *Profiles in Action*, London, Further Education Unit.

Introduction

The early 1980s saw a great deal of innovation and change in the area of educational assessment, and alongside the development work for GCSE there were a variety of profiling, graded test and graded assessment schemes emerging. In many respects these schemes, which were often local rather than national, were as concerned with supporting specific curricula as they were with any assessment issues. However, in this next article Desmond Nuttall, along with his close friend and collaborator over many years, Harvey Goldstein, stand back from these new developments and attempt to assess their technical qualities. Having themselves been associated with similar critiques of examinations, tests and other assessment approaches that pre-dated profiles and graded tests, they are at pains to point out that technical deficiencies of one kind or another are almost inevitable in assessment schemes that are relevant, practical and usable. Their argument that finding a good assessment scheme usually depends upon trading off one type of deficiency against another kind of relevance, is a crucially important one.

More assessment schemes tend to break the fundamental principles of measurement theory by adding together quantitative measures of different aspects of educational achievement. Desmond Nuttall's quote from White (1974) in Paper 2 sends up this common failing in a humorous way. However the price of reporting a number of separate scores or grades in a profile of achievement is that the reliability, validity and comparability of those separate scores may be fairly low when compared with global scores, arising from a more extensive battery of assessments.

In many contexts, argue Desmond Nuttall and Harvey Goldstein, the impact that different assessment schemes have on the curriculum, both taught and experienced, far outweighs the need for those same assessments to have immaculate psychometric (or educational measurement) properties. It does, however, depend somewhat upon who is intending to use the assessment results and what they are likely to infer from them.

A further important aspect of this paper is the way it calls for more assessment-related research that attends to the curriculum and practical classroom implications of different assessment methods. These authors were among a number who were highly influential in moving a good deal of assessment research away from the rarefied preoccupation with statistics, internal consistency measures, and the like that had stultified educational assessment research in the UK during the 1960s and 1970s. Desmond Nuttall in particular was to go on to be associated with a number of large scale evaluations of assessment innovations (such as the PRAISE project), which successfully placed their major emphasis on the wider educational implications of such changes, and wrestled assessment research free from the clutches of those who saw it simply as a branch of psychometrics.

PROFILES AND GRADED TESTS: THE TECHNICAL ISSUES

We shall review first, but briefly, what seems to be the current state of profiling; the aims and controversies which are being discussed. We shall then identify what seem to us to be the key technical issues which have yet to be solved before profiles can be accepted widely as satisfactory additions or alternatives to other forms of assessment. Then we shall describe and evaluate the graded test movement. Finally we shall link together graded testing and profile reporting and discuss the relationship between them. On all these topics we have been able to find little written about technical matters, and very little relevant empirical research, and in this article we therefore discuss the major technical issues in the hope of facilitating a more informed debate.

Current Activity

The last few years have seen a considerable interest in profile reporting in education. An early report from the Scottish Council for Research in Education (SCRE, 1977), has stimulated a variety of others both at the school level in the work of the Schools Council (Balogh, 1982; Goacher, 1983) and even more vigorously at the FE level in the work of the Further Education Unit

(FEU) (FEU, 1982a) and the related City and Guilds of London Institute (CGLI) development work (Stratton, 1982a).

There is general agreement that the disaggregated nature of the information in a profile is of greater potential use to students, lecturers and employers who wish to understand the specific strengths and weaknesses of an individual, rather than some average assessment. There is also a general recognition of the need to distinguish formative profiles which are produced during a course from summative ones which represent a final assessment and are typically based on an amalgamation over time of the formative set of assessments. Formative profiles are designed to be part of the learning process, to be discussed by lecturer and student together, while the summative kind are designed for the outside world and selection for employment. These two broad purposes may be often in conflict and affect the need for comparability and reliability in the assessments, as we shall demonstrate.

There is also conflict among the motives of the advocates of profiles. At one extreme, in the words of Broadfoot (1982), herself a collaborator in the SCRE work, profiles provide a viable alternative to the powerful 'anti-educational' constraint of public examinations. At the other is the Associated Examining Board's new 'A' level geography examination which provides a profile by means of a separate grade for each of four papers, to yield more information from existing examinations, a development reviewed in detail by Harrison (1983). In between, in the mainstream of development, is the FEU and CGLI approach and that of SCRE and many of the schools studied in the Schools Council work, which see their profiles as existing alongside centralized examinations. In the case of the pre-vocational courses stimulated by the FEU, the intention seems to be that profiles should become a dominant element in assessment, while in schools there seems to be a recognition that public examinations will remain the dominant element for some time to come.

One feature common to most profiles, in contrast to examinations, is their inclusion of personal and social skills alongside so-called basic skills and more conventional attainments. Sometimes the personal and social skills are reported simply as records of activity, without judgment, but often they are assessed and graded (by the lecturer alone, or by the lecturer and student in partnership). In the CGLI Vocational Preparation course (365), for example, there are four ratings for each of the abilities 'to be self-aware' and 'to cope with problems', as well as for 'calculating' and 'reading and writing'. Simple rating scales of this kind are widely used; each point is accompanied by a description of the ability or attainment level it represents. While it is usually admitted that some of these ratings will be more 'subjective' than others, the common aim appears to be to remove this element as far as possible by providing careful verbal descriptions, training the assessors carefully and carrying out periodic 'quality control' checks on their work. Some more open-ended schemes use 'comment banks', consisting of comments whose placing on the scale has had prior agreement (Black and Dockrell, 1981).

This present article is largely concerned with some of the key technical

issues which have received too little serious attention in the discussion up to
the present. Such references as there are admit to the existence of problems of
reliability and indeed validity, but fail to probe them in any depth (MacIntosh,
1982; Harrison, 1983). In our view, however, there do exist serious technical
problems and, unless these can be solved satisfactorily, profiles will rest on
insecure foundations. We are concerned largely with the 'mainstream' developments, although we do recognize other strands to profiling. For readers
who want a more detailed discussion of the general educational aspects of
profiling the reports by Balogh (1982), Goacher (1983), Burgess and Adams
(1980), the Scottish Vocational Preparation Unit (1982) and the FEU publications mentioned above will be useful.

Norm versus Criterion-referencing

This article does not provide the space to present a detailed discussion of this
issue, but some general remarks are relevant. This is because, for both profiles
and graded tests, criterion-referenced assessment is commonly advocated.
Further, since criterion-referenced assessment has often been regarded as not
amenable to quantitative manipulation in the same way as norm-referenced
assessment, there is the possibility that some important technical problems
will be ignored.

Firstly, it is extremely difficult to imagine a criterion-referenced assessment that is totally independent of norm levels. If a criterion point is to be
useful it must obviously distinguish between individuals, so that the possibility exists that some will reach it and others will not. We can know whether
this is the case only by collecting data on how many individuals do so — thus
estimating a norm. Since, in fact, 'cut off' points are at choice, if not actually
arbitrary, this 'norming' information will typically be used in determining
them, at least initially. The difference between criterion-referenced and norm-
referenced tests lies in their methods of construction, intended use and interpretation. In terms of construction, criterion-referenced tests are designed
consciously to avoid the psychometric models of norm-referenced tests, and
in terms of use they employ fewer categories but ones which are designed
to convey educationally meaningful information. In the case of profiles, the
important issue is that of providing assessments that are both accurately
related to the profile elements and comparable across individuals. This is not
easy to achieve.

A central thrust of the profiles movement has been the attempt to relate
assessment more closely to the curriculum than public examinations typically
do (Mansell, 1982). Thus, teachers and lecturers have collaborated in the design
and testing process, and assessments are intended to be made in the context
of curriculum activities. If curricula differ, a comparabilility problem is immediately raised, since there is then no guarantee that consistent interpretations
can be made. To overcome this problem, much effort has been put into an

attempt to develop context-free assessments. The SCRE profile, for example, has one skill level for number which is described as 'Can handle routine calculations with practice', and the amplification is provided 'Fairly accurate but slow; is able to calculate percentages and money calculations etc.'

The difficulty with such out-of-context descriptions is that they are too poorly defined to ensure comparability, and the more precisely defined they become the more rooted in a context they become. Thus the above definition would need to specify what was meant by 'routine' so that such a calculation could be recognized. It would need to specify the order of difficulty of the 'percentages' referred to and make much more precise the phrase 'Fairly accurate but slow', and so on. Eventually, for a high degree of comparability to be achieved, the description would have to be so precise that we would be very nearly back with the classical test situation where everyone is administered effectively the same set of items — i.e., a highly specific context for the assessment. Of course such tests need not be paper-and-pencil ones. They could be imaginative practical or work-related assessments, but still be context-bound, and thus would encounter the same problems as all traditional tests; namely not being equally relevant to each of a wide diversity of curricula.

It seems clear, therefore, that there is an inbuilt contradiction here that is not only unresolved, but also hardly discussed in the recent literature. Moreover, given the difficulty, if not the sheer impossibility, of achieving comparability between existing public examination boards because of the differences between the syllabuses and courses it is difficult to see a more satisfactory solution emerging for profiles (Goldstein, 1982).

If profiles are to be faithful to a curriculum, then they will presumably have to sacrifice the aim of comparability across curricula, and cease striving to become context-free. This raises the possibility that some (key) elements of the profiles will be 'centralized' and others 'localized'. In the circumstances it seems very likely that the former will come to assume greater importance than the latter. It is interesting to note that government policy on the 17+ is that in 'key' areas (English, science, maths) performance will be 'externally assessed or moderated' while at the same time the policy generally supports profiles (DES, 1982a). Whether the assessments are norm-referenced or criterion-referenced is secondary.

Before leaving this topic, it is worth pointing out that the skill descriptions used in profiles so far developed for the school or further education system presuppose, because of the context-free requirement, that there really are abilities or skills which can be applied equally within different contexts. Thus, in mathematics, skills are defined in terms of symbolic *mathematical* operations so that a child who can 'calculate a percentage', for example, presumably can do so in all practical contexts. What many researchers have realized is that such symbolically defined skills do not necessarily transfer from one situation to another, since performance depends upon disposition and motivation, for example, as well as competence, and indeed that the autonomous existence of a 'skill' is itself rather a slippery notion. It is arguable that this issue is fundamental to skill assessment and that if profiles ignore it their relevance will be greatly diminished.

This discussion has been mainly in terms of comparability, which is an attribute of assessment principally required by the selector (for employment, further or higher education) who wants to compare one individual with another. With formative profiles, comparison with others is less important; the record can then concentrate upon what the student has done, and under what conditions, so that the context is specified. The record can be cumulative, so that development of skills or their application in new contexts can be observed and discussed: the comparison is with the individual's own past and not with others' current performance. Reliance upon grades and grids is no longer necessary, and some schemes like the Record of Personal Experience (for details, see Burgess and Adams, 1980) consist only of the students' own accounts of their experiences (validated by an adult), without comment or judgment by the teacher.

In those schemes where a common framework is needed for the recording of judgments, valid, reliable and comparable assessment can be achieved only if assessors are trained to interpret the concepts used. Discussions of what is meant by the concept, the contexts or occasions in which it might manifest itself, and the evidence that would allow judgments to be made about the degree to which it is present, are all essential. Discussion followed by ratings of particular examples can generate a calibrated comment bank that will allow others to be trained more quickly in the use of a particular scale. (For more information about comment banks see Black and Dockrell, 1981). Nevertheless, as pointed out above, once assessments are required to reflect learning contexts, true comparability becomes elusive. This will almost certainly happen if individual teachers or lecturers rate their own students.

There have been few studies of the degree to which the different scales in the profile are assessing separate attributes. In Scotland it was found that teachers were reluctant and often unable to make distinct assessments of personal qualities like honesty (SCRE, 1977), while Stratton found that improvements on one attribute were almost invariably matched by improvements on another (for example, 'working with authority' and 'self awareness') though his findings were not consistent across his two samples of raters (Stratton, 1982a). While more studies of this kind would be useful, one must accept that lack of discrimination between attributes may arise through the 'halo' effect, that is, the tendency of a rater's overall impression (favourable or unfavourable) of the student to influence all the individual ratings. More training of raters, especially more discussion of specific examples of behaviour, may well reduce the 'halo' effect and so convey more real information.

Scaling of Profile Elements

Whilst not all profile systems scale, if an employer or a teacher is offered a profile in which a number of disparate elements are each rated on a scale of

1–4 say, there is a clear invitation to compare the ratings. A student might be rated 1 (high) on 'planning a task' and also 1 on 'working with colleagues'. Yet if the former is applicable only to say 5 per cent of the population and the latter to 25 per cent it is difficult to see how the two ratings can be equated. Indeed, the only method of satisfactorily equating them is to define the ratings as applying to the same population percentages. Thus this would imply a direct 'norm-referencing' of the grades, and is again an issue which has been very little discussed. It is relevant to note the public examination boards' experience with equating grades in different subject areas. After some early work in the 1970s (Nuttall, Backhouse and Willmott, 1974) the attempt was abandoned once it was realized that this could be done only on a strictly norm-referenced basis as described above, thus violating the principle that the grading systems should not be solely norm-referenced.

There seems to be no good reason why there should be the same number of steps for each element. The number should be determined through experience and discussion so that the lowest should be in reach of all, and the highest, neither a ceiling which all reach nor a level which few reach. In some cases, there may be room for several intermediate steps, in others for one or even none. The Scottish Vocational Preparation Unit (1982) has drawn attention to the giant and uneven steps in many schemes, which could be avoided if the definitions of the scale points were generated by experienced practitioners familiar with the range of attainment in the population and using real examples of student behaviour.

Scaling done in this manner, leading to an appropriate number of steps for each element rather than forced into a uniform mould, might be less prone to invite inappropriate comparisons between ratings while, at the same time, leading to more attainable goals for students and lecturers.

Weighting and Combining Profile Elements

The grid type of profile tends implicitly to give equal weight to each element, leaving the user to choose the subset on which she or he wishes to concentrate. Once this subset is selected, however, there is still an implied equal weighting so that the user, in the absence of specific guidelines, presumably will attach equal weight to the selected elements. Yet, for a variety of reasons this may be inappropriate. Some elements may be measured with low reliability (see later), some skills may effectively appear several times in slightly different guises, some assessments may have stronger validity than others, etc. In other words, the user generally needs more information about the profile other than the profile itself, just as the traditional test user should have access to information on reliability, validity, norms, etc. Yet, given the already large quantity of data supplied in some profile systems, the provision of such extra information seems somewhat daunting. Some research to study users' needs and the way in which they use the information supplied would be welcome.

The weighting problem becomes of crucial importance if a user is to aggregate all or a subset of the elements. Not only will the above considerations apply, but the user will have her or his own relative weights and some guidance would be useful. In the absence of such guidance, there is a danger that many users will, often inappropriately, average in some simple fashion the ratings, grades or scores.

Weighting and combining elements is particularly tempting if performance is recorded quantitatively, and the temptation to make inappropriate combinations might be less in schemes where numbers are not attached to the descriptions of behaviour or evidence. The temptation to weight and combine elements is also reduced if each element does not have the same number of scale points.

Reliability

Quite a lot has been written about the reliability of grading systems, especially in public examinations (Willmott and Nuttall, 1975; Murphy, 1982) and it is now widely recognized that quite large measurement errors exist, so that there is a reasonably high probability that a student with a particular grade could have obtained a grade one or even two removed on a parallel examination, for example, one with a different set of questions or with a different marker. The reliability of the elements of a typical profile, often assessed subjectively or perhaps by means of a short skills test, could be very low, much lower than that of a public examination. Yet there is a negligible amount of serious effort devoted to studying this problem. Of course, as MacIntosh says, validity is fundamental and we have already said something about that. However, if a very unreliable profile is interpreted too literally by a user, serious mistakes can occur. Consider, for example, the SLAPONS profile designed to communicate arithmetic skills to employers (Pratley, 1982). Each element has a 'score' of from 0 to 5, yet as with many conventional examinations, there is little indication of whether a difference of 1 or 2 or 3 score points between students or between elements is to be treated as meaningful or could be within 'measurement error'.

It is, of course, quite difficult to obtain estimates of measurement error (the standard error of measurement as it is known in the context of standardized tests) and the most popular traditional methods seem of little use (Ecob and Goldstein, 1983). The measurement errors can arise from a number of sources. There are differences between assessors or raters. There is variation in the tasks on which students are judged and there is variation in the response given by the student from day to day or situation to situation. Also, in a profile, some of these measurement errors may be correlated and their effects thus compounded.

Stratton (1982b) studied the agreement between raters by asking them to place examples of behaviour on the profile scale. There was consensus for 71 per cent of the examples, though for about a third of these the consensus may have been spurious. A sound consensus therefore emerged only with just less than half the examples. The raters were, however, inexperienced, and Stratton concluded that agreement might be much higher among trained, experienced raters. But this study shows the magnitude of error that may arise from just one source, and reinforces the need for considerable careful research in order to provide some indication of measurement error. For example, a set of confidence intervals, based on rough estimates, one for each element, could be devised so that judgment of differences would occur only for non-overlapping intervals. These could also, in principle, be incorporated visually onto a profile chart, as is often provided with standardized test batteries, and we would suggest that those who are preparing profiles pay particular attention to this possibility.

Drawing attention to measurement error is particularly important with summative profiles because of the importance of the decisions that might be made in the light of the information contained in them. With formative profiles, where irrevocable decisions can be avoided, lower reliability might be tolerated if an increase in reliability can only be achieved at the expense of validity. But it is likely that the techniques used to enhance reliability, like more training, the use of two or more raters or gathering more evidence, are also those that will enhance validity by promoting clarification and deeper understanding of each element in the profile. Thus we again return to the importance of collaborative development and operation of profile systems, in which training occurs through discussion and rating of examples, and where the possibilities and limitations of a profile system can be illuminated.

Whither Profiles?

We have, quite deliberately, emphasized the current technical shortcomings of profile research and implementation. We do so not because we wish to argue against profiling as such, in fact quite the contrary because we believe that profiles do have interesting potential. It is because we are concerned that a too ready acceptance of a technically weak system will ultimately be counter-productive when its deficiencies become apparent during use. As we have indicated, in the well-established area of public examinations there are still considerable technical problems to overcome and in the sophisticated area of statistical test theory and psychometrics these controversies over fundamentals continue to rage. In both these areas, part of the case against the assessment techniques has rested on technical inadequacies. We are quite clear that the technical problems surrounding profiles are just as difficult as in these other areas and to ignore them would seem to be folly.

In our view, it would be wise to spend time now reflecting on these technical matters before too widespread and too rigid systems are developed.

From a research point of view there is no doubt that there are considerable challenges, and in the areas of reliability, scaling, weighting and studying 'skills' it should be possible to make useful progress.

Graded Tests

The graded tests movement shares many of the aims of the profiling movement, for example, a desire that education and assessment are seen as positive rather than negative experiences for all students, and a determination to put the curriculum first. Well-established in sport, music and other performing arts, graded tests are relatively recent arrivals in mainstream subjects of the secondary school curriculum, but have already made a dramatic impact upon the teaching and learning of modern languages and, in the Kent/Schools Council Mathematics Project, upon mathematics.

The basic idea of graded tests is not new and might be considered part of normal good practice. Phase tests in Technician Education Council (TEC) units, and indeed the TEC system of units at progressively higher levels (for example, maths 1, maths 2, maths 3), are straightforward examples of graded tests, where progress to the next level is contingent upon success at the previous level (a success that comes to most, if not all, students).

Yet graded tests have suddenly begun to attract a good deal of attention. The Cockcroft Report (DES, 1982b) has given graded tests — called 'graduated' tests there — further respectability and, in response to its recommendations, the DES has announced a substantial programme of research and development on graded tests in mathematics, principally for low attainers. Some of the modern language schemes are also designed principally for low attainers, but others are for the full ability range, as are most of the schemes in sport and the performing arts.

Perhaps the best known scheme (and certainly the oldest, founded some 100 years ago) is run by the Associated Board of The Royal Schools of Music. It attracted nearly 350,000 entries from the UK and Eire in 1980, an average of over 50,000 for each of the first five grades and sharply fewer (below 20,000) for the top three grades which involve a theory component as well as a practical. Each of the grades is designed to represent a defined standard of performance while the grades together form a progressive sequence of development in practical musicianship. The examination can be taken several times a year and the grades are not tied to particular ages, so that the scheme is tailored to the progress of each individual. Furthermore, as with sports, the choice of test items or pieces tends to be limited, with many elements, such as scales, known in advance.

Similar features, apart from the last, are characteristic of virtually all graded test schemes. In his review of graded tests (the most comprehensive and useful that is currently available), Harrison (1982) encapsulates the essence of a typical graded test scheme in modern languages in three features:

that it is progressive, with short-term objectives leading on from one to the next; that it is task-oriented, relating to the use of language for practical purposes; and that it is closely linked into the learning process, with pupils or students taking the tests when they are ready to pass.

The curricular side of the schemes is especially significant in modern languages, where the movement is known as Graded Objectives in Modern Languages (GOML) to emphasize that the guiding principle is in the development of a well-defined progression of educational objectives (building from the bottom upwards) rather than in the tests themselves.

Advocates of GOML schemes (of which there were about sixty in 1981, according to Harrison) point to the increased motivation of their pupils, with tangible proof given by dramatic increases in the proportion of third-year pupils opting for modern language courses in their curriculum in the vital fourth and fifth years. They also report that pupils and parents value the certificates issued for each grade.

Nevertheless, in most of what has been written about graded tests (as about profiles) there is little dispassionate evaluation, and it is therefore difficult to analyze what the key ingredients of their success in motivating pupils really are. One is almost certainly the short-term nature of the objectives allied to the principle of mastery learning and testing by way of criterion-referenced tests, which more than 90 per cent will pass in modern languages (and more than 80 per cent in music): that is, positive reinforcement, coupled with a tangible reward, at relatively frequent intervals (in contrast to public examinations where reward is stored until the end of five years of secondary education, and then is granted to the few rather than the many).

Another key ingredient is the enthusiasm of the teachers, sparked off, it would seem, by the curricular innovations of GOML. GOML schemes tend to be local and the teachers using the schemes have the chance to be involved in the further development of the schemes and in the assessment of their own pupils. This professional commitment is reminiscent of the early days of the Certificate of Secondary Education (CSE) examination, and may well be dissipated (as many would say has happened in the CSE) as the schemes become routine or are taken up by those who have not been party to the original development. In Oxfordshire, HM Inspectorate judged that in many schools there was still far to go in thinking about appropriate objectives for the less able, which stresses how difficult it is to translate laudable aims into effective classroom practice (HMI, 1983).

The most common type of problem raised by GOML teachers in the survey conducted by Harrison was organizational, for example, a lack of secretarial help, additional demands on time or the organizing of the oral test themselves. But it is apparent that the organizational problems posed by individual rates of progress have largely been ducked by teachers, who have used the expedient of testing all pupils at about the same time. HMI are critical of this failure to meet what most would regard as one of the cardinal principles of masterly learning:

> On the whole, however, it (the use of Oxfordshire's graded test scheme) tends to be confined to the less able pupils who all take the test at the same time . . . Even where groups have this measure of homogeneity it is clear that some pupils are being faced with too easy a test which for others is still too difficult . . . Thus, while the original intention of a high pass-rate is achieved, the timing of testing is more often related to the age of the pupils than to their linguistic readiness.

Sport and the performing arts tend to be taught either individually or in small groups as closely linked to age as school year groups, and therefore avoid the problem of modern languages. But that problem is likely to be as acute in mathematics and other subjects for which graded tests are currently being proposed, namely science and English.

It is clear that the individualization of learning, something that is likely to be accelerated by the microprocessor, creates organizational problems for an individual teacher or lecturer within the normal institutional constraints. Those concerned with whole institutions, such as principals, heads and LEAs, need to consider the implications of the widespread introduction of graded tests, and at least one Chief Education Officer has already welcomed the implied break with the tradition of grouping pupils by age and the possibility of grouping by attainment level or developmental stage instead (Brighouse, 1982).

The Curriculum and Graded Tests

Mansell remarked that 'profiling forces assessment into the learning process' ('A burst of interest' in *Profiles*, FEU, 1982); the worry of many is that graded tests will force assessment into the learning process not in the constructive way hoped for by Mansell, but in a destructive way that will lead to an excess of testing and to a backwash effect throughout the secondary school or further education curriculum that will make the backwash effect of the much maligned systems of examinations at 16+ look mild in comparison. *Curriculum-led assessment may be a splendid concept when the agreed curriculum commands enthusiasm and support*, as it manifestly does in modern languages, but where there is no agreed curriculum or where the field of study is not so vast that several different curricula are equally acceptable (as is the case of English), the particular subject curriculum that comes to lead the graded tests may be viewed by many teachers as a straitjacket. On the other hand, Pearce (1983) sees graded testing acting as a stimulus to sort out some of the problems of curriculum diversity:

Graduated testing on any scale would expose the flaws in our position with painful clarity. The real need is a machinery to enable teachers to negotiate agreed curricula and institutionalize those agreements with a necessary minimum of validation. That is what has happened with BEC, and to a different extent with TEC, with on the whole very encouraging consequences as well as the inevitable protests of those in whom the loss of their chains induces a state of terror.

One way to guard against the worst sort of backwash is to ensure that the assessment procedures validly measure the full diversity of curricular objectives. That requirement almost certainly demands an impressive array of oral, practical and written assessments, as well as course work, projects and other extended exercises so that we should talk of graded assessments rather than graded tests. Couple these assessments with the need for at least two formal occasions of testing each year at each grade level, and one arrives at a substantial assessment industry that is viable only if the teachers themselves accept a major role in the assessment of their own pupils.

The technical issues in assessment of pupils by teachers have been studied extensively (Cohen and Deale, 1977) and can be summed up in the two concepts of reliability and comparability. With criterion-referenced graded tests, achieving agreement about the criteria for marking among all those involved might be simpler than it is within traditional public examinations, but the variation in the conditions under which the tests are given and the variation in the tasks from school to school, and occasion to occasion, may wipe out any enhanced reliability of marking. Since there is a ready opportunity to retake a graded test, it might be argued that reliability of assessment is not as important as it is within the public examination system but this will depend upon the significance of the decisions made as a consequence of the test result.

There is a further fundamental difficulty which arises particularly acutely when a test can be retaken, namely the opportunity to learn, or teach to, the test itself, so that the curriculum will become distorted. To avoid this problem, tests would have to be changed between administrations and a moment's reflection will indicate the enormity of the task of continually developing new tests and equating then with the old, where testing takes place two or three times a year. The investment of time and expertise that this process requires is well represented in Holland and Rubin (1982). We are not aware that this issue has been faced seriously by the advocates of graded tests.

If mastery is in fact essential before a student can successfully work at the next level, then a false positive (a pass given when a fail should have been) may be as damaging as a false negative, which denies a student who is ready to move up the opportunity to do so. The consequences for individual students, especially at higher levels, where the results are more obviously for external consumption, may lead to too great an emphasis on striving for high reliability. As with public examinations, the fear would then be that the demand for high reliability will overide the demand for validity. This tension appears to be a common feature of assessment systems, and the direction in which it is resolved tends to be a function of the significance of the decisions made on the test results. Open entry to higher education, for example as in the Open University, would reduce the significance of 'A' level grades.

Similar concerns arise with the pressure for comparability. The more standardization that is imposed on the quest for reliability and comparability, the greater the threat to the key features of graded tests. One area in which comparability might reasonably be sought is over the number of levels in a graded test scheme designed principally for the age range 11 to 16. Most of the modern language schemes have five levels, and the Cockcroft Report suggests between four and six. But in the first case, the five levels span the full ability range and five years of secondary education, while in the second the target is just low attainers from the age of 14 upwards.

Determining Grade Levels

What considerations are important in the choice of the number of levels and their positioning or spacing? Educational theorists are not in sufficient agreement in most fields to provide an answer, and so the choice will be guided largely by practical considerations such as balancing the value of frequent feedback to students with the desire to avoid excessive testing. How the grades of the graded tests might be linked to the grades of public examinations, most obviously those at 16+, if indeed such a link is either desirable or feasible, is also a matter for much discussion in the GOML movement as more and more schemes develop level 4 and 5 material (for more detail about these issues, see Harrison, 1982, and Kingdon, 1983).

Of more fundamental concern is whether the concept of *progression* from one grade to the next makes sense in many subjects of the curriculum. While almost all subjects are taught on a broad principle of progress, this progress is not tied to the linear development of an unvarying set of objectives and there are many different ways of progressing through the same syllabus. Mastery of the objectives at one level may, therefore, not be essential to the study of the objectives at the next level, and graded tests could easily become simply modular tests, that is, tests on self-contained content that can be taken in any order and whose material can be forgotten without apparent penalty after the test has been taken.

In practice, the lack of differentiation and individualization in education (and the Oxfordshire modern language schemes are probably typical in this respect) probably serves to make the *graded* part of GOML tests relatively insignificant: the important things are teacher enthusiasm and pupil rewards. A modular scheme might serve just as well. The most precious ingredient, therefore, becomes teacher enthusiasm, which puts a premium on local self-determination and involvement and argues against making national or regional comparability so important that the development of graded tests becomes simply another centralized assessment activity.

Another issue is whether attainment of a grade or level, particularly when specified in criterion-referenced terms, can satisfactorily be determined at the gross level of a subject or has to be at a much more disaggregated level as we have discussed earlier in the case of profiles. In public examinations Orr and Nuttall (1983) *argue that true criterion-referencing and aggregation are incompatible*, and the same arguments would seem to apply to graded assessments. Harrison (1982) draws attention to the uneasy compromise between global certification and criterion-referencing that seems to be arising in some of the GOML schemes. Dealing with more narrowly defined skills or domains may help to make the progression through the grades more obvious, and allows for some skills to be put into cold storage at some levels while new ones are introduced, thus adding more flexibility in those cases where there is no single route of progress. At the same time, reasonably reliable separate assessments of many skills at each level may magnify the testing load unbearably, especially for the assessor.

Profiles and Graded Assessments

Thus there are a number of common, or very similar, issues facing profiles and graded assessments. In particular, the choice of the elements or dimensions that should be assessed deserves much deeper thought and investigation. At present, the dimensions have been chosen for sound educational (curriculum-led) reasons but without much subsequent exploration of overlap and redundancy. Sometimes a single dimension embraces multiple objectives that are better separated. More careful specification of the objectives and the evidence needed to determine whether they have been successfully or partially achieved would clearly be beneficial, and could be followed after the event by the straightforward analyses used by Stratton (1982a) to detect redundancy (or possible 'halo' effect).

Deciding upon the number of reporting levels and the size of the steps is also a shared problem. Its solution must be rooted in the experience of teachers and lecturers whose knowledge of the typical performance and the range of performance in the particular population of pupils or students is vital. But too great a reliance on the norms of the past should be avoided; both profiles and graded assessments have stimulated unexpected improvements in motivation and attainment, and the definition of the steps should therefore be carried out in action rather than determined in advance.

This leads to the suggestion that more needs to be established about the effects of profiles and graded assessments upon students and lecturers. It was suggested above that the notion of 'grades' or 'progression' might be relatively unimportant and that the key ingredients were public rewards for the students and the enthusiasm of the teachers, but this is still speculative. Investigations of profile schemes in action (following Goacher, and Stratton) and evaluation of the new graded test developments are essential. This is particularly important where graded test schemes are being devised only for the 'low attainers', since the dangers of labelling in this procedure are only too obvious; there are, in any case, considerable but rarely discussed problems in actually defining, for example, the 'lowest 40 per cent of the ability range'.

Both profiles and graded tests make the curriculum that leads them much more obtrusive than the system of conventional examinations. The consequence is that, if lecturers and teachers are to preserve their freedom in choice of teaching strategy and examples relevant to the local context, both kinds of developments must be local rather than national (though a national *framework* is, of course, not ruled out). The inherent limitations in the concept of comparability must be exposed so that the advantages of formative assessment can be permitted to flourish (Goldstein, 1982; Orr and Nuttall, 1983). But by putting emphasis on the local, the pressing need for training of assessors is also emphasized and made more urgent.

Although some profile schemes imply that each dimension is judged in the same way on a four-point scale, the evidence for the judgments can be of very different kinds, ranging from single subjective appraisals of personal qualities to cumulative test-based assessments of numerical skills. In the latter case, there is potentially a very obvious marriage of profiles and graded assessments.

It comes as no surprise, then, that profiles and graded tests are being brought together. The Cockcroft Report envisaged that performance in the graded tests might contribute to the kind of profile described above, an idea that has rapidly been taken up by a number of LEAs and examining bodies. For example, the ILEA is proposing a 'London Record of Achievement', a portfolio containing details of examination passes, other achievements in school and a profile compiled by teachers, parents and the pupils themselves (reported in Education, 19 November 1982). The portfolio will also contain the results of graded tests in mathematics, English, a foreign language (European or Asian), science, and design and technology, though development work has begun only in mathematics, English and science.

Even more advanced are the plans for the Oxford Certificate of Educational Achievement (OCEA), run by the Oxford Delegacy of Local Examinations (also responsible for GCE examinations) in conjunction with a number of LEAs including Oxfordshire, and the University Department of Educational Studies. The Certificate will have three components:

(i) the P-component, a personal record or report of achievements;
(ii) the E-component, a record of public examination grades;
(iii) the G-component, a record of graded assessments in English, mathematics, modern languages and science (Oxford Delegacy, 1983a and 1983b).

The principal contrast between graded assessments and profiles (anyway, in their record form rather than the grid form) lies in their stance towards quantification and measurement. Graded assessments are firmly within the psychometric tradition of tests and examinations, while the advocates of profiles are often against measurement and the reductionism and trivialization that all too often accompany measurement. So, in the union of profiles and graded assessments, we see the exciting prospect of bringing together the humanistic and quantitative traditions in educational assessment. From this could emerge a most fruitful collaboration that could give a new rigour to humanistic assessment while preserving the pre-eminence of validity and curricular relevance.

To achieve this, action research is essential, integrating the development with the evaluation, and analyzing the processes of selection, judgment and interpretation in the development and use of the assessments within the context of the college, school and workplace. While the technical issues we have discussed also need to be studied, what is *not* needed is the sort of detailed technical research of the type that has been done for fifty years on existing examination systems, largely atheoretical and motivated by a desire to provide merely technical answers to essentially educational problems. Just as the accent in assessment moves to stress its formative value rather than its summative use, so the research should develop so as to be sensitive to such changes.

Acknowledgments

We gratefully acknowledge the constructive comments on an earlier draft of this paper made by Geoff Bardell, Tricia Broadfoot, Bob Fairbrother, Derek Foxman, Andrew Harrison, Keith Kimberley, Mike Kingdon, Jack Mansell, Peter Mortimore, Malcolm Skillbeck, Stephen Steadman and Alison Wolf.

References

BALOGH, J. (1982) *Profile Reports for School Leavers*, London, Longman for the Schools Council.

BLACK, H.D. and DOCKRELL, W.B. (1981) *Diagnostic Assessment in Secondary Schools*, Hodder and Stoughton for the SCRE.

BRIGHOUSE, T. (1982) Article in *Education*, 24/31 December, p. 491.

BROADFOOT, P. (1982) 'The pros and cons of profiles', *Forum*, 24, pp. 66–9.

BURGESS, T. and ADAMS, E. (Eds) (1980) *Outcomes of Education*, London, Macmillan Education.

COHEN, L. and DEALE, R.N. (1977) *Assessment by Teachers in Examinations at 16+*, Schools Council Examinations Bulletin 37, London, Evans/Methuen.

DEPARTMENT OF EDUCATION AND SCIENCE (1982a) *17+: A New Qualification*, London, HMSO.

DEPARTMENT OF EDUCATION AND SCIENCE (1982b) *Mathematics Counts* (The Cockcroft Report), London, HMSO.

ECOB, R. and GOLDSTEIN, H. (1983) 'Instrumental variable methods for the estimation of test scoring reliability', *Journal of Educational Statistics*, fall, 8, 3.

FEU (1982a) *A Basis for Choice* (2nd edn), London, FEU.

FEU (1982b) *Profiles*, London, FEU.

GOACHER, B. (1983) *Recording Achievement at 16+*, London, Longman for the Schools Council.

GOLDSTEIN, H. (1982) 'Models for equating test scores and for studying the comparability of public examinations', *Educational Analysis*, 4, 3, pp. 107–18.

HARRISON, A.W. (1982) *Review of Graded Tests*, Schools Council Examinations Bulletin 41, London, Methuen Educational.

HARRISON, A.W. (1983) *Profile Reporting of Examination Results*, Schools Council Examination Bulletin 43, London, Methuen Educational.

HMI (1983) *A Survey of the Use of Graded Tests of Defined Objectives and Their Effect on the Teaching and Learning of Modern Languages in the County of Oxfordshire*, London, DES.

HOLLAND, P. and RUBIN, D. (Eds) (1982) *Test Equating*, New York, Academic Press.

KINGDON, J.M. (1983) 'Graded tests', paper presented at an informal seminar at the University of London Institute of Education.

MACINTOSH, H.G. (1982) 'A 17+ package: A View from the School', *Profiles*, London, FEU.

MANSELL, J. (1982) 'A burst of interest', *Profiles*, London, FEU.

MURPHY, R.J.L. (1982) 'A further report of investigations into the reliability of marking of GCE examinations', *British Journal of Educational Psychology*, pp. 58–63.

NUTTALL, D.L., BACKHOUSE, J. and WILLMOTT, A.S. (1974) *Comparability of Standards Between Subjects*, Schools Council Examinations Bulletin 29, London, Evans/Methuen Educational.

ORR, L. and NUTTALL, D.L. (1983) *Determining Standards in the Proposed Single System of Examining at 16+*, London, Schools Council.

OXFORD DELEGACY (1983a) *Oxford Certificate of Educational Achievement Newsletter, Issue Number 1*, Oxford, Oxford Delegacy of Local Examinations.

OXFORD DELEGACY (1983b) *Oxford Certificate of Educational Achievement Newsletter, Issue Number 2*, Oxford, Oxford Delegacy of Local Examinations.

PEARCE, J. (1983) 'The future of graded tests', *Education*, 17 June, pp. 465–6.

PRATLEY, B. (1982) 'Profiles in practice', *Profiles*, London, FEU.

SCOTTISH COUNCIL FOR RESEARCH IN EDUCATION (1977) *Pupils in Profile*, Hodder and Stoughton for the SCRE.

SCOTTISH VOCATIONAL PREPARATION UNIT (1982) *Assessment in Youth Training: Made-to-measure?*, Edinburgh, Jordanhill College.

STRATTON, N. (1982a) *An Evaluation of a Basic Abilities Profiling System Across a Range of Education and Training Provision* (interim report for CGLI Profiling Project 3), London, CGLI.

STRATTON, N. (1982b) 'Reliability of basic skills profiles', paper given at the annual meeting of the British Educational Research Association, St Andrews.

WILLMOTT, A.S. and NUTTALL, D.L. (1975) *The Reliability of Examinations at 16+*, London, Macmillan Education.

Nuttall, D.L. (1986a) 'What can we learn from research on testing and appraisal?' in Dockrell, B. *et al.* (Eds) *Appraising Appraisal* (report of a conference organized by the British Educational Research Association at Sheffield, 11 March), Kendal, BERA.

Introduction

Teacher appraisal was one of a number of management techniques imported into the education service during the 1980s. Although much in harmony with the Thatcher Government's emphasis on market principles to achieve greater efficiency, quality and hence, productivity in education, the idea was not of its creation. Rather it was an idea of growing international currency which, as Desmond Nuttall points out in this paper, had already been the subject of three decades of research in the industrial context, especially in the USA. As far as UK education was concerned, however, it was an idea whose time had come. As Nisbet and Broadfoot (1980) suggest, research typically starts to influence policy and practice in education after a period of slow incremental growth and only when the ideas match the policy-climate of the day. Teacher appraisal is a classic example of this. Sir Keith Joseph, who was Secretary of State for Education and Science in the early 1980s, was an ardent protagonist of market principles. A keen Thatcher supporter, he was quick to seize on the idea of assessing teacher quality as a way of weeding out incompetents from the profession. As a highly intelligent and experienced politician he was, however, quick to recognize his mistake as the backlash of teacher disquiet and resolute teacher union opposition forced him to adopt a less simplistic view of the matter and to begin to consider possible alternative approaches. The pioneering Suffolk LEA experiment in particular was to establish the alternative idea of appraisal as a formative technique designed to enhance teaching quality through professional development for all rather than the dismissal of a few incompetents.

These two different conceptions of the purpose of teacher appraisal were to dog the developing debate on the matter throughout the 1980s (Hartley and Broadfoot, 1987). It is a tension that is clearly evident in this article in which Desmond Nuttall explores some of the key issues informing the debate. In particular, he questions how the reality of classroom practice might be added to the rhetoric of discussion, a problem that has continued to dog the progressive implementation of teacher appraisal as it throws up all sorts of technical issues concerning how best such observation may be conducted.

Desmond Nuttall's discussion of teacher appraisal in the light of available research findings leads him to conclude, once again, that giving teachers scope for the operation of an autonomous, collaborative professionalism is one of the keys to raising the overall standard of pupil learning. Subsequent experience has vindicated this view — at least as far as teacher appraisal is concerned, experience which could be informing other assessment policy debates but, sadly, is not.

WHAT CAN WE LEARN FROM RESEARCH ON TEACHING AND APPRAISAL?

Introduction

The purpose of this paper is to look at research into teaching and appraisal to see what we might learn about good practice and potential pitfalls. Research on teaching is, of course, a vast field — a recent annotated bibliography (Powell and Beard, 1984) lists no fewer than 3041 studies of teacher effectiveness — and, when coupled with the rapidly expanding field of school effectiveness, cannot possibly be comprehensively surveyed in the space of this paper. But I hope to be able to draw a few lessons that are relevant to the practice of teacher appraisal.

Research on appraisal is well established in industry, commerce, the Civil Service and other public sector organizations (which from this point I simply label industry) on both sides of the Atlantic (see, for example, Fletcher and Williams, 1985). Although I think many would agree with Taylor (1976) that there are dangers in importing industrial approaches into schools and classrooms, I believe that many of the lessons painfully learnt in three decades of research into appraisal in industry do have relevance for education, as I shall attempt to show later. And there is a growing body of research into teacher appraisal, mainly in the USA but increasingly here as well.

The Current State of the Art

Teacher evaluation is now mandated in more than half the states of the USA, though in most cases the responsibility is simply placed upon the local school districts to develop a scheme. In almost every case, the primary purpose is considered to be 'teacher improvement' but pressures for accountability have often meant that schemes also have summative purposes (tenure decisions, promotion, merit pay). The conflicts that arise from combining summative and formative purposes are a constant theme in the literature (see, for example, Darling-Hammond *et al.*, 1983; and Stenning and Stenning, 1984).

From a survey of thirty-two well-developed schemes in the USA, McLaughlin (1982) provides a characterization of a typical scheme: a pre-evaluation conference, classroom observation, followed by a post-evaluation conference leading to a written action plan whose implementation is monitored. Nevertheless, there is 'a general lack of integration between teacher evaluation and staff development or district curriculum guidelines'. There is also little agreement about 'instrumentation' (and hence criteria) and the role of the teacher in the process.

Research in this country (for example, HMI, 1985a; James and Newman, 1985; Suffolk Education Department, 1985; Turner and Clift, 1985) paints a rather different picture. Emerging schemes, as devised by individual schools, are almost exclusively formative, but geared primarily to identifying desires for in-service activities or for other kinds of experience (for example, a spell as acting unpaid second deputy head of year) that might enhance career development. The predominant model is the industrial one of an interview centred on target-setting and the evaluation of targets set on previous occasions, coupled with an identification of appropriate career development plans and training needs. Indeed, the Identikit picture of a British appraisal system in industry given by Fletcher and Williams (1985) could almost serve as an Identikit picture of a British teacher appraisal scheme. Classroom observation is rarely a part of British schemes, and the survey by James and Newman (1985) indicates that schemes currently being devised by schools are less likely to involve classroom observation than those already established. There are exceptions, of course: schemes being fostered, often on a pilot basis, by LEAs tend to combine summative and formative purposes and to be rather more comprehensive (Butterworth, 1986), and some school-devised schemes include classroom observation (sometimes by peers in co-observation), or are based on departmental review which combines classroom observation and individual appraisal with organizational and curricular review (Turner and Clift, 1985). Most of these schemes have not been in existence long enough for their effects to be well documented, and in many cases the Hawthorne effect is noticeable or the honeymoon is yet to be over. Inevitably the studies of HM Inspectorate (HMI, 1985a) and Duncan Graham and his colleagues (Suffolk Education Department, 1985) were short-term, while the detailed and longer term case studies of my colleagues, Phil Clift and Glenn Turner, and of James and Newman at

Bath are not yet complete. So it is difficult to speak with any authority about the effects of British appraisal schemes.

The Assessment of Teaching Performance

Before turning to the lessons of research and experience about good practice, I would like to raise a few issues about teaching performance that have to be grappled with in any discussion of teacher appraisal. As I do so, I would ask you to bear in mind the criteria for a good appraisal scheme put forward by John Nisbet, namely that it should be beneficial, fair, comprehensive, valid, open, effective in producing changes and, last but by no means least, practicable.

The Place of Classroom Observation

All the speakers here today are agreed that the way to improve the quality of teaching and learning must lie to a very large extent in what goes on in classrooms. HMI (1985a) share that view: 'Without classroom observation appraisal will lack real evidence of teaching skill and provide little that can be built upon to secure improvement'. Other commentators are harsher: 'The appraisal interview leaves in abeyance the gaps between rhetoric and reality' (Adelman, 1985). One can speculate as to the reasons why so many British schemes do not include classroom observation, and some reasons might not reflect too well upon the professionalism of teachers. But I suggest that in part the mismatch may be due to teachers' needs for job satisfaction, job enrichment and career development in a climate where mobility and promotion prospects have dramatically declined, while commentators are more interested in the quality of student learning.

What Criteria?

Another possible reason for caution on the part of teachers about observation of classroom performance is the lack of agreement about the criteria to be used in assessing performance. Without specified and known criteria, there is the fear of subjectivity and nepotism, but even with specified criteria the judgment of performance may not be valid. Criteria for judging teaching have evolved over a century, as Grace (1985) shows: for a long time, as in industry, personal traits like reliability and leadership predominated, but stimulated by McGregor's famous article in 1957 the accent is now on performance, the attainment of targets and 'can-do' skills (as it is in the field of student assessment).

HMI (1982 and 1985b) have become more explicit about their criteria, which for their survey of probationary teachers were grouped under the head-ings of: the relationship developed with the pupils, the match of work to the pupils' capabilities, the use of language in the classroom, and the choice and exploitation of teaching materials. Taylor (1985) believes that the extensive work on teacher effectiveness has at last begun to bear fruit, though the qualities of a good teacher (for example, the promoting of active learning and active learning time and the use of praise) are not straightforward or easily assessable (see also Kyriacou, 1985). Ed Stones would fully agree about the complexity of the teacher's task; he has based his work on teaching primarily on what we know about learning, and has been very critical of the variety and crudity of the assessment of teaching practice (Stones and Morris, 1972). Although much teacher effectiveness research can be criticized on methodo-logical grounds (Elliott, 1985; Stones, 1975; Turner, Nuttall and Clift, 1986), at least two messages come through loud and clear: the complexity of the task, and the importance of context. A teacher who is effective with one group of students at one level in one school is not necessarily equally effective with another group. Any teacher appraisal scheme has to be sensitive to this point, as HMI claim to be but without offering substantiation or example (HMI, 1982). They found quite a significant negative correlation between ratings of quality of teaching performance and the constraints outside the teacher's control (for example, lack of resources): −0.43 in the primary phase and −0.38 in the secondary. But we do not know how they made allowances for constraints in their ratings of quality.

The difficulty of securing agreement upon criteria (that should, of course, vary from job to job within teaching, by level, phase, subject and role) should not be underestimated. The criteria employed embody particular views of teaching — as labour, as a craft, as a profession or as an art — on which there may be little consensus, and their validity may be suspect. Capie (1985) argues that the State of Georgia is almost unique in employing criteria of teacher competence that have demonstrated empirical relationships with pupil learn-ing; in most other cases, validity is just assumed. Moreover, the approach encourages concentration on individual criteria or competencies; Peaker (1986) points to the frequent absence of any holistic assessment and Doyle (1984) argues that 'some excellent teachers will be missed if the present body of knowledge about effective teaching is used as a profile to select master teachers'. As Taylor (1985) said in another context, 'Effectiveness requires the right mix, not just the right ingredients'.

Doing Classroom Observation

Even if we have agreement on the criteria to use in the classroom, our prob-lems are not over. Methodology and instrumentation are not value-free (Burgess, 1985a), and even with the most structured of observation schedules, observers will not always agree. For example, with detailed criteria but not fully structured observation, HMI (1982) found that their ratings of teaching performance correlated only to the extent of 0.44 (primary) and 0.38 (secondary) with Heads' more general ratings of quality. We would be foolish, too, to ignore all that we have learned about methodology from qualitative, less structured classroom observation (see, for example, Burgess, 1985b).

So, even if we agree that we must assess teaching performance by observation of classroom practices, we still face a major debate about how we do it fairly, comprehensively, validly and constructively.

The Qualities of a Good Appraisal Scheme

I now turn to what research has to say about what makes (or at least facilitates) a good appraisal scheme, that is one that will, by and large, meet John Nisbet's criteria. There is much common ground in the literature, though my list is not identical with any of those in my principal sources (Darling-Hammond *et al.*, 1983; Fletcher and Williams, 1985; HMI, 1985a; Stiggins and Bridgeford, 1984; Suffolk Education Department, 1985). I also note that most of the qualities are those advocated for successful institutional self-evaluation (see Nuttall, 1981 and forthcoming).

First, there is the facilitating effect of a tradition of institutional self-evaluation and constructive self-criticism. More generally, a climate of trust among the staff, and between head and teachers, a good professional self-image, high morale and a commitment to appraisal and to acting upon its results, especially from the top, are all helpful. Commitment from the top is perhaps best demonstrated by a willingness to be the first to undergo appraisal: in the light of the Education Bill, the first candidate for appraisal is obvious.

Secondly, there is a general consensus that an effective scheme *cannot* serve formative and summative purposes simultaneously. Industry has learnt this lesson, and usually has separate systems for the two sets of purposes; conversely, experience from the USA shows that in a dual-purpose scheme, summative considerations usually prevail, resulting in negligible teacher improvement. Furthermore, as Stiggins and Bridgeford (1984) point out, summative procedures usually have to be hammered out by collective bargaining and therefore tend to be standardized and bureaucratic, when what is needed is responsive, flexible schemes. I have to say, though, that the work of colleagues and myself on institutional self-evaluation demonstrates that formative and summative purposes can co-exist within the same scheme (Nuttall, forthcoming). I also wonder whether there are enough resources and time for separate schemes for different purposes, and whether one can ensure that information derived during the course of formative appraisal is not used, indirectly if not directly, when summative decisions are being made.

Thirdly, a good scheme must link the results of appraisal to appropriate action — one of John Nisbet's criteria. Promises must be kept, and the resources for appropriate staff development activity (inside and outside the institution) must be made available. More than that, though, the nature and the quality of the feedback given after classroom observation and in the appraisal interview deserve careful consideration: critical comment should be limited and balanced with recognition of success (or relative success). A joint problem-solving approach that focuses on the job and its problems rather than on the individual and his or her characteristics also helps. But all of this has to be seen not as offering universal rules but considerations to be adapted in the light of individual and institutional circumstances. (I particularly recommend the book by Fletcher and Williams, 1985, on this topic of feedback.)

Fourthly, and perhaps most crucially, there is the importance of involving those who will be appraised in the process. At one level, this means involving them in the development of any scheme, rather than imposing it upon them. At a deeper level, it means ensuring that self-appraisal is an important component (if it cannot be the only component for reasons of credibility or comparability). Self-appraisal has long been advocated in industrial schemes (McGregor, 1957) but I must note the view expressed by Heron in 1981 (cited by Fletcher and Williams, 1985) that people need help with self-appraisal because 'our educational institutions do not equip people with either the expectations or the skills of self-appraisal — assessment is something that is handed down from above throughout schooling (and that, perhaps, is the root of some of the defensive reactions to appraisal)'. Maybe that accusation will be easier to rebut when profiling and student-centred reviewing become fully established in our schools and colleges. The contribution of critical self-appraisal to the improvement of classroom practice has been well demonstrated by people like Elliott and Adelman, especially in the Ford Teaching Project, and promoted not least by the Open University in its courses on curriculum evaluation (P234, *Curriculum in Action*, and E364, *Curriculum Evaluation and Assessment in Educational Institutions*). I therefore believe that the case for self-evaluation has been overwhelmingly demonstrated, but in a manner that is demanding of time and effort and that is responsive and context-specific (i.e., not guided by preordained criteria). We are back to the models of teaching and the teacher embodied in different approaches to appraisal.

This leads to my fifth nostrum: a good scheme must give the teacher some autonomy. Glasman and Paulin (1982) show that the acceptability of schemes to teachers depends upon their having some continuing control over the process. Given all the evidence about the degree to which teacher effectiveness is specific to the context, any scheme must be responsive to particular circumstances: leaving some control in the hands of the individual teacher can guarantee a measure of responsiveness, and a greater feeling of ownership of the criteria and hence greater confidence in their validity. The extent to which different standards might be applied to different individuals or in different circumstances has also to be considered, as John Nisbet argues.

My sixth point bears on this issue: a shared understanding of both criteria and processes among all parties is essential, which also means that there must be a clear understanding of the role each party plays. This is particularly important when the teacher being appraised has some control over the criteria or the standards employed (or both).

My next two points refer mainly to procedures. First, schemes which employ more than one observer or appraiser gain reliability and validity, as well as credibility, particularly if peers are involved as well as superiors (Peaker, 1986). For appropriate phases of education, one can extend this point to embrace the views of students: Murray (1984) has shown how ratings by university students of their lecturers' performance, when appropriately combined with other evidence, can contribute to improved teaching performance. Secondly, research in industry has shown the value of using ipsative rating scales, that is, scales that ask raters to compare the performance of the individual on one dimension with his or her performance on the other dimensions to indicate *relative* strengths and weaknesses (rather than normatively against the performance of the 'average' teacher which risks the demotivating effects of a straight E profile).

Finally, *none* of these desirable qualities can be realized without adequate training. This point has been made so often that I will not elaborate upon it, save to say that training must embrace not only particular skills (such as those of observation, interviewing and counselling) but also more general managerial skills *and* a discussion of values and assumptions.

I have created a daunting list, I am aware, but I think it would be hard to meet John Nisbet's criteria without satisfying most of them. Similarly, they are necessary conditions to meet two of the minimal conditions specified by Darling-Hammond *et al.* (1983) (and quoted by Stiggins and Bridgeford, 1984) for a successful teacher evaluation system:

> All participants understand how [the] criteria and processes relate to the basic goals of the organization; ie, there is a shared sense that the criteria reflect the most important aspects of teaching, that the evaluation system is consonant with their educational goals and conceptions of teaching.
>
> Teachers perceive that the evaluation procedure enables and motivates them to improve their performance; and principals perceive that it enables them to provide instructional leadership.

The Effects of Appraisal

As I said earlier, the effects of appraisal schemes are not well researched, especially in this country; furthermore, research is usually concerned with the appraisees' *perceptions* of the effects rather than with more independent observations. In comparative studies in industry, Fletcher and Williams (1985) report that 30 per cent (of nearly 6000 appraisees) reported that their job satisfaction had been increased by the appraisal interview and 40 per cent thought that their job performance had improved (or was likely to improve) as a result of their interview. (The best figures achieved by an organization were 40 and 54 per cent respectively.) In education, Suffolk Education Department (1985) noted an enhanced professionalism among teachers, an open, welcoming ethos in schools and a willingness of teachers to discuss their appraisal cycle. But some of these may have been pre-existing conditions rather than effects. Geoffrey Samuel (1984) detects the creation of 'an atmosphere of openness and honesty that is conducive to genuine professionalism' as a result of the appraisal scheme introduced in his own school. HMI (1985a) make similar points about openness, and the enhancement of teachers' professionalism, particularly greater awareness and understanding of curricular and organizational aims; they even indicate that in many cases there is improved performance on the part of individual teachers. Only occasionally, then, do we get a hint that pupils might be gaining as a result of the appraisal of their teachers.

Perhaps it is inevitable that the predominance of the appraisal interview within and outside education in the UK couped with the absence of observation of job performance mean that the satisfaction of the appraisees becomes the principal criterion for judging the effectiveness of appraisal schemes. Indeed it is a reasonable hypothesis that, to put it simply, the happiness of teachers leads to improved learning on the part of children. But I, for one, would like to explore the mechanisms of this hypothesis rather more rigorously since like Bill Taylor (1985) I believe that 'the ultimate test of any policy or initiative is whether it secures real improvement at the level where it really counts . . . Improvement starts and ends with quality of pupil learning'.

References

ADELMAN, C. (1985) 'Teacher appraisal', paper for the Fourth Cambridge Conference on Educational Evaluation.

BURGESS, R.G. (1985a) 'A problem in search of a method or a method in search of a problem? A critique of teacher appraisal', paper for the Fourth Cambridge Conference on Educational Evaluation.

BURGESS, R.G. (Ed) (1985b) *Strategies of Educational Research: Qualitative Methods*, Lewes, Falmer Press.

BUTTERWORTH, I.B. (1986) 'The appraisal of teachers', Educational Management Information Exchange Paper, Slough, NFER.

CAPIE, W. (1985) 'Coming of age: Systematic performance evaluation', *Educational Measurement: Issues and Practice*, 4, 3.

DARLING-HAMMOND, L., WISE, A.E. and PEASE, S.R. (1983) 'Teacher evaluation in the organizational context: A review of the literature', *Review of Educational Research*, 53, 3.

DOYLE, W. (1984) 'Effective teaching and the concept of the master teacher', paper presented at the annual meeting of the American Educational Research Association, New Orleans.

ELLIOTT, J. (1985) 'Evaluating teaching quality', *British Journal of Sociology of Education*, 6, 1.

FLETCHER, C. and WILLIAMS, R. (1985) *Performance Appraisal and Career Development*, London, Hutchinson.

GLASMAN, N.S. and PAULIN, P.J. (1982) 'Possible determinants of teacher receptivity to evaluation', *Journal of Educational Administration*, 20, 2.

GRACE, G. (1985) 'Judging teachers: The social and political contexts of teacher evaluation', *British Journal of Sociology of Education*, 6, 1.

HMI (1982) *The New Teacher in School*, London, HMSO.

HMI (1985a) *Quality in Schools: Evaluation and Appraisal*, London, HMSO.

HMI (1985b) *Education Observed 3: Good Teachers*, London, DES.

JAMES, C.R. and NEWMAN, J.C. (1985) 'Staff appraisal schemes in comprehensive schools: A regional survey of current practice in the South Midlands and the South West of England', *Educational Management and Administration*, 13, 3.

KYRIACOU, C. (1985) 'Conceptualising research on effective teaching', *British Journal of Educational Psychology*, 55, 2.

MCLAUGHLIN, M.W. (1982) *A Preliminary Investigation of Teacher Evaluation Practices*, Santa Monica, CA, The Rand Corporation.

MCGREGOR, D. (1957) 'An uneasy look at performance appraisal', *Harvard Business Review*, 35.

MURRAY, H.G. (1984) 'The impact of formative and summative evaluation of teaching in North American universities', *Assessment and Evaluation in Higher Education*, 9.

NUTTALL, D.L. (1981) *School Self-Evaluation: Accountability with a Human Face?* York, Longman for Schools Council.

NUTTALL, D.L. (Ed) (forthcoming) *Studies in School Self-Evaluation*, Lewes, Falmer Press.

PEAKER, G.T. (1986) 'Teacher management and appraisal in two school systems in the southern USA', *Journal of Education for Teaching*, 12, 1.

POWELL, M. and BEARD, J.W. (1984) *Teacher Effectiveness: An Annotated Bibliography and Guide to Research*, New York, Garland.

SAMUEL, G. (1984) 'A formal assessment of performance', *Education*, 5, October.

STENNING, W.I. and STENNING, R. (1984) 'The assessment of teachers' performance: some practical considerations', *School Organization and Management Abstracts*, 3, 2.

STIGGINS, R.J. and BRIDGEFORD, N.J. (1984) 'Performance assessment for teacher development', paper presented at the annual meeting of the American Educational Research Association, New Orleans.

STONES, E. (1975) 'How long is a piece of string?' in *How Long is a Piece of String?*, London, Society for Research into Higher Education.

STONES, E. and MORRIS, S. (1972) 'The assessment of practical teaching', *Educational Research*, 14, 2.

SUFFOLK EDUCATION DEPARTMENT (1985) *Those Having Torches . . . Teacher Appraisal: A Study*, Ipswich, Suffolk Education Department.

TAYLOR, W. (1976) 'The head as manager' in PETERS, R.S. (Ed) *The Role of the Head*, London, Routledge and Kegan Paul.

TAYLOR, W. (1985) 'The task of the school and the task of the teacher' paper for the DES Conference *Better Schools: Evaluation and Appraisal*, Birmingham.

TURNER, G. and CLIFT, P.S. (1985) *A First Review and Register of School and College Based Teacher Appraisal Schemes*, Milton Keynes, Open University School of Education.

TURNER, G., NUTTALL, D.L. and CLIFT, P.S. (1986) 'Staff appraisal' in HOYLE, E. and A MCMAHON, A. (Eds) *World Yearbook of Education 1986*, London, Kogan Page.

Nuttall, D.L. (1986b) 'Problems in the measurement of change' in Nuttall, D.L. (Ed) *Assessing Educational Achievement*, Lewes, Falmer Press.

Introduction

This next paper is taken from a book, entitled *Assessing Educational Achievement*, which Desmond Nuttall edited for Falmer Press in 1986. The papers in that book were all updated versions of ones which had appeared in a special issue of the journal *Educational Analysis* in 1982. The collection spans the breadth of Desmond Nuttall's assessment interests, bringing together the work of sociologists, psychologists, statisticians and educational administrators each working on different aspects of assessment change within the UK, along with contributions from Australia, Canada and the USA. Desmond Nuttall's paper also demonstrates that breadth as he analyzes a variety of approaches that have been applied to the measurement of educational change in the UK as well as internationally.

Within an education system that has often been accused of being excessively introverted and navel-gazing, Desmond Nuttall always stood out as someone who was knowledgeable about developments overseas. His regular quoting of evidence from the USA, Canada, Sweden, Australia etc., revealed another significant part of the body of evidence upon which he based his judgments. All of this required extensive networking, at which he was exceptionally good. As Harvey Goldstein stated in an obituary, published in *Research Intelligence* in 1993:

> It was amazing how Desmond seemed to know almost everybody working in education, and not merely in Britain. One would continually discover new people he was advising or working with, whether in Lancashire, Mauritius or Boston. (p. 40)

This paper, as well as portraying Desmond Nuttall's breadth of perspective on measurement of change methodologies, also puts forward a rigorous critique of psychometric latent-trait solutions, which have in the past been assumed to hold the key to solving difficult assessment comparisons. This chapter was followed by two further papers in both the journal and book versions of the collection by Harvey Goldstein and Bob Wood, which Desmond Nuttall modestly referred to in both introductions as 'the most important and most enduring in the collection'. These three scholars together have between them in fact presented a consistently good case for starting to treat educational assessment as a field requiring its own theories and techniques of analysis, rather than as a sub-set of psychometrics. This is a challenge that others are now taking up in the mid 1990s (see for example Gipps, 1994).

PROBLEMS IN THE MEASUREMENT OF CHANGE

The essence of education is change, the acquisition of mental processes, skills and attitudes that were not present before, or the development and improvement of existing ones. It follows that the assessment or measurement of this change is important in education, both to chart the development and to match teaching strategies to the individual's changing needs. A good example of instruments designed for this purpose are the checklists focussing on children's development in scientific thinking developed by Harlen *et al.* (1977). This formative use of assessment is becoming more widely recognized and promoted, as Black's chapter in this volume demonstrates.

But the measurement of change is fraught with problems, especially in the common research strategy using pre-test — post-test designs yielding gain scores (see, for example, Harris, 1963). Cronbach and Furby (1970) go as far as to argue that 'gain scores are rarely useful, no matter how they may be adjusted or refined' (p. 68) and offer some recommended procedures that obviate the need to estimate change scores for individuals. The reanalysis by Aitken, Bennett and Hesketh (1981) of Bennett's (1976) study of teaching styles and pupil progress avoids the use of gain scores, and by working at the level of classrooms rather than individuals largely circumvents the key problem of the unreliability of the pre-test and post-test scores. But the focus of most longitudinal studies is on the individual; in such cases, statistical modelling taking into account the errors of measurement as set forth by Goldstein (1979a) and Kessler and Greenberg (1981) becomes essential.

This chapter is principally concerned, however, not with the problems of measuring change in individuals, but in the performance of national educational systems and sub-systems, a subject that has been gaining prominence on both sides of the Atlantic over the last fifteen years or so (Husen, 1979). In Britain, there has been a persistent campaign, most obviously in the Black Papers on education and fully documented and evaluated in the Open University (1981a), to discredit so-called progressive methods of education by pointing to an alleged decline in standards of educational performance, especially in reading and mathematics.

Such allegations, coupled with the wider issues of accountability and effective policy-making based on sound information, have led to the establishment of national (or regional) testing programmes designed to collect information about educational performance and to chart changes in the levels of performance. The idea of measuring change was not ostensibly important in the establishment of the Assessment of Performance Unit (APU) in England and Wales: the Unit's terms of reference are 'to promote the development of methods of assessing and monitoring the achievement of children at school, and to seek to identify the incidence of under-achievement'. The tasks amplifying these terms of reference make no reference to the measurement of change but, as Gipps points out in her chapter in this volume, the publicity material produced by the APU in its early years carried the clear message that the APU's role was to monitor in order to provide information on standards and how these change over time.

There was never any doubt that the National Assessment of Educational Progress (NAEP) in the USA should measure changes in educational attainment over time (Forbes, 1982). The evaluation of NAEP by Wirtz and Lapointe (1982) reaffirms the importance of this particular aim, and links it to public expectations:

> The assessment also identifies changes in student achievement levels over periods of time, characteristically four-year or five-year periods. There are some who challenge the reliability of such comparisons and others who question their value. Whether something is better or worse than it used to be seems less important than whether the present condition is good or bad, satisfactory or unsatisfactory. Yet the popular attraction of comparisons is plain, and the assessment's titular claim to measuring 'progress' reflects a widely accepted value. (p. 8)

In Canada, the provincial assessment systems were heavily influenced by NAEP and the measurement of change is an explicit aim in at least two provinces (Alberta and British Columbia) and probably in most, if not all, as McLean demonstrates elsewhere in this volume.

The emergence of these large-scale assessment systems designed, in part at least, to measure changes in the level of educational performance, has led to a considerable debate in Britain (but apparently not in the USA) about the most appropriate techniques for measuring change, if indeed it is sensible to attempt such measurement at all. There are two basic strategies, the use of the same tests (or items) on the different occasions and the use of different tests, in the latter case spawning a variety of techniques. These strategies are critically examined in turn below.

The Use of the Same Tests

One of the best-known examples of this strategy is the series of studies of reading comprehension between the 1940s and the 1970s (Start and Wells, 1972). Two tests were used (the Watts-Vernon and the NS6), the second also being used in the first APU survey of language development (DES, 1981), thus linking the older series of studies with the new. Although on the authors' own admission the 1970/71 studies were deficient on a number of counts (caustically elaborated upon by Burke and Lewis, 1975), the apparent decline in scores seen in those studies was sufficient to stimulate the establishment of a Government Committee of Enquiry that reported in 1975 (DES, 1975) and was one of the triggers for the establishment of the APU.

One of the most telling criticisms of the study by Start and Wells is that the tests were becoming increasingly dated in the language used. Words such as 'mannequin' and 'wheelwright' were not uncommon when the tests were developed, but are virtually unheard today. Any decline in test score might therefore not be reflecting a decline in the literacy of schoolchildren when faced with realistic and relevant text but a change in the difficulty of certain of the test items and thus of the test itself. What is ostensibly the same test, relied upon as an unchanging yardstick, is in reality slowly changing its nature. Much social and educational research over time is prone to similar problems: one example is in the changing rates of various types of crime (see the Open University, 1981b). Crime may appear to be increasing, not because the number of criminal incidents alters, but because there is a greater willingness on the part of the public to report them, sometimes just because of changing social attitudes but on other occasions as a result of changing social policy and law (such as the change that allowed rape victims to remain unnamed in court).

In the period up to 1983 when NAEP was administered by the Education Commission of the States in Denver, its strategy was also to make direct comparisons through re-use of the same items (administered in as similar a manner as possible) in successive surveys (for more detail of the method see Nuttall, 1983). A high proportion of items are released after each survey, so that the proportion of questions that can be used in more than three successive surveys (spanning twelve or so years) is negligible. As events transpired, NAEP in Denver was never obliged to devise a strategy for measuring changes in performance over longer periods, though some sort of chaining of surveys would, of course, have been possible (the first with the second and third, the second with the third and fourth, and so on). The risk of cumulative chaining error would become progressively greater, but linguistic and social factors are less likely to disturb item difficulty if the 'lifespan' of an item remains limited to little more than a decade.

One drawback of the original NAEP strategy is the limited number of questions on which direct comparisons were possible. Questions were (properly) chosen for release after each survey more or less at random, except where it was obvious that they might date (as was the case with some questions in social studies). There was some risk, nevertheless, that the questions common to two surveys were not representative of the questions in either survey.

The domain defined by the common questions may therefore be narrower than the domain of interest in any given year. This was clearly so in the British Columbian comparison of 1977 and 1981 mathematics surveys, as described by McLean in this volume. The Change Categories, comprising items used in both 1977 and 1981, though carefully constructed, did not themselves represent the whole domain of mathematical achievement that was considered worthy of assessing in 1981. As McLean says, domain definition is crucial to the measurement of change; one might add that changes in domain definition (to be expected in the light of curriculum development) undermine the measurement of change. This point is elaborated below. The use of the same tests (or items) is therefore difficult to defend because inevitable curricular, social and linguistic change will convert what appears to be an unchanging yardstick into a piece of elastic. Moreover, the use of the same tests (which become increasingly dated) may increase the difficulties of allowing national assessment systems to address today's and tomorrow's educational problems in line with their other aims — what one evaluation of NAEP characterized as the dangers of 'an unholy alliance with the past' (quoted by Wirtz and Lapointe, 1982, p. 70). Wirtz and Lapointe themselves warn of the dangers of concentrating too much upon techniques that permit comparisons over time, to the extent that broader educational goals that might lead to the raising of standards are neglected.

The Use of Different Tests

Beside these important educational objections to the continuing use of the same tests, practical reasons resulting from the release of questions in published reports make reliance upon the same items effectively impossible over any substantial period (as with NAEP).

Latent Trait Theory

One obvious candidate to solve the measurement problem created by a changing item pool is latent trait theory. For the APU, the one-parameter (Rasch) model was favoured — there being no guessing problem with the items — and strongly advocated by those concerned with the monitoring of mathematical and language development. In the latter case, the rating scale and possible differences between raters necessitated a generalization of the model (DES, 1981). But the criticisms (Goldstein and Blinkhorn, 1977; Nuttall, 1979a; Goldstein, 1979b and 1980) were such as to lead to the virtual abandonment of latent trait models by the APU. Criticisms were at two interacting levels: the technical and the educational. The technical criticisms are now by-and-large well known, and common to most psychological and educational applications. A most thorough and trenchant evaluation of these criticisms is given by Traub and Wolfe (1981), focusing particularly on dimensionality and goodness of fit. Goldstein's (1980) demonstration of estimation bias in the fixed-effects model is also a very telling contribution to the swelling literature of the limitations of latent trait models.

But these technical criticisms pale into insignificance beside the educational criticisms. The essence of the process of education is to achieve change in behaviour, change that is (in practice if not in theory) not identical in each individual. The invariance of item parameters (apart from a scaling constant) implied by the Rasch model sits unhappily with the notion of educational change. This proposition is at its most obvious when the order of difficulty of items is compared across groups receiving different kinds of, and amounts, of teaching.

The APU's testing strategy means that some students will face items on topics that they have never been taught (topics A and B, say). For them, such items will appear relatively harder than items on topics (C and D, say) which they have been taught; for a group of students taught topics A and B but not C and D, the relative difficulty of the items is reversed, and the latent trait model breaks down. Ostensibly, a simple solution would be to apply the model separately within each domain (A + B, and C + D) but in practice the number of possible combinations of topics studied and not studied by different groups of students is so large that analysis by each topic would almost certainly degenerate into analysis item by item — the *reductio ad absurdum* foreseen by McDonald (1981).

The measurement of change over time further highlights the inapplicability of latent trait models in the context of the work of the APU. Not only must the item pool be replenished (to make up for items released to the public) but it must be maintained relevant to the curriculum. This implies that the domain specification is changing, and that some items will be discarded as being no longer appropriate. One obvious operationalization of this concept of item inappropriateness is that the difficulty of the item changes relative to the other items in the pool; in other words, an item that once fitted that latent trait model no longer fits it. This again exposes the inherent contradiction between parameter invariance and educational change. These sorts of considerations led Traub and Wolfe (1981), echoing Goldstein, to conclude

... we view as potentially dangerous the practice of applying latent trait scaling over time and over educational programs where instruction varies. (p. 380)

Despite these strictures, the new management of NAEP at Educational Testing Service (ETS) is actively investigating the use of latent trait methods, especially the three-parameter model, for the study of changes in performance over time (Messick, Beaton and Lord, 1983). ETS has been in the vanguard of the development and application of latent trait theory (under the leadership of Lord) and is increasingly using the theory in its vast programme of test equating, especially for new forms of the Scholastic Aptitude Test (Holland and Rubin, 1982). Messick *et al.* (1983) acknowledge some of the technical limitations of the theory, particularly the crucial assumption of unidimensionality, but indicate how with the new procedures for the sampling of items (Balanced Incomplete Block Spiralling) it becomes possible to estimate item covariances and hence to explore the dimensionality of the data in a way that was not possible with matrix sampling. They state that they will 'determine how the exercises in a skill area can be subdivided into subareas that are roughly unidimensional . . . If a few exercises do not fit this procedure, they will be removed from the IRT (latent trait) analysis and analyzed by conventional methods such as proportion-correct' (*ibid.*, pp. 44–5).

On the educational criticisms of latent trait theory, the ETS proposals are silent and the quotation above suggests that technical considerations like fit to the model — itself a highly contentious issue as the review by Nuttall (1983) shows — will prevail over educational judgments concerning the validity and comprehensiveness of the areas and subareas. Given the debate that has taken place in the UK over the last few years (a debate that is not unfamiliar in the US through papers such as Goldstein's (1983) and personal contacts), the fervent advocacy of latent trait methods by ETS is somewhat surprising. But their position is quite clear: the perceived advantages 'make IRT scaling not only ideal for NAEP purposes, but essential' (Messick *et al.*, 1983, p. 85).

In fairness, it must be said that ETS is not planning to rely exclusively upon latent trait methodology. Messick *et al.* describe two major approaches to trend analysis that will be used. The first is at the level of the exercise or item (implying the re-use of the same ones over time), analysing the interactions 'subpopulation x item x years' which if they existed would negate the use of the Rasch model. The second is at the level of the scale (for example, reading comprehension, computation) and will similarly explore interactions: it is not wholly clear how the scale scores will be derived and latent trait methods might well be used.

This account demonstrates an interesting and contrasting change in attitudes towards the use of latent trait models. In England and Wales they were strongly advocated in the mid-1970s and used in the early stages of the work of the APU, but in response to much criticism their use has all but been abandoned in national and local monitoring. In the USA, the first years of national monitoring eschewed their use (but not apparently for the reasons that they have been rejected for in the UK), whereas in the mid-1980s their use is now being ardently and apparently rather uncritically promoted.

Generalizability Theory

The APU science monitoring team rejected the Rasch model because of their expectation of high student x item interaction, particularly likely because of their process model of the curriculum and curricular differences between schools. Johnson (1982) cites the study of Hively *et al.* (1968) in which they found student x item effects (admittedly confounded with other interactions and the residual) accounting for some 45 to 50 per cent of the total variance for various kinds of arithmetic test. In her own work on science tests, she found percentage contributions varying between 45 and 64 for the pupil x question interaction (unconfounded).

Johnson and her co-workers (Johnson and Hartley, 1981; Johnson and Bell, in press) have therefore been advocating an approach based on generalizability theory (Cronbach *et al.*, 1972). As its practical use has not been fully reported yet, it is difficult to evaluate, but two immediate criticisms suggest themselves. The key to the approach is the estimation of sampling variance when different samples of items are drawn from the same pool: but is the universe of items well enough defined (i.e. is the domain well enough specified) and are the items in the pool well enough prepared to allow us to assume that the items in the pool are a random sample from the universe? The more general controversy over this issue is well summarized by Shavelson and Webb (1981). On the one hand Loevinger (1965) argues that sampling cannot be random unless one can catalogue or display all possible members of the population (at least in principle). On the other hand, the concept of exchangeability put forward by de Finetti (1964) allows one to consider simply whether the actual items are exchangeable with other potential items without the necessity to catalogue the whole population. This less stringent criterion may still be hard to meet in the early stages of the development of an item pool, as Johnson and Bell (in press) implicitly acknowledge.

The second criticism concerns changes in the domain specification (and hence the definition of the universe of items) and in item difficulty: generalizability theory, like latent trait theory, cannot cope with changing domains or universes, or with items that change in difficulty for cultural reasons. Johnson and Bell (in press) acknowledge this in their concluding sentence:

> But there will always remain a potential risk to unambiguous interpretation of the resulting temporal data if the dynamic question pools from which survey questions are selected are ill-defined *and* allowed to change in nature during updating.

The Subjective Approach

The complexity of the interpretation of changes in test scores and the wide variety of social, cultural, educational and curricular factors that influence the changes are widely acknowledged. For example, Wirtz *et al.* (1977) pointed to the educational and social changes that complicated the interpretation of the significance of the decline in Scholastic Aptitude Test scores over the last twenty-five years. Austin and Garber (1982) similarly stress the need to view educational test score changes 'within the context of a *changing* educational and social milieu, whereas vocal critics view the context as unchanging' (p. 248). Farr and Fay (1982) begin to propose a way in which the broader changes might be taken into account:

> Any responsible comparison of achievement test scores from different time periods must consider a host of factors that may operate on the groups tested and that may vary across time. Such factors involve educational, demographic, economic and other societal factors which act as uncontrolled variables. Events, situations and attitudes unique to time periods ought to be included and studied among such factors.
>
> Since such factors can interact in highly complex ways, most cannot be mathematically removed from the test scores and, so, must be weighed subjectively. While this should not inhibit recognition of a study's potential importance, conclusions and implications of any trend study are open to question and to interpretation from numerous perspectives. The achievement trend analysis which ignores such factors, however, is much more limited than one which takes them into account. (p. 136)

Subjective judgment has always played a large part in the principal achievement testing activity in Britain, the systems of public examinations. These systems customarily make public all the questions used each year and therefore constantly have to face the problem of relating performance on different sets of questions over time (as well as between the examinations in the same subject set by different boards and schools, or by the same board on alternative syllabuses, in the same year). Typical procedures (and possible solutions to the problems of the maintenance of grading standards) are described by Christie and Forrest (1981).

The basic approach is simply to ask a panel of subject experts (the awarders) to 'carry' a notion of a fixed level of performance (for each level of achievement publicly certified) and to apply that notion to performance on any appropriate set of questions constituting an examination in that subject. On many occasions, when the syllabus remains unchanged from year to year, the sets of questions will be roughly parallel but, when the domain specification undergoes revision, the awarders are obliged to do their best to translate the fixed level of performance to a comparable level of performance defined by new criteria. Translated into the context of the APU, Nuttall (1979a and 1981) has proposed that the method might be applied thus: samples of completed test booklets (objective by objective, or domain by domain) at scores representing the 5th, 25th, 50th, 75th and 95th percentiles would be drawn for each of the years involved in the comparison. The task of the panel of experts would be to judge whether the samples at each percentile point represented a similar or a different standard of performance.

There have been many formal investigations of the comparability of public examination standards, with cross-moderation (that is, the remarking and regrading of work by other examiners) being the method currently favoured. All methods have revealed the complexity of the problem of comparability, one of the most difficult aspects hinging on the difficulty of comparing tests with different domain specifications (Bardell *et al.*, 1978; Nuttall, 1979b; Orr and Nuttall, 1983; Goldstein, in this volume).

One merit of the panel approach is that the panel has the option of declaring the comparison invalid, as happened in effect in one of the most sophisticated British studies of examination standards over time (Christie and Forrest, 1980). The domain specification of chemistry at GCE advanced level had changed so much over the period under review (1963 to 1973) that a direct comparison of standards was impossible. Moreover, on those occasions when a panel considers that direct comparison remains possible, they can make subtle adjustments for change in the content or coverage of the test (and assign less weight to skills or topics that are declining in importance, and more to those that are increasing in importance). A further advantage is that a panel would be likely to detect and draw attention only to differences that are of some educational significance.

Introducing subjectivity into the process of measuring changes in performance thus has a number of potential advantages over more mechanistic, and seemingly more objective, processes, but is, of course, not without its problems. Even professionally trained judges have difficulty in assessing the likely performance of students on tests or specific items as the studies by Thorndike (1982) and Black *et al.* (1984) show; the latter warn how societal and professional expectations can be inconsistent as well as inaccurate. It is clearly necessary for subjective accounts to be as reflexive as possible, to avoid keeping hidden the sort of assumptions that are too readily hidden in technically complex methodologies like latent trait and generalizability analyses.

The use of panels to comment upon the findings of surveys (as opposed to judging changes in performance levels) is already an established practice in North America. Wirtz and Lapointe (1982) praise the relatively recent introduction of this practice at NAEP at Denver, and McLean (in this volume) cites three Canadian provinces — British Columbia, New Brunswick and Alberta — that employ panels. The use of panels to comment upon results raises a final very important issue about attempts to measure change in standards, namely the gathering of suitable data about policy and practice in the schools that might help to explain changes in standard. Gardner (1982) points to the very many competing explanations that were offered for the decline in SAT scores; most of these explanations were conjectural, necessarily so in the absence of hard information about social and curricular changes.

Nuttall (1980) argues that attempts to measure change in performance without measuring changes in important educational variables at the level of local authorities and schools (for example, resource provision, staffing standards) and at the level of classrooms (at the very least using a measure of opportunity-to-learn) is pointless and likely to be fruitless, though even if such concomitant educational changes are measured cause-and-effect relationships will be hard to establish in surveys of this kind. Farr and Fay (1982), Wirtz and Lapointe (1982), Messick *et al.* (1983) and McLean (in this volume) also argue for more efforts to be made to collect educationally important background variables so that the results of surveys can be more easily interpreted and put to use.

Conclusions

The main conclusion is that the measurement of change in the level of performance of educational systems is not possible as there is no way of establishing an unchanging measuring instrument over any length of time. Indeed, there are dangers in attempting to do so because such a measuring instrument cannot adapt to meet current needs or concerns. Procedures claiming to meet the need for the domain specification to vary over time while reporting results on an unchanging scale have also been shown to be inadequate.

If public expectation obliges some comparisons over time to be made, then a method involving panels along the lines described above offers a more sensitive and adaptable way that might prevent chalk being compared with cheese. Alternative strategies have also been offered by Goldstein (1981 and 1983). The first draws upon experience of longitudinal studies (Goldstein, 1979a) and proposes using the school as the basic unit of analysis, sampling in such a way that a proportion of schools would recur in each time sample. This approach also appeals to Messick *et al.* (1983), though they note substantial practical problems. The second is to chart changes in relative *differences* between sub-groups over the years, rather than to attempt direct comparisons between years. These proposals are currently being refined and developed, and are the topic of a research project at the National Foundation for Educational Research (Gipps, in this volume). But whatever strategy is adopted, the exercise will be pointless unless important educational variables other than performance are also systematically assessed.

At the time of writing (mid-1984), the debate about methods continues but major reports using most of the major approaches discussed in this chapter have yet to be published. The reports of the APU surveys, covering the first two or three years in each field (mathematics, language and science), have said little or nothing about comparisons between years (though the reports reviewing the first five years in which surveys were conducted annually will surely do so). The work of NAEP at ETS and, with a few exceptions, the work of the Canadian provinces (see McLean in this volume) is too recent to have yielded published comparisons over time.

Once these reports begin to appear, the debate will inevitably hot up again. Meanwhile almost all experts in Britain, and most in Canada, take the view that strong assumptions of invariance in the way that items behave or are interpreted are unwarranted in education where change is of the essence of the process, if not its *raison d'être*. Change in the items and the domain specifications must therefore be explicitly acknowledged and subjectively allowed for.

References

AITKEN, M., BENNETT, S.N. and HESKETH, J. (1981) 'Teaching styles and pupil progress: A re-analysis', *British Journal of Educational Psychology*, 51, 2, pp. 170–86.

AUSTIN, G.R. and GARBER, H. (1982) 'The implications for society' in AUSTIN, G.R. and GARBER, H. (Eds) *The Rise and Fall of National Test Scores*, New York, Academic Press.

BARDELL, G.S., FORREST, G.M. and SHOESMITH, D.J. (1978) *Comparability in GCE*, Manchester, Joint Matriculation Board.

BENNETT, S.N. (1976) *Teaching Styles and Pupil Progress*, London, Open Books.

BLACK, P., HARLEN, W. and ORGEE, T. (1984) *Standards of Performance — Expectations and Reality*, APU Occasional Paper No. 3, London, Department of Education and Science.

BURKE, E. and LEWIS, D.G. (1975) 'Standards of reading: A critical review of some recent studies', *Educational Research*, 17, pp. 163–74.

CHRISTIE, T. and FORREST, G.M. (1980) *Standards at GCE A-Level: 1963 and 1973*, London, Macmillan Education.

CHRISTIE, T. and FORREST, G.M. (1981) *Defining Public Examination Standards*, London, Macmillan Education.

CRONBACH, L.J. and FURBY, L. (1970) 'How we should measure "change" — or should we?', *Psychological Bulletin*, 74, 1, pp. 68–80.

CRONBACH, L.J., GLESER, G.C., NANDA, H. and RAJARATNAM, N. (1972) *The Dependability of Behavioral Measurements*, New York, Wiley.

de FINETTI, B. (1964) 'Foresight: Its logical laws, its subjective sources' in KYBURG, H.E. and SMOKLER, G.E. (Eds) *Studies in Subjective Probability*, New York, Wiley.

DEPARTMENT OF EDUCATION AND SCIENCE (1975) *A Language for Life* (the Bullock Report), London, HMSO.

DEPARTMENT OF EDUCATION AND SCIENCE (1981) *Language Performance in Schools: Primary Report No. 1*, London, HMSO.

FARR, R. and FAY, L. (1982) 'Reading trend data in the United States: A mandate for caveats and cautions' in AUSTIN, G.R. and GARBER, H. (Eds) *The Rise and Fall of National Test Scores*, New York, Academic Press.

FORBES, R.H. (1982) 'Testing in the USA', *Educational Analysis*, 4, 3, pp. 69–78.

GARDNER, E. (1982) 'Some aspects of the use and misuse of standardized aptitude and achievement tests' in WIGDOR, A.K. and GARNER, W.R. (Eds) *Ability Testing: Uses, Consequences, and Controversies*, Part II, Washington, D.C., National Academy Press.

GOLDSTEIN, H. (1979a) *The Design and Analysis of Longitudinal Studies*, London, Academic Press.

GOLDSTEIN, H. (1979b) 'Consequences of using the Rasch model for educational assessment', *British Educational Research Journal*, 5, 2, pp. 211–20.

GOLDSTEIN, H. (1980) 'Dimensionality, bias, independence and measurement scale problems in latent trait test score models', *British Journal of Mathematical and Statistical Psychology*, 33, 2, pp. 234–46.

GOLDSTEIN, H. (1981) 'Measuring trends in test performance over time', paper presented to the APU Invitational Seminar on Monitoring over Time, London, June.

GOLDSTEIN, H. (1983) 'Measuring changes in educational attainment over time: Problems and possibilities', *Journal of Educational Measurement*, 20, 4, pp. 369–77.

GOLDSTEIN, H. and BLINKHORN, S. (1977) 'Monitoring educational standards — an inappropriate model', *Bulletin of the British Psychological Society*, 30, pp. 309–11.

HARLEN, W., DARWIN, A. and MURPHY, M. (1977) *Match and Mismatch: Raising Questions*, Edinburgh, Oliver and Boyd.

HARRIS, C.W. (Ed) (1963) *Problems in Measuring Change*, Madison, W1, University of Wisconsin Press.

HIVELY, W., PATTERSON, H.L. and SAGE, S.H. (1968) 'A universe-defined system of arithmetic tests', *Educational Measurement*, 5, pp. 275–90.

HOLLAND, P.W. and RUBIN, D.B. (Eds) (1982) *Test Equating*, New York, Academic Press.

HUSEN, T. (1979) *The School in Question*, Oxford, Oxford University Press.

JOHNSON, S. (1982) 'Monitoring science performance: Comparability and reliability considerations', paper presented to the Fifth International Symposium on Educational Testing held at the University of Stirling, Scotland, June/July.

JOHNSON, S. and BELL, J.F. (in press) 'Evaluating and predicting survey efficiency using generalizability theory', *Journal of Educational Measurement*, summer 1985.

JOHNSON, S. and HARTLEY, R. (1981) 'Generalizability theory and national monitoring of science performance', paper presented to the APU Invitational Seminar on Monitoring over Time, London, June.

KESSLER, R.C. and GREENBERG, D.F. (1981) *Linear Panel Analysis: Models of Quantitative Change*, New York, Academic Press.

LOEVINGER, J. (1965) 'Person and population as psychometric concepts', *Psychological Review*, 72, pp. 143–55.

McDONALD, R.P. (1981) 'The dimensionality of tests and items', *British Journal of Mathematical and Statistical Psychology*, 34, pp. 100–17.

MESSICK, S., BEATON, A. and LORD, F. (1983) *A New Design for a New Era*, Princeton, NJ, ETS/NAEP.

NUTTALL, D.L. (1979a) 'A rash attempt to measure standards', Supplement to *Education*, 21 September, pp. ii–iii.

NUTTALL, D.L. (1979b) 'The myth of comparability', *Journal of the National Association of Inspectors and Educational Advisers*, 11, pp. 16–18.

NUTTALL, D.L. (1980) 'Will the APU rule the curriculum?', Supplement to *Education*, 6 June, pp. ix–x.

NUTTALL, D.L. (1981) 'Assessing changes in performance over time', paper presented to the APU Invitational Seminar on Monitoring over Time, London, June.

NUTTALL, D.L. (1983) 'Monitoring in North America', *Westminster Studies in Education*, 6, pp. 63–90.

OPEN UNIVERSITY (1981a) *E200: Contemporary Issues in Education, Unit 15, Approaches to Teaching*, Milton Keynes, Open University Press.

OPEN UNIVERSITY (1981b) *E200: Contemporary Issues in Education, Unit 17, Schools and Deviance*, Milton Keynes, Open University Press.

ORR, L. and NUTTALL, D.L. (1983) *Determining Standards in the Proposed Single System of Examining at 16+*, London, Schools Council.

SHAVELSON, R.J. and WEBB, N. (1981) 'Generalizability theory: 1973–1980', *British Journal of Mathematical and Statistical Psychology*, 34, pp. 133–66.

START, K.B. and WELLS, B.K. (1972) *The Trend of Reading Standards*, Slough, National Foundation for Educational Research.

THORNDIKE, R.L. (1982) 'Item and score conversion by pooled judgment' in HOLLAND, P.W. and RUBIN, D.B. (Eds) *Test Equating*, New York, Academic Press.

TRAUB, R.E. and WOLFE, R.G. (1981) 'Latent trait theories and the assessment of educational achievement', *Review of Research in Education*, 9, pp. 377–435.

WIRTZ, W. *et al.* (1977) *On Further Examination: Report of the Advisory Panel on the Scholastic Aptitude Test Score Decline*, New York, College Entrance Examination Board.

WIRTZ, W. and LAPOINTE, A. (1982) *Measuring the Quality of Education: A Report on Assessing Educational Progress*, Washington, D.C., Wirtz and Lapointe.

Goldstein, H. and Nuttall, D.L. (1986) 'Can graded assessments, records of achievement, modular assessment and the GCSE co-exist?' in Gipps, C.V. (Ed) *The GCSE: An Uncommon Exam* London, Institute of Education/ Heinemann.

Introduction

The advent of the GCSE examination in 1987 incorporated much of the novel assessment thinking that emerged during the 1980s. The exam was based on a more criterion-referenced approach to reporting achievement and to this end, sets of national criteria were developed for each subject to inform the preparation of individual syllabuses by the newly-formed examining groups. Desmond Nuttall was closely involved in these developments. He was asked to advise in a variety of policy-making arenas and worked with the examining groups themselves to help implement that policy. Of particular significance was the key role he played at the Open University which had the contract for developing training materials — manuals and videos — for each subject which could be used for the massive 'cascade' programme designed to induct teachers into the new procedures.

Conscious as this article and others (for example, Paper 9) show him to have been of the limitations of the new GCSE, Desmond Nuttall questions the potential of the other assessment procedures which were emerging at that time to break the mould. As he and Harvey Goldstein suggest, there was very little serious attempt at the time to relate any of the current initiatives to existing educational philosophies — or to indicate the outline of a new one. So caught up were those involved in the various assessment movements of that time with the goal of changing practice, that the building of a more solid and collective rationale for the initiatives was relatively neglected. There is a certain irony in the fact that the intensification of the assessment debate during the 1990s has prompted the search for such a new assessment philosophy in a way that was much less necessary in the optimistic and open climate of the 1980s. The pressure to use assessment not only for selection — which Goldstein and Nuttall identify as a major inhibitory factor on new developments — but also to raise overall learning standards prompted a more explicit articulation of an alternative assessment philosophy, a philosophy that emphasizes assessment rather than measurement; learning rather than certification.

Goldstein and Nuttall's paper foreshadows many of the issues which would be more fully articulated in later years. The tensions they identify concerning the realization of a truly mastery-oriented, criterion-referenced assessment system were ones that were to figure again and again in Desmond Nuttall's work. The problems of comparability in particular, which had preoccupied Desmond Nuttall throughout his professional life, were exacerbated by these new approaches to assessment through their tendency to produce more complex, disaggregated results. The problems posed in this respect by records of achievement, for example, with their emphasis on broadly-based, positive assessment including affective dimensions, were matched by those inherent in modular assessment schemes where some assumption of equivalence had to be made if they were to be capable of aggregation into a qualification.

Goldstein and Nuttall's exploration of the common strands informing the various assessment initiatives discussed in this paper is as lucid as it is significant. The article challenges us to answer the fundamental question concerning what assessment is for. It challenges us to consider ways of reconciling the selection imperative on the one hand and the teacher-initiated informal assessment of learning on the other. It challenges us to consider how we may fairly and effectively assess 'practical' skills and affective characteristics; to question whether the traditional elevation of abstract, theoretical thinking really does deserve its long-standing elite status. It demands that we ask ourselves how long we will tolerate the iron grip of external examinations concerned with selection, curriculum control and existing hierarchies of knowledge.

CAN GRADED ASSESSMENTS, RECORDS OF ACHIEVEMENT, AND MODULAR
ASSESSMENT CO-EXIST WITH THE GCSE?

Philosophical Considerations

The other chapters in this volume describe and evaluate various aspects of the GCSE. Here we look at the relationship between the aims of the GCSE and those of other major assessment initiatives — graded assessments and records of achievement. Furthermore, since the focus of this volume is the GCSE, we do not consider the possible operation of graded assessments or records of achievement independent of GCSE or as the dominant modes of assessment, although this is not to deny that either (or both in partnership) might eventually predominate at least at some levels of education.

We shall describe each of four types of assessment (graded assessments, records of achievement, modular assessments and the GCSE) in terms of their educational justifications, followed by an analysis of the implicit and explicit educational philosophies embodied in these justifications. From there we shall draw out the similarities and conflicts between the types, and hence the issues likely to emerge in any simultaneous implementation of one or more of the types of assessments in the same educational environment alongside GCSE.

A major difficulty we have found in discussing philosophical or theoretical foundations is that there is very little serious attempt to relate any of the current initiatives to existing educational philosophies or to indicate the outline of a new one. Thus, the graded assessment movement draws much of its inspiration and rhetoric from graded tests in other areas, notably in artistic and sports fields, but with minimum critical analysis of the similarities and differences between those areas and general education in schools. Records of achievement are commended to us as providers of a wider portfolio of information, without addressing the question of the optimum amount of information that is required for different purposes. In similar vein, the new GCSE, as might be anticipated from an essentially bureaucratically driven exercise, deals with the notion of 'standards' by abandoning a critical definition in favour of metaphor.

Part of our task, therefore, has been to infer key features of the frameworks within which advocates of the different assessments implicitly seem to operate. Yet our aim is not to engage only in philosophical argument, but to use that to prepare a practical critique. If the result appears unduly critical, then we make no apology but rather invite those who do not share our conclusions to join us in a debate we feel is long overdue. We should also make it clear that we accept that the very fact of change often produces new perspectives and hence important innovations in curriculum and teaching. Undoubtedly this is true of new assessment approaches. Our concern here, however, is to examine the specific claims of these approaches rather than their effects, which are often beneficial if sometimes unplanned or unexpected.

Graded Assessments

The early discussion of graded testing or assessment often involved reference to graded examinations in music or grade certificates awarded for swimming, etc. (see, for example, Harrison, 1982). The advantages of such assessments were said to be in the short-term 'positive' motivation provided by relatively clearly defined tasks to be 'mastered', or competencies to be demonstrated. The term 'positive' refers to the reinforcement provided by a high probability of 'passing' a grade, which in turn implies that students are not entered unless they are perceived to have a high probability of passing. Thus the 'positive' nature of the assessment resides in appropriate entry decisions rather than in the assessment itself, and so depends upon the actions of teachers and others. If this is so, then at the very least we need to have an understanding of how the mechanism works, if indeed it does, in other parts of the curriculum. Furthermore, what are the procedures whereby pass rates are maintained and how do these react upon teaching and learning? Such questions lead to broader ones about the relationships between tutor and student, about whether there is an inherent link between this relationship and the form of assessment, and about whether the assessment method can be 'lifted' from one context to another. Of particular interest is the question of how 'negative' achievement or 'failure' is dealt with. We shall return to these issues, and also what we call context-related assessment, below.

The second common aspect of graded assessments is the acceptance of the idea of 'mastery'. Because of its often close association, or even identification, with the notion of criterion-referencing we shall be discussing the two together below. We note, however, that both notions relate explicitly to a body of educational writing largely concerned with the formulation of detailed, and usually behavioural, educational goals and methods of assessing the achievements of those goals (for example, Bloom, Hastings and Madaus, 1971). In practice, however, this literature tells us little about how to operationalize notions of mastery in relation to broad-based curricula as opposed to narrow definitions of skill; consequently, the development of graded assessments has been *de novo*, rather than part of any systematic extension or application of the existing theory of mastery learning and assessment.

The use of the results of graded assessments does not seem to have been fully thought through. Apart from their obviously redundant use in deciding whether to proceed to the next 'level' of assessment (given the policy governing entry decisions), the results of many graded assessments are to be equivalenced to a grade level of GCSE. This has been unashamedly justified in order to achieve acceptance and 'respectability' for graded tests, and there has been little examination of the consequences of such equivalencing. It is tacitly assumed that it can be done without prejudicing existing aims, but this is not guaranteed and we shall examine this further when we discuss the nature of assessment instruments when they are required to perform a selection function.

Finally, an issue which afflicts all assessment procedures (perhaps more in the United Kingdom than elsewhere in the world) is that of *comparability* — across time as the content of the assessment changes, across institutions such as schools which use different content and contexts to assess the same objectives, and across domains or subjects. The only known areas where comparability or equating can be said to work are very narrowly defined cases involving costly norm-referenced procedures, hardly applicable to the schemes being developed (see Holland and Rubin, 1982; Goldstein, 1986). Yet the descriptions of graded assessment schemes are predicated on a common understanding of what each level 'means'. What is unclear is the epistemological basis for such meaning — is the intention to 'objectify' it in terms of mathematically-defined relationships as in test equating, or to refer it to expert judgment, or perhaps simply to ignore the problem by pretending it does not exist? We shall have more to say about this later.

Records of Achievement

A principal distinguishing feature of records of achievement (or profiles) is their incorporation of explicit and separate assessments of a much wider range of achievements than other modes of assessment, especially in the affective domain. It is, however, worth remarking that there appears to be no reason why such achievements should not be incorporated into the other three forms of assessment. That this appears not to have been seriously considered reflects the provenance of graded assessments, modular assessments and the GCSE and their primary concern with the same set of issues. The main appeal of profiling is to the notion of education for the whole person, to a desire to give positive value and status to affective and other non-academic achievements. For many, the real value of this appeal is to the teacher and above all to the student himself or herself and lies in the *process* of education, and the control of teacher and student over the assessment. But few deny (albeit reluctantly in some cases) that status can be conveyed only by means of a permanent, observable record negotiated between student and teacher. It is this record which, along with the other kinds of assessment, would be 'used' . . . by whoever wants to use it. Clearly, to achieve value for non-cognitive activities, knowledge of them has to be of use to someone. Yet we find little explicit discussions of who that person (other than the student) is, but there seems to be a general presumption, as in the Oxford Certificate of Educational Achievement (OCEA), that it is a selector of sorts — an employer, perhaps, or a Youth Training Scheme (YTS) managing agent. So again we find an instrumental end-product, raising the issue we mentioned above of the way in which the use of an assessment interacts with its initial philosophy. A fundamental question is how far the ideal of honest and objective recording is compatible with the reality of knowing that such recording may have a role in determining life chances. This is hardly a novel question, but it still deserves a considered response.

Two other important issues arise with records of achievement which have counterparts in the other forms of assessment. The first is made explicit in many of the profiling systems (for example, those of the City and Guilds of London Institute) that consist of graded descriptions of each of a wide range of achievements. A key feature of these is their out-of-context formulation, that is, their phrasing in terms that sound very much like general 'skills' or 'abilities' presumed to exist independently of any particular context. Here, a direct line of descent can be traced from a traditional and widely held belief in such concepts as 'intelligence', though this belief is one that has increasingly been questioned. Yet if such descriptions convey little real information, is it then possible to generate records of achievement in terms of context-specific descriptions?

The second issue is again that of 'positive' achievement. If negative comment is to be eschewed (as the Department of Education and Science, 1984, advocates), 'negative' achievement presumably becomes that range of possible achievements which are not mentioned in the record. There would seem to be a clear invitation to read between the lines, and this leaves us wondering what the term 'positive' achievement really signifies.

Modular Assessment

A number of different arguments are put forward for breaking up a course of study into relatively small units or modules, and assessing achievement at the end of each. One argument is for curricular flexibility (and sometimes organizational flexibility) so that students can have more choice, and a greater variety of potentially valuable courses can be created. But where the modules are being combined to create courses for the GCSE examination (as is the case in many TVEI schemes), the national criteria tend to create a straitjacket and much of the curricular flexibility is lost because only a very limited number of combinations of modules will be acceptable as a GCSE course in physics, say.

Some modular schemes (such as those operated by the Business and Technician Council and the Open University) consist of modules that are studied over a period as long as a year. Other schemes (for example, Inner London Education Authority, 1984) advocate modules that can be completed in as little as six or eight weeks, so that students receive relatively rapid public feedback about performance. In this they resemble graded assessments, but the assumption is that the students will be assessed when their group completes the module, rather than when they are individually ready. Many will therefore fail (or show modest achievement); the consequence that many students will have more negative than positive reinforcement does not seem to have been faced.

Modular schemes often share many of the features of the other assessment initiatives, such as criterion-referencing and the specification of detailed objectives or assessment criteria that are independent of context. But modular schemes experience the problems of comparability in a much more acute form than other types of assessment when aggregated for the purpose of some global award like a degree or a GCSE grade. If curricular flexibility is to be encouraged, then students will present a great variety of different combinations of modules, but the assumption will usually have to be made that a grade 2, say, in one module is equivalent to a grade 2 in any other module. The more that choice is constrained (as it will be in GCSE, as argued above), the more the problem is alleviated, but the greater the loss in flexibility.

The GCSE

At the heart of the GCSE proposals is the aim of specifying curriculum content and pedagogy by a suitable specification of the examination system (for the detailed argument see Nuttall, 1984). Of course, for any examination system to be able to succeed in this task, it must possess sufficient muscle to have its way. Historically, in Britain, there has been little doubt, even among its bitterest opponents, that the public examination system really matters to parents, students, teachers, further and higher education, and employers; that same cultural assumption has clearly been inherited by the GCSE. As we have already said, at least two of the other forms of assessment currently being developed look to the GCSE to legitimize their own status.

We should make it clear that we do not take a value position when we talk of examinations determining aspects of curriculum and pedagogy. We believe that there should be a debate on the extent to which this is desirable, and about other approaches to curriculum determination and control (described, for example, by Broadfoot, 1979). That debate is not being held now and may well be irrelevant once the GCSE is in place.

Other contributions to this volume analyze the significant features and innovations of the GCSE. Here, then, we summarize their effects upon schools, teachers and students. The aims, objectives and content of examination courses are determined (with varying precision in different subjects) by the national criteria (Department of Education and Science, 1985). Although there is provision in the criteria for their regular review and for their temporary suspension to allow for promising curricular developments to be tried, they will be difficult and time-consuming to modify. (At the time of writing, the criteria have been suspended only for one subject, SMP mathematics, a subject dear to the hearts of the top brass of the Secondary Examinations Council.) The advent of grade criteria would lead to a tightening of the specification of the curriculum. Curricular and classroom organization will be determined partly by the need to prepare students for a particular 'level' of the examination in many subjects (see Gipps's chapter above), somewhat in the present manner of choosing CSE or GCE, but possibly with a finer gradation; partly by the need for coursework and its assessment (see MacIntosh's chapter); and partly by the grade criteria (see Murphy's chapter). Pedagogy stands to be influenced by the increased involvement of teachers in the process of assessment (see Torrance's chapter). Because of the requirement for comparability and the consequent need for some kind of moderation of teachers' and pupils' work, the traditional role relationship of teacher and learner seems destined to be nudged in the direction of formal assessor and candidate, with possibly profound implications for traditional roles and with penalties for departures from the new role. We shall return to all of these core issues when discussing practical implications.

Selection and Assessment

In common with existing 16+ examinations, the principal use of the GCSE is as a selection device, whether for employers or as a requirement for training courses or advanced educational studies. The primacy of this function has particular consequences. We have mentioned already the way in which the other forms of assessment, directly or indirectly, aspire to gain a share of the action and we have alluded to the way in which this changes their role. The role of the 16+ examination itself reflects the deeper commitment of the secondary education system to selection and much of past and present debates can be said to be concerned with the tension between the selective and other functions of education (see Broadfoot, 1979). What seems to be emerging at the end of the 1980s, however, is a willingness on the part of those concerned with devising new modes of assessment to concede that the credibility of these new modes is dependent upon accommodating to the GCSE and to the demands of the user outside the school gates — in effect, to concede the primacy of selection, albeit with extreme reluctance and distaste in some cases. It is because of the many ways in which graded assessments, modular schemes and records of achievement are having to make compromises that we feel that their initial beneficial effects within schools and classrooms cannot yet be taken as established.

In many ways, graded assessment and profiling are attempts to formalize much of the teacher-initiated informal assessment of learning which takes place as an inherent part of teaching. Such informal assessment may take a variety of guises, but its aim is formative which distinguishes it from assessment for selection, which is invariably summative. Indeed, the policy of some schools and teachers is consciously to postpone as far as possible the time at which the latter mode of assessment begins to dominate. This leads us to ask what we believe is a key question underlying all current developments, namely how far the acceptance of the supremacy of the idea of 'assessment for selection' militates against any change in the nature of teaching and learning in schools. It is not our purpose to offer speculative answers to this question, but rather to place it onto an agenda for debate. It is, of course, the striving for fairness in selection that puts such emphasis upon comparability and reliability, and permits the down-grading of what should be pre-eminent, namely validity.

Criterion Referencing

The notion of criterion-referenced assessment has acted as a principal legitimating device for the GCSE and to a lesser extent for graded assessment and records of achievement. The idea that the result of an assessment enables you to say 'what a student can do' rather than 'how a student is ranked in relation to her peers' is seen as an attractive one, and has inspired much research and debate over the past twenty years. Much of this debate has been concerned with the relationship between assessment and the curriculum, the clear specification of assessment objectives, the predictive generalizability of such assessments and the problem of defining a suitable criterion 'level' for deciding whether the 'can do' description can be awarded, and in what contexts.

It could be argued that the clear specification of assessment objectives is a desirable feature of all assessment procedures, as is an understanding of the predictive usefulness of an assessment (as one aspect of validity). In the development of graded assessments there seems to have been much concern with criterion or mastery levels, so that the probability of passing is high enough to be encouraging, but clearly not 100 per cent which would make the assessment redundant. In fact, the decision as to cut-off point is ultimately determined by considerations of student motivation, resources and so forth, rather than by some inherent logic of curriculum, pedagogy or the assessment. Hence the 'can do' skill is defined effectively in terms of the characteristics of those students who actually pass the assessment, so that to understand the meaning of 'can do' would require a detailed study of those students and the conditions under which they learnt it.

Which brings us to the issue of context. A study of the draft grade criteria for the GCSE, profile descriptors and the descriptions of levels in many graded assessment schemes shows that almost all do not specify the context in which the assessment is demonstrated. For example, one of the draft grade criteria for English in the domain of writing requires candidates to be able to 'describe a scene or character as the task requires'. There is no localization of the kind of task (perhaps the candidate can do this with some tasks and not with others), nor any attempt to elaborate on what an 'acceptable' description might be.

Such general descriptions follow inevitably from the stated aims of the assessment. Not only would context-specific descriptions be very lengthy, but they would also be impossible to examine exhaustively. Moreover, the more specific the context, the less apparently generalizable the achievement. Since all forms of assessment are inevitably limited to a *sampling* of achievements, a high level of generality is imposed upon the descriptions. This is even more necessary in the GCSE since grade criteria have to be equally applicable to diverse syllabuses in the same subject offered by different examining groups. Yet such general, out-of-context, descriptions can only be valid on the assumption that they relate to demonstrable achievements. Thus we need to assume the existence of a high level competency, such as 'the ability to describe a scene', whose attainment an assessment system is designed to elicit. It is clear, however, that the real existence of such an ability, just like the reality of something called general intelligence, is an assumption, with important consequences. In particular, if the assumption is incorrect, then it is difficult to see what the utility of the description might be.

Suffice it to say that the degree to which achievements are genuinely context-free is very much a matter for debate. There is considerable empirical evidence challenging the notion of context-free assessment (Wolf and Silver, 1986; Nuttall, 1986). It must therefore be of some concern that graded assessments, profile descriptions and the GCSE grade criteria are all predicated on a particular view of the context-independent nature of performance descriptions.

Comparability

We have already referred to the difficulty of finding an 'objective' procedure for ensuring comparability within each form of assessment as well as between them. The experiences of the examining boards in the 1970s is salutary in this respect. They effectively abandoned the search for a foolproof procedure and settled for expert examiner judgment, in addition to a large measure of norm referencing, with all the problems of subjectivity and lack of objective reference which that implies (see Schools Council, 1979; Bardell, Forest and Shoesmith, 1978). In fact such a system resembles a cross between comparability by fiat and comparability on the basis of a strongly shared value-system. An interesting variant is the 'equivalence' between CSE Grade 1 and a GCE O-level 'pass' — an equivalence purely by fiat. No doubt something similar can be put together for the GCSE, although the increased amount of teacher assessment and the differentiated papers will make this more difficult; as a result we may see rather more equivalencing by fiat. An order of magnitude still more difficult is the equivalencing of graded assessments and modular assessment to the GCSE. While it may be possible to specify equivalence by fiat between performance on modules and the GCSE, this will not do for graded assessments in those cases where students are assessed both by graded assessments and by the GCSE. (In other cases, the graded assessments may be accepted as the GCSE assessments.) If an equivalence is established between GCSE grades and levels of the graded assessment in a subject, then it cannot be acceptable for significant proportions of students to pass a graded assessment level and subsequently fail to achieve the equivalent GCSE grade. Yet from all that we know about the unreliability of examinations, it is almost certain that such apparent 'anomalies' will arise. This will expose both the unreliability of the assessments and the impossibility of a consistent one-to-one equivalence. Nor would it be acceptable to eliminate the problem by raising the criteria for the achievement of a given level of the graded assessment, since this will lead to even more students achieving the 'equivalent' GCSE grade but not the graded assessment level than formerly, with a perceived and presumably unacceptable fluctuation in 'standards'. Similarly, if large numbers of students also took separate modular assessments in addition to the GCSE, the same problems would rise. We note that this problem is not a new one in equating; it merely becomes apparent because large numbers of students are exposed to both 'equivalent' forms. It thus represents a major incompatibility which, if not resolved either by decoupling the equivalence or by allowing graded assessments (rigidly controlled by the national criteria) to replace GCSE, will presumably lead to the eventual discrediting of the system and perhaps to the demise of graded assessment.

Usage

There seems to be little discussion and even less evidence about the ways in which the several forms of assessment are to be used in conjunction. To a large extent the equivalencing of graded assessment and modular assessment to GCSE solves the problem (while raising others), but it remains with records of achievement. The Oxford Certificate of Educational Achievement, for example, is planned simply to be an extensive document containing public examination results as well as evidence of other cognitive and non-cognitive achievements. This presentation of detailed information is more likely to be informative than a summary, but in practice it may well be summarized into a single score or grade in different ways before being used, so that its potential utility is negated. The importance of this can be seen within the GCSE itself where the proposals for grade criteria envisage that separate domain grades will be presented *in addition to* a summary grade over domains. This invites the use of the summary grade as the principal selection device, as occurs at present when employers and higher education selectors simply add up separate grades to form an overall score. When dealing with the more disaggregated information in records of achievement, users may tend to ignore everything other than those things which can easily be summarized into a score or grade or a picking-out of isolated and unreliable pieces of information. Here we see an incompatibility in mode of presentation of results and their likely use which, unless resolved, could lead to a downgrading of much of the information in records of achievement.

Conclusions

We have argued, in a general way, that there are both compatibilities and incompatibilities between the different forms of assessment that will determine the progress of each. We have also argued that the GCSE is the 'prestige' form to which the others are being forced to accommodate and against whose requirements their success will be judged. We have not addressed the intriguing question of whether this needs to be so, nor whether it is the result of contingencies related to sources of funding, the dominance of assessment for selection or other aspects of the educational environment. There is, however, one final issue which we feel, in the long term, is of more importance than the form of the particular kinds of assessment that survive.

All the new forms of assessment have shown at least some concern with objectives and content not previously assessed formally. Thus GCSE has raised the visibility of 'practical' assessment, and records of achievement the visibility of affective characteristics. What has not been questioned, however, is the relative status of different kinds of achievement. Put simply, our present assessment systems embody a hierarchy in which abstract, theoretical achievement is almost always accorded a higher status than the practical and the affective, and this status is intended to reflect what is believed, in the tradition of the 11+ and 'intelligence', to influence life chances. We find little explicit in the new proposals that presents a real challenge to this view. Thus, while the GCSE pays homage to practical achievement, it is a very puny attempt to rehabilitate the status of practical knowledge and skills, and may readily be subverted. While we are witnessing some substantial changes in the *manner* of doing assessment, we remain sceptical that they will induce any major change in the *aims* of education, and in its fundamental relation to the rest of society. Rather, we can easily envisage a process whereby the flagship of the assessment fleet, the GCSE, actually reinforces those aspects of present public examinations that are concerned with selection, with curriculum control and with the existing status hierarchies of kinds of knowledge.

References

BARDELL, G.S., FORREST, G.M. and SHOESMITH, D.J. (1978) *Comparability in GCE*, Manchester, JMB on behalf of the GCE Boards.

BROADFOOT, P.M. (1979) *Assessment, Schools and Society*, London, Methuen.

BLOOM, B.S., HASTINGS, J.T. and MADAUS, G.F. (1971) *Handbook on Formative and Summative Evaluation of Student Learning*, London, McGraw-Hill.

DEPARTMENT OF EDUCATION AND SCIENCE (1984) *Records of Achievement: A Statement of Policy*, London, DES.

DEPARTMENT OF EDUCATION AND SCIENCE (1985) *GCSE: The National Criteria*, London, HMSO.

GOLDSTEIN, H. (1986) 'Models for equating test scores and for studying the comparability of public examinations' in NUTTALL, D.L. (Ed) *Assessing Educational Achievement*, Lewes, Falmer Press.

HARRISON, A.W. (1982) *Review of Graded Tests*, Schools Council Examinations Bulletin 41, London, Methuen Educational.

HOLLAND, P. and RUBIN, D. (Eds) (1982) *Test Equating*, New York, Academic Press.

INNER LONDON EDUCATION AUTHORITY (1984) *Improving Secondary Schools* (The Hargreaves Report), London, ILEA.

NUTTALL, D.L. (1984) 'Doomsday or a new dawn? The prospects of a common system of examining at 16-plus' in BROADFOOT, P.M. (Ed) *Selection, Certification and Control*, Lewes, Falmer Press.

NUTTALL, D.L. (1986) 'The validity of assessments', appendix to WOLF, A. and SILVER, R. *Work Based Learning: Trainee Assessment by Supervisors*, Sheffield, Manpower Services Commission.

SCHOOLS COUNCIL (1979) *Standards in Public Examinations: Problems and Possibilities*, London, Schools Council.

WOLF, A. and SILVER, R. (1986) *Work Based Learning: Trainee Assessment by Supervisors*, Sheffield, Manpower Services Commission.

Nuttall, D.L. (1987) 'The validity of assessments', European Journal of the Psychology of Education, II, 2, pp. 109–18.

Introduction

This next article is certainly one of Desmond Nuttall's classic contributions to furthering the conceptualization of educational assessment. Arising out of work he was asked to do by the Manpower Services Commission (a Government quango whose role was to enhance the contribution of education and training in preparing individuals for employment), the paper was published in the *European Journal of the Psychology of Education*. This may explain why it has not been quoted as much as one might expect, as that is not a journal that is widely read by those working in this field in the UK.

The article wrestles with some of the key concepts of effective educational assessment. What is assessment for? When can an assessment be regarded as a valid assessment? How far should one generalize from assessment results based upon sample performances? How far can one expect performance in one context to be a good indicator of the likelihood of that type of performance being repeated in other contexts? Should educational assessment involve an attempt to record optimum performances of individuals? If so is this likely to require different circumstances for different individuals?

Many assessment debates have ignored key questions such as these, and have run into difficulties as a result. The fundamental nature of some of these questions is such that real improvements in the practice of educational assessment can only occur if they are faced and resolved. An example of this happening in practice is to be found in Gipps and Murphy's (1994) recent volume on equity in educational assessment. One of the reasons they give for such slow progress in sorting out equal opportunities issues in educational assessments, is the lack of clarity that exists about what could constitute a 'fair test' for male and female students, for example. The need to relate assessment to 'the experience of the individual', and to present 'tasks that are perceived as relevant to the current concerns of the student', two key elements of Desmond Nuttall's conclusions, are at the heart of Gipps and Murphy's (1994) recommendations for improving the fairness of educational assessments.

The influence of context on performance is readily observable in everyday life. We all find it easier to relax in certain situations rather than others, and football teams tend to perform better in front of their home crowd rather than in away fixtures. The psychological research of Margaret Donaldson (1978) and many others has demonstrated very clearly how much contextual changes influence children's performance in developmental tests. Despite all of this those responsible for designing educational assessments often treat the context for those assessments as an arbitrary factor. A major conclusion of Desmond Nuttall's analysis in this paper is that the validity of any assessment, for any individual, for any particular purpose, will depend profoundly on the appropriateness of the context in which the assessment occurs.

THE VALIDITY OF ASSESSMENTS[1]

The paper reviews the concept of validity, and adopts the formulation that validity is the extent to which the results of an assessment can be generalized. The evidence about the validity of paper-and-pencil tests is then examined, leading to the conclusion that the relationship between performance on such tests and criteria of occupational performance is generally very modest. Research about the factors influencing performance on assessment tests is reviewed, and the three main categories of factor found to be motivation, the conditions of assessment and the way in which the task is presented. In conclusion, the responsibility of the assessor to elicit the candidate's best performance is contrasted with the responsibility to ensure the validity of the results of the assessment, and hence to ensure that the sample of behaviour assessed is representative of the universe of interest.

The Concept of Validity

Every assessment is based upon a *sample* of the behaviour in which we are interested; we intend to generalize from the particular sample of behaviour we observe to the universe of that behaviour. To take an example: when a classroom test of mental arithmetic is given, the teacher is not simply interested in the answers to her questions, she is interested in what the answers tells her about the children's grasp of particular knowledge and processes (for example, the multiplication tables) and what she therefore needs to do in the way of further teaching. Occasionally it is possible to be comprehensive (for example, one could test every one of the tables up to twelve) but much more often it is impossible: one cannot test a child on every possible addition sum, let alone on every possible reading passage. So to say that a child has mastered addition or can read fluently, one is bound to be making a generalization from limited evidence.

But the generalization is not necessarily only to the domain of the behaviour defined in an abstract way. Having tested a child on the two times table, to conclude from a flawless performance that he therefore knows all his tables is obviously a faulty inference. But equally if the child had been tested by an unknown adult visitor to his classroom and found incapable of reciting his tables, it might be inappropriate to conclude that he didn't know his tables; if his mother or his teacher had asked him, he might have recited them confidently. The universe of the behaviour of interest has therefore to be carefully defined and will embrace the conditions and occasions of assessment as well as the content.

The fidelity of the inference drawn from the responses to the assessment is what is usually called the *validity* of the assessment. In practice, an assessment does not have a single validity; it can have many according to its different uses and the different kinds of inference made, in other words according to the universe of generalization. This is a slightly different formulation of the term 'validity' from the one offered in many textbooks of which the definition given by Nuttall and Willmott (1972) is typical: 'The extent to which a test or examination does what it was designed to do'. The formulation is, however, consistent with it and accords with modern views, such as those of Messick (1984):

'Elsewhere I have maintained that test validity is an overall evaluative judgment of the adequacy and appropriateness of inferences and actions based on test scores (Messick, 1980). As such, validity is an inductive summary of both the existing evidence for and the potential consequences of test interpretation and use' (p. 231).

As Rogoff (1981) points out, it is not clear where we should draw the boundaries of our generalizations. He gives the example of the conclusions that might be drawn from successful performance on a syllogism problem: the individual (a) will do well on the next syllogism; (b) will do well on other kinds of logic problems; (c) will be logical in many situations; or (d) is smart. The specification of the domain of the behaviour in which we are interested is thus critically important; I return to this issue later.

The formulation of validity put forward here tends to embrace another desirable characteristic of good assessment, namely reliability. Only if the assessment is repeatable, using another assessor or on another occasion, is it of any value. This is another aspect of generalization — across assessors or occasions — as the formulation of generalizability theory by Cronbach and his colleagues (1972) recognizes.

Different aspects of generalizability are sometimes in tension, since the pressure for standardization and uniformity arising from the need for generalizing across assessors and occasions can conflict with establishing conditions that will allow a faithful sampling of the behaviour of interest. A third desirable quality of good assessment, namely utility, can also be in conflict with validity and reliability. Utility embraces the convenience, flexibility and inexpensiveness of the assessment, inevitably considerations of some importance. It was mainly lack of utility that led to the demise of specially mounted practical science tests in examinations taken by 16-year-old students in the UK; no one felt that experimental investigation was unimportant. The National Criteria for science in the examinations being introduced in 1988 require the assessment of the skills involved in experimental investigation, and the examination boards are already pointing to the cost implications, while accepting that science examinations will become more valid.

Ways of Assessing Validity

If we accept validity as meaning the degree to which the responses to the assessment can be generalized, the way to explore it is through the relationship of these responses to other assessments of the same behaviour (and of different behaviours as well to check that our assessment is not unduly contaminated). In the textbooks this type of validation would be known as construct validation, and in the minds of many psychometricians it subsumes or replaces all the other kinds of validation that textbooks list, for example, face, instructional, content and so forth (see, for example, Angoff, 1986).

In an applied setting, we may have a very clear idea of what it is we are trying to assess (the construct). For example, in selecting applicants for university places, we are interested in predicting how well they will 'do', which is usually interpreted to mean how they will fare in their final examinations. It is relatively straightforward to examine the statistical relationship between tests and examinations taken by university applicants and the first-year or final results of those admitted. Research in Europe and North America (Mitter, 1979) has shown that attainment at the end of schooling is the best predictor of university examination performance, better than aptitude tests and ratings from interviews but not particularly good (in the sense that some who do well at 18 will not do very well in their finals, and vice versa). But many would argue that success at university should not be measured just in terms of final examination performance, but in other ways (for example, student politics, journalism, drama and sport). To decide upon the criterion of success is often difficult in occupational settings as well; should salespersons be judged in terms of volume of sales or customer satisfaction, or by some global rating by supervisors (which may be contaminated by 'halo effect')? Often, then, there is no single criterion or, in other words, the universe of the behaviour in which we are interested is difficult to describe. This is particularly true in education or non-specific training. The variety of circumstances in which we hope that the education or training may be valuable is almost impossible to describe. If we cannot define the universe, we can hardly be expected to judge how representative the sample of behaviour we assess, actually is. So validation is a difficult process in all but the most straightforward selection procedures, and is impossible if we do not have a clear idea of what it is we are trying to assess.

Evidence About the Validity of Assessments

Assessments (through tests, interviews, examinations, performance appraisals, simulations and so forth) are in daily use for educational and occupational selection, and there have been many studies of their predictive validity. (It might be argued that there have not been enough studies: in the UK, school examination results are widely used in selection for employment without any evidence that they do predict performance on the job. In the USA, validation of selection procedures has been done much more rigorously to establish that they do not have adverse impact, i.e. that they do not discriminate unfairly between groups such as ethnic groups, the sexes or different age groups.)

Ghiselli (1966) conducted a very comprehensive review of the validity of occupational aptitude tests, almost all paper-and-pencil tests, some general such as reasoning or intelligence tests, others rather more specific like clerical aptitude or mechanical reasoning tests. The validity of these predictors was modest with a median correlation coefficient of .19 when criteria of job proficiency were used. When criteria obtained during the training phase were used (often tests and examinations more similar in type to the selection tests than were the job proficiency measures), the median correlation coefficient rose to about .30. This resembles the value often achieved in educational selection (for example, attainment at 18+ against university performance (see Mitter, 1979), and examinations at 16+ against performance in technical education (see Williams and Boreham, 1971)).

Another comprehensive review was carried out by Samson, Graue, Weinstein and Walberg (1984). They summarized studies relating academic performance to subsequent occupational performance (using criteria such as income, job satisfaction and effectiveness ratings) in professional fields. The mean validity coefficient of the educational predictors was only .155. The highest coefficients were found in the fields of business and nursing, middle values in engineering and teaching, with negligible values among medical doctors and PhDs.

It is fair to conclude that paper-and-pencil tests and examinations have very modest predictive validity against criteria of occupational performance. When the criteria are themselves paper-and-pencil tests or examinations, the validity is somewhat higher, but the experience of organizations that allow open entry and self-selection is that much talent is wasted by relying on conventional selection devices (see various contributions in Mitter 1979, and also Nuttall, 1983, for a summary of the experiences of the Open University).

Less is known about the predictive validity of other kinds of assessment used in selection, but the validity of more job-specific assessments tends to be higher. For example, Jones (1984) reports:

> The types of (selection) tests used (in the USA) have tended to be-come more specifically job-related. The general tests of reasoning have proved much more difficult to validate. (Appendix L, p. 8)

The general consensus is that performance assessments and simulation (for example, work samples and trainability tests) have higher predictive va-lidity than paper-and-pencil tests (Hecht, 1979; McClelland, 1973; Monjan and Gassner, 1979; Priestley, 1982; Robertson and Downs, 1979; Spencer, 1983).

Priestley (1981) concludes that practice has shown that the more closely the sample of behaviour assessed resembles behaviour on the job and the more the criteria of occupational success are justified (for example, by job analysis and job relevance), the stronger is the basis for validity, though it must of course be demonstrated in any particular application. Analysis of the job and the skills it requires allows the devising of appropriate assessments so that there is a point-to-point correspondence between the assessment and the cri-terion (Robertson and Downs, 1979), but sometimes, once a skill is present in sufficient amount to allow the job to be done, improvements in that skill do not necessarily lead to enhanced job performance. In such circumstances, Spencer (1983) argues that one should attempt to identify the factors or skills that differentiate the person who is good at the job from the person who is exceptional. Not all the skills that appear in the job analysis will necessarily differentiate the excellent from the good.

Factors Influencing Performance

Examples given below show how in some circumstances an individual may be able to demonstrate his or her mastery of a mathematical operation, for example, while in other circumstances he or she cannot. The notion of a distinction between *competence* (the basic ability to perform) and *performance* (the demonstration of the competence on a particular occasion or under par-ticular circumstances) has become increasingly important in examining the factors that influence performance especially when that performance is being assessed. A fuller statement of the distinction between competence and per-formance comes from Messick (1984):

Competence refers to what a person knows and can do under ideal circumstances, whereas performance refers to what is actually done under existing circumstances. Competence embraces the structure of knowledge and abilities, whereas performance subsumes as well the processes of accessing and utilizing those structures and a host of affective, motivational, attentional and stylistic factors that influence the ultimate responses (Flavell and Wohlwill, 1969; Overton and Newman, 1982). Thus, a student's competence might be validly revealed in either classroom performance or test performance because of personal or circumstantial factors that affect behaviour. (p. 227)

It should be noted that this definition of competence, widely accepted in the psychological literature, differs from that used in the world of occupational training. One current definition from that world is 'the ability to perform a particular activity to a prescribed standard' (see FEU, 1986).

The psychological construct is a very slippery notion, of course (see Wood and Power, 1984) and we have to find a way of operationalizing it. Dillon and Stevenson-Hicks (1983) propose that the operational definition of competence should be the level of performance obtained under elaborative procedures beyond the performance level obtained under standard conditions. There have been many attempts to develop elaborative procedures particularly among the retarded, often using training procedures (for example, Feuerstein, 1980). Another approach is collaboration between tester and student to help the student to produce his or her best performance. This has affinities with Vygotsky's (1978) concept of the zone of next development, which represents the gap between the present level of development and the potential level of development, identified on the basis of what he or she can already do provided that he or she receives the best possible help from an adult.

It is not clear, however, that the operational definition proposed by Dillon and Stevenson-Hicks is particularly helpful. They are, in effect, simply proposing a different universe of generalization, albeit one that reminds us of our responsibility to attend to the influences upon performance. Research on the conditions that facilitate or hamper performance has not always been very systematic but it is growing in importance, as two examples from the work of Hudson (1966 and 1968) show. He worked with 17-year-old students using tests of divergent thinking (for example, How many uses can you think of for a brick?) One example is anecdotal: Hudson entered a class and was rather angry and aggressive with the group of students who were about to take the test. Their performance was significantly higher than on a previous occasion (unlike other groups who were retested). The second example arose from more systematic work. Hudson found that 17-year-olds specializing in the study of science offered fewer responses to divergent thinking tests than arts specialists. Yet, when he invited science specialists to imagine that they were a bohemian artist called McMinn (for whom a character sketch was supplied) and to answer the test in the role of McMinn, he found that the science specialists then gave as many (and as bizarre) responses as the art specialists. In other words they were capable of producing more responses than they chose to under standard conditions.

A study of cross-cultural research (for example, Laboratory of Comparative Human Cognition, 1982; Cole and Means, 1981), research among the retarded or the socially deprived (for example, Wallace, 1980; Zigler and Seitz, 1982) and more general work on task presentation (for example, Donaldson, 1978; Bell, Costello and Kuchemann, 1983) suggests that the following inter-related factors are particularly significant in affecting performance under conditions of assessment:

(a) motivation to do the task and interest in it (influenced by the personal experience and the instrumental value of performing it);

(b) the relationship between the assessor and the individual being assessed and the conditions under which the assessment is made;

(c) the way in which the task is presented, the language used to describe it, and the degree to which it is within the personal experience of the individual being assessed.

The first, motivation, is so obvious that it merits little discussion, though that is not to dismiss its importance. Performance will never be as good if the individual sees no point in performing, and it is a real challenge to the teachers of many alienated young people to convince them that there is a point in studying subjects like history and geography. The enhanced motivation of young people in post-compulsory education and training schemes to which many educators and supervisors testify is generally attributed to the obvious relevance of the activities to employment and wage-earning. Other motivating factors are the enthusiasm of the teacher for the subject ('infectious enthusiasm') and tangible and accessible rewards (for example, certificates) to which the success of the graded test movement is often, but still rather uncertainly, attributed (Nuttall and Goldstein, 1984).

The relationship between assessor and student is important in many ways. Among the first to elaborate the competence-performance distinction were the sociolinguists who found that minority groups and deprived young people would show very limited vocabulary and speech forms with middle-class white investigators while having very rich conversation among themselves. Many characteristics of the assessor (for example, ethnic origin, sex, status) can affect students' performance, as can the degree to which the assessor provides support, encouragement and help, and the quality of such support and feedback. An assessor known to the student can often elicit a higher level of performance (provided that the relationship between them is good), but there are qualifications to this generalization. Hudson's anecdotal finding has already been mentioned and can be seen as an example of how challenge and competition can fire enhanced performance in conformity with the Yerkes-Dodson Law: too little or too much anxiety leads to lower performance than if one is moderately anxious. More generally, the conditions of testing can be influential: Seitz, Abelson, Levine and Zigler (1975) found that young children tested in the home performed worse than another group tested in a classroom, contrary too expectation. Observations suggested that maternal anxiety about the child's performance inhibited that performance. Moreover, it is a common finding that performance during a course of study (assessed continuously by the teacher) is better than performance in the examination (see, for example, Cohen and Deale, 1977). It is often concluded that teachers are overgenerous in their assessments; an alternative conclusion is that the conditions under which course work was conducted and assessed elicited or facilitated genuinely better performance.

The effect of the way in which the task is presented has been studied extensively. In reviewing the findings of the first Assessment of Performance Unit surveys of mathematical performance, Eggleston (1983) concluded: 'The significance of differences in presentation seems to be unquestionable' (p. 6). This may be as simple as presenting the same numbers for addition vertically or horizontally; in the latter case 20 per cent fewer 11-year-olds could give the correct answer. But the task is not identical; an extra step (lining up the columns appropriately) is needed when the numbers are presented horizontally. Yet both tasks are on the topic of addition. This small example reinforces the point made at the beginning: a careful specification of the domain of behaviour of interest is necessary. Not only does one have to specify the addition of three numbers (containing up to three digits) but also how those are to be presented physically; alternatively, if the physical presentation is not specified, the assessor must vary it to ensure that the sampling of behaviour is representative of the whole domain of addition. And should the presentation be in mathematical (i.e. abstract) form or as a problem in words? Again, Eggleston (1983) gives examples of how the same mathematical task presented in different forms leads to different levels of performance, concluding that 'the success rate is, in general, diminished when the mathematical performance is embedded in an everyday "problem" formulation' (p. 9). The format of the question can also have an effect; for example, the fact that the answer to a multiple-choice question can be guessed correctly can lead to an incorrect inference about competence (Wood and Power, 1984). And simply changing the position of a question in a test can make the question appear easier or harder (Leary and Dorans, 1982).

Bell, Costello, and Kuchemann (1983) summarize the results of a wide range of studies in mathematics under five categories of factors influencing performance:

(a) context (especially familiar or unfamiliar);
(b) readability (including all sorts of linguistic factors);
(c) size and complexity of numbers (mentioning the striking feature that complicated numbers appear to make it more difficult to *recognize* which operation is needed);

(d) number and type of operations and stages (of which vertical and horizontal addition provide a simple example);

(e) distractions (including superfluous information).

There is similar work in the field of Piagetian psychology which shows how children's capacities have often been underestimated because of the way in which the problem has been presented (for example, Brown and Desforges, 1979; Bryant, 1974; Donaldson, 1978). For example, Greenfield (1966) found that her African subjects showed conservation-of-liquids when they were allowed to pour the liquids themselves, but not when she did all the manipulations.

The conclusion is inescapable: the way in which the task is presented, the presenter, and the perceived significance of the task to the student — factors which might be termed the 'context' of the task in a broader sense than that used by Bell *et al.* above — can all have a major effect on the performance of the person presented with the task. Assessment (like learning) is highly context-specific and one generalizes at one's peril.

Conclusions

It seems appropriate to sidestep the psychological construct of competence and to think simply in terms of the conditions that elicit the individual's best performance. Modern educational assessment is beginning to strive to permit those assessed to show their best performance, and to take account of the factors that might prevent the best performance from being demonstrated (Messick, 1984; Wood, 1986). Research, as usual, has no unambiguous answers about how this can be achieved but features of the task and the conditions of assessment that seem to be elaborative are:

(a) tasks that are concrete and within the experience of the individual;

(b) tasks that are presented clearly;

(c) tasks that are perceived as relevant to the current concerns of the student;

(d) conditions that are not unduly threatening, something that is helped by a good relationship between the assessor and the student.

The goal of releasing the best performance from people being assessed seems highly desirable in human terms as well as psychologically illuminating, but does it contribute to improving the validity of the assessment? One hypothesis about why performance assessments are better predictors of occupational competence than paper-and-pencil tests is that paper-and-pencil tests have fewer elaborative features than performance assessments. But a more plausible hypothesis is that it is due to the lack of match between the nature of the tasks in a paper-and-pencil test and on the job, and between the context of testing and normal occupational performance. A paper-and-pencil test taken under very formal standardized conditions is about as unlike real life as you can get. The magnitude of the generalization from the performance assessment to occupational performance is very much more limited.

Consequently it does not automatically follow that eliciting best performance improves validity. One is most likely to improve validity by improving the sampling of tasks and contexts from the universe of interest — and that means defining the universe very much more carefully than we have done in the past. If the successful employee needs arithmetical skills, then the nature of the skills and the conditions under which they have to be deployed need to be spelt out so that appropriate tasks and appropriate conditions can be devised. If it is difficult to specify the universe (because, for example, the trainee might be employed in so many different circumstances), a wide range of tasks should be administered under a wide range of conditions. If the job requires the task to be done under pressure, then the assessment should put the trainee under similar pressure, even if that means that best performance is not elicited. (In the longer run it might be more fruitful to change the job so that best performance can be utilized.)

With the benefit of hindsight, it seems strange that so much effort should have been put into the development and validation of general paper-and-pencil tests, when everything points to their artificiality, their remoteness from the nature of any normal job and their unelaborative conditions of administration. It seems likely that considerations of utility and reliability have prevailed over considerations of validity. The signs are now that validity is claiming its rightful pre-eminent position, and that the careful specification of the universe of generalization is helping to stimulate improved conditions of assessment and more thought about evoking an individual's best performance.

Note

1 The writing of an earlier version of this paper was funded by the Manpower Services Commission and was published as an appendix to Wolf and Silver (1986). I acknowledge with thanks the comments of Alison Wolf, Martyn Hammersley and Harvey Goldstein on that earlier version, and the support of the Manpower Services Commission.

References

ANGOFF, W.H. (1986) *Validity, An Evolving Concept*, Princeton, NJ, Educational Testing Service (mimeo).

BELL, A.W., COSTELLO, J. and KUCHEMANN, D. (1983) *A Review of Research in Mathematical Education* (Part A: Research on Learning and Teaching), Windsor, NFER-Nelson.

BROWN, G., and DESFORGES, C. (1979) *Piaget's Theory: A Psychological Critique*, London, Routledge and Kegan Paul.

BRYANT, P.E. (1974) *Perception and Understanding in Young Children*, London, Methuen.

COHEN, L., and DEALE, R.N. (1977) *Assessment by Teachers in Examinations at 16+*, (Schools Council Examinations Bulletin 37), London, Evans/Methuen Educational.

COLE, M., and MEANS, B. (1981) *Comparative Studies of How People Think*, Cambridge, MA, Harvard University Press.

CRONBACH, L.J., GLESER, G.C., NANDA, H. and RAJARATNAM, H. (1972) *The Dependability of Behavioural Measurements*, New York, Wiley.

DILLON, R.F., and STEVENSON-HICKS, R. (1983) 'Competence vs. performance and recent approaches to cognitive assessment', *Psychology in the Schools*, 20, pp. 142–5.

DONALDSON, M. (1978) *Children's Minds*, London, Fontana.

EGGLESTON, S.J. (1983) *Learning Mathematics* (APU Occasional Paper 1) London, Department of Education and Science.

FEU (1986) *Assessment, Quality and Competence*, London, Further Education Unit.

FEUERSTEIN, R. (1980) *Instrumental Enrichment*, Baltimore, MA, University Park Press.

FLAVELL, J.H. and WOHLWILL, J.F. (1969) 'Formal and functional aspects of cognitive development' in ELKIND, D. and FLAVELL, J.H. (Eds) *Studies in Cognitive Development*, New York, Oxford University Press.

GHISELLI, E.E. (1966) *The Validity of Occupational Aptitude Tests*, New York, Wiley.

GREENFIELD, P.M. (1966) 'On culture and conservation' in BRUNER, J.S., OLIVER, R.P. and GREENFIELD, P.M. (Eds) *Studies in Cognitive Growth*, New York, Wiley.

HECHT, K.A. (1979) 'Current, status and methodological problems of validating professional licensing and certification exams' in BUNDA, M.A. and SANDERS, J.R. (Eds) *Practices and Problems in Competency-based Education*, Washington, DC, NCME.

HUDSON, L. (1966) *Contrary Imaginations*, London, Methuen.

HUDSON, L. (1968) *Frames of Mind*, London, Methuen.

JONES, J.E.M. (1984) *The Uses Employers Make of Examination Results and Other Tests for the Selection of 16–19 year olds for Employment*, Reading, University of Reading (unpublished M. Phil thesis).

LABORATORY OF COMPARATIVE HUMAN COGNITION (1982) 'Culture and intelligence' in STERNBERG, R.J. (Ed) *Handbook of Human Intelligence*, Cambridge, Cambridge University Press.

LEARY, L.F. and DORANS, N.J. (1982) *The Effects of Item Rearrangement on Test Performance: A Review of the Literature* (Research Report RR-82–30), Princeton, NJ Educational Testing Service.

MCCLELLAND, D.C. (1973) 'Testing for competence rather than for intelligence', *American Psychologist*, 28, pp. 1–14.

MESSICK, S. (1980) 'Test validity and the ethics of assessment', *American Psychologist*, 35, pp. 1012–27.

MESSICK, S. (1984) 'Test psychology of educational assessment', *Journal of Educational Measurement*, 21, pp. 215–37.

MITTER, W. (Ed) (1979) *The Use of Tests and Interviews for Admission to Higher Education*, Windsor, NFER Publishing Co.

MONJAN, S.V. and GASSNER, S.M. (1979) *Critical Issues in Competency-based Education*, New York, Pergamon.

NUTTALL, D.L. (1983) 'Unnatural selection', *Times Educational Supplement*, 18 November, p. 19.

NUTTALL, D.L. and GOLDSTEIN, H. (1984) 'Profiles and graded tests: The technical issues' in *Profiles in Action*, London, Further Education Unit.

NUTTALL, D.L. and WILLMOTT, A.S. (1972) *British Examinations: Techniques of Analysis*, Slough, NFER.

OVERTON, W.F. and NEWMAN, J.L. (1982) 'Cognitive development: A competence/utilization approach' in FIELD, T. *et al.* (Eds) *Review of Human Development*, New York, Wiley.

PRIESTLEY, M. (1982) *Performance Assessment in Education and Training: Alternative Techniques*, Englewood Cliffs, NJ, Educational Technology Publications.

ROBERTSON, I. and DOWNS, S. (1979) 'Learning and the prediction of performance: Development of trainability testing in the United Kingdom', *Journal of Applied Psychology*, 64, pp. 42–50.

ROGOFF, B. (1981) 'Schooling and the development of cognitive skills' in TRIANDIS, H. and HERON, A. (Eds) *Handbook of Cross-cultural Psychology* (Volume 4), Boston, MA, Allyn and Bacon.

SAMSON, G.E., GRAUE, M.E., WEINSTEIN, T. and WALBERG, H.J. (1984) 'Academic and occupational performance: A quantitative synthesis, *American Educational Research Journal*, 21, pp. 311–21.

SEITZ, V., ABELSON, W.D., LEVINE, E. and ZIGLER, E. (1975) 'Effects of place of testing on the Peabody Picture Vocabulary Test scores of disadvantaged Head Start and non-Head Start children', *Child Development*, 46, pp. 481–6.

SPENCER, L.M. (1983) *Soft Skill Competencies*, Edinburgh, Scottish Council for Research in Education.

VYGOTSKY, L.S. (1978) *Mind in Society*, Cambridge, MA, Harvard University Press (first published in Russian in 1934).

WALLACE, J.G. (1980) 'The nature of educational competence' in SANTS, J. (Ed) *Developmental Psychology and Society*, London, Macmillan.

WILLIAMS, I.C. and BOREHAM, N.C. (1971) *The Predictive Value of CSE Grades in Further Education* (Schools Council Examinations Bulletin 24), London, Evans/Methuen Educational.

WOLF, A. and SILVER, R. (1986) *Work-Based Learning: Trainee Assessment by Supervisors*, Sheffield, Manpower Services Commission.

WOOD, R. (1986) 'The agenda for educational measurement' in NUTTALL, D.L. (Ed) *Assessing Educational Achievement,* Lewes, Falmer Press.

WOOD, R. and POWER, C. (1984) 'An enquiry into the competence-performance distinction as it relates to assessment in secondary and further education', South Australia, Flinders University (unpublished report).

ZIGLER, E. and SEITZ, V. (1982) 'Social policy and intelligence' in STERNBERG, R.J. (Ed) *Handbook of Human Intelligence*, Cambridge, Cambridge University Press.

Nuttall, D.L., Goldstein, H., Presser, R. and Rasbash, H. (1988) 'Differential school effectiveness', *International Journal of Educational Research*, 13, 7, pp. 769–76.

Introduction

When Desmond Nuttall moved from the Open University to become Director of the Research and Statistics Branch of the Inner London Education Authority in 1986, this gave him the chance to contribute to one of the most highly respected educational research groups in the UK. Among his predecessors in this post were Marten Shipman and Peter Mortimore both of whom were, and still are, extremely well known academics and educational researchers, who not only contributed to building up the ILEA Research and Statistics Branch but who also went on to hold prestigious senior professorial posts in university educational research centres.

Desmond Nuttall's interest in the ILEA post characterized his concern for the application of research findings directly to influence educational policy and practice. The ILEA was an education authority highly committed to doing just that. It provided an environment in which Desmond Nuttall could become fully immersed in the cut and thrust of everyday policy-making and implementation, founded on the goals of the ILEA to improve the effectiveness of its educational provision for all pupils. At the heart of this work was a concern for disadvantaged groups, and much of the ILEA research was used to explore ethnic, social class and gender differences, in order to consider ways in which educational disadvantages could be countered.

This paper provides a good example of the type of analyses that the ILEA Research and Statistics Branch was able to undertake. The size of the samples used, and the sophistication of the analysis that could be used were often beyond those which were available to other educational researchers, and as such the ILEA research had a particularly powerful impact on national and international debates-for example about school effectiveness. Later work on ILEA examination results, which directly followed up the evidence presented in this paper, was able to refute the findings of Smith and Tomlinson (1989), that differences in examination results between ethnic groups were small, and very much smaller than the differences between schools. The ILEA research in this respect provided quite unprecedented analyses of the performance of children from different ethnic backgrounds in different ILEA secondary schools. The use of multi-level modelling (Goldstein, 1987) in these analyses allowed a detailed picture to emerge of the contribution of ethnic background differences, alongside an account of the influence of gender differences and verbal reasoning levels.

The contribution of work such as this to the debate about school effectiveness has been significant. Simplistic league tabling of schools on the basis of raw examination results, totally ignores the context within which individual schools are operating. Results such as those reported in this paper allow us to consider school effectiveness in relation to contextual factors such as the composition of a school's intake analysed in terms of gender, ethnic grouping, social class, and verbal reasoning levels. Thus a school which appears from raw results to be ineffective may actually be very effective once the nature of its intake is understood and a 'value-added' approach is taken. Even more significantly, the results encourage us to think not of 'school effectiveness' as a unitary trait, but rather to think about different types of school effectiveness, by revealing evidence of, for example, relative effectiveness in relation to children from particular ethnic backgrounds or within a particular verbal reasoning band on intake. Such analyses take us well beyond ritualistic political drum beating about 'failing schools', towards an understanding of school effectiveness that is well informed, insightful and constructive. The ILEA Research and Statistics Branch is sadly no longer with us, but the inheritance that it has left is a rich one, and one which deserves to be cherished.

DIFFERENTIAL SCHOOL EFFECTIVENESS

Abstract

Studies of school effectiveness are briefly reviewed, pointing to the need to study effectiveness for sub-groups within each school as well as overall. The results of a multilevel analysis of a large dataset covering the years 1985, 1986 and 1987 and using examination performance as the outcome measure are presented, revealing substantial differences between ethnic groups. The findings also show that the effectiveness of a school varies along several dimensions, and that there is also variation over time. The implications of these findings are discussed.

Introduction

This chapter describes preliminary analyses of a large dataset held about secondary schools in inner London. It explores an issue of great concern to policy-makers, teachers and parents, namely whether some schools are more effective than others not only in a general sense, which is now well established in the literature, but also in the sense of being equally effective for all groups (for example, boys and girls, ethnic minority groups and so on). In this chapter, the effectiveness of schools is measured in terms of their students' success in public examinations at age 16. The Inner London Education Authority, currently the largest education authority (school district) in the UK; with 140 secondary schools, serves an inner city, multiracial community as well as more affluent suburbs; the differences between the schools it controls are very marked in terms of their social and ethnic composition. Its twin aims are to improve the quality of education, and to ensure equality of opportunity.

The issue of measuring and describing the effectiveness of schools has become even more significant in England and Wales after the passing of the 1988 Education Reform Act. Among other things, this Act requires each school to publish a wide range of performance measures based on a series of tests and assessments across the curriculum (TGAT, 1988a and 1988b), as well as a diverse set of performance indicators as a result of the devolution of financial control to the schools. The proposals require that these indicators should be published without statistical adjustment to reflect the different characteristics of the intakes of the schools, though the publication of adjusted results in addition is not prohibited. Fair and comprehensible ways of presenting performance indicators in context, and to reveal differences between subgroups of students, are therefore urgently needed.

Background

School effectiveness has been extensively studied, and the two most influential studies in England are Rutter, Maughan, Mortimore and Ouston (1979) and Mortimore, Sammons, Stoll, Lewis and Ecob (1988), for secondary schools and primary schools respectively. Both used schools in the area of ILEA. The ILEA has also analyzed school effectiveness routinely, and published ratings of the effectiveness of all its secondary schools on two occasions (ILEA Research and Statistics, 1986 and 1987a). 'Effectiveness' is taken to be the difference between the actual 'output' of the school and the 'output' expected (in the statistical sense) of a school with identical student characteristics. The measure of output used was the aggregated public examination results of students aged 16. A variety of measures of the characteristics of pupils attending each school were investigated using aggregate level multiple regression analyses; three factors consistently emerged as significant in analyses over the years. First was the proportion of the age group in each school eligible for free school meals (a measure of economic deprivation); the second was the proportion of pupils in VR Band 1, which is a London-wide measure of performance at age 11 generating norms of 25 per cent of the population in VR Band 1, 50 per cent in VR Band 2 and 25 per cent in VR Band 3 over the ILEA area as a whole (allocation of individuals to each band is carried out by the head and teachers at each primary school on the basis of their judgment of the pupils' overall attainment; the *number* in each band in each school is assigned by the ILEA on the basis of the *number* of pupils scoring on each quartile on a test of verbal reasoning administered throughout the Authority). The third factor was the proportion of girls in the age group in each school, reflecting the fact that nearly half the secondary schools in London are for girls only or boys only, leading to sex imbalance in many of the co-educational schools, as more parents prefer single-sex education for their daughters than for their sons.

The more recent of the two routine reports (ILEA Research and Statistics, 1987a) noted a number of significant limitations to the analyses and the ILEA agreed to suspend the publication of ratings of effectiveness for each secondary school while the methodology was improved. The most significant limitation was the use of aggregated data for each school, rather than data on each individual student, for example, his or her sex. Woodhouse and Goldstein (1988) have shown the dangers of relying on aggregated data in the context of the analysis of examination results for local education authorities in the UK, and have advocated the use of multilevel models (Goldstein, 1987). The methodological literature now shows that these models are universally preferred in the study of school effectiveness (see, for example, Aitkin and Longford, 1986; Bryk and Raudenbush, 1987; Mortimore *et al.*, 1988).

Two major issues concern methodological investigators in the field of school effectiveness at the present time. The first issue is the stability of effects across time. The second issue is of greater social and educational significance. Recent studies (for example, Hallinger and Murphy, 1986; Cuttance, 1988a; Teddlie, Stringfield, Wimpleberg and Kirby, 1989) show that the characteristics of effective schools are not necessarily the same for schools in areas of very different socioeconomic status, while the work of Gray, Jesson and Jones (1986), and Cuttance (1988b) shows that some schools are more effective with some sub-groups (for example, those of high attainment on entry) than with others (for example, those of low attainment on entry).

The ILEA Junior School Project (Mortimore *et al.*, 1988) found that some schools were more effective with particular sub-groups than other schools. For example:

> These results suggest that, in general, schools which had a positive effect in promoting reading progress for one sex also tended to have a positive effect for the other, whilst those which were ineffective for one sex were likely to be ineffective for the other. Nonetheless, there was some variability. Although for the majority of schools (twenty-nine) effects for girls and for boys were in the same direction (positive for both or negative for both) the results were discrepant in 12 schools. In eight of these schools, effects on reading progress were positive for boys, but negative for girls. (p. 210)

This chapter presents a more detailed investigation of these issues, for ILEA secondary schools rather than junior schools; it might be expected that secondary schools, as much larger organizations, could show greater diversity in their differential effectiveness. Moreover, because of the larger numbers of students in secondary schools and because many more schools are included in the present sample, better estimates of sub-group differences can be made.

Method

The dataset comprises the results of public examinations taken at, or about the age of 16 for three cohorts of ILEA students, those attaining the age of 16 in the school years ending in 1985, 1986 and 1987 respectively. These examination results are readily available and have to be published in aggregated form by each school as a requirement of the 1980 Education Act.

The examination results were made available for each student within each secondary school by the examining bodies. Schools were asked to provide information on the sex, VR band on entry to secondary school (as described above), and the ethnic background on each student in the cohort. Two basic ethnic categories were used: 'black' and 'white'. Within 'black', the sub-categories were: African, African-Asian (in 1985 only), Arab, Bangladeshi, Caribbean, Indian, Pakistani, South-East Asian and other black; the 'white' sub-categories were: Irish, English/Scottish/Welsh (although in 1985 those two categories were merged), Greek, Turkish, other European white and other non-European white. Some groups were small, and the results for such groups are not always shown in the analyses discussed below. Full information about the samples in 1985 and 1986 are given in ILEA Research and Statistics (1987b), and the 1987 sample was very similar. Not all 140 secondary schools provided student-based data on ethnicity in each year; the number of schools where complete data are held for all three years is sixty-four, but all 140 provided data in at least one year. Certain other information about the

Table 1: Fixed Effect Estimates

Coefficient	Estimate	Standard error
Constant (intercept)	17.8	—
Girls minus boys	2.5	0.2
VR Band 1 minus Band 3	19.0	0.3
VR Band 2 minus Band 3	8.2	0.2
Ethnic group[a]		
African	4.0	0.5
Arab	4.4	1.1
Bangladeshi	4.7	0.7
Caribbean	−0.4	0.2
Greek	4.6	0.7
Indian	7.3	0.5
Pakistani	6.0	0.6
SE Asian	8.3	0.6
Turkish	3.7	0.4
Other	3.8	0.4
Year	1.4	0.2
Boys schools minus mixed schools	0.8	0.3
Girls schools minus mixed schools	1.4	0.3
Church of England schools minus county	1.2	0.4
Roman Catholic schools minus county	2.4	0.3
Free school meals (FSM) proportion	−0.41	0.04
FSM percentage squared	0.003	0.0004

[a] Each ethnic group is contrasted with the English, Scottish and Welsh group.

schools has also been incorporated into the analyses; for example whether each school is mixed or single sex, and whether it is fully maintained by ILEA (i.e., a county school) or voluntary (i.e., supported by the Church of England or the Roman Catholic Church). Additional information about the schools, including aggregated data about the student body, is available from other databases and will be included in more extensive analyses still being carried out.

The data were analyzed with multilevel modelling software (Rasbash, Prosser and Goldstein, 1989), using three levels: between students, within schools/between years, and between schools.

Results

The multilevel model provides estimates both of the fixed or average effects, such as the difference in the performance of boys and girls overall, and of the random effects, such as the variation in the boy–girl difference across co-educational schools. The model can also provide estimates of such differences for each school (Goldstein, 1987, chapters 2 and 3). Table 1 provides estimates of the fixed effects in the three-level analysis (using data from three consecutive years involving 140 schools and 31,623 students).

Apart from the constant term (or 'intercept' estimate), the estimates refer to differences between groups: for example, the difference between the performance of girls and boys is 2.5 score points in favour of girls, with a standard error of 0.2. The largest differences are between students in the three VR bands. It should be noted that a score of seven points is awarded to a grade A in the GCE 'O' level examination, so that the average difference of nineteen points between students in VR Bands 1 and 3 amounts to nearly three grade As. The performance of the different ethnic groups is in each case compared with that of the students of English, Scottish, Welsh and (in 1985 only) Irish backgrounds (ESWI), who form the largest single group. All ethnic groups perform significantly better than the ESWIs, except those of Caribbean background who perform slightly but not significantly worse.

The relationship between examination score and time is 1.4 points increase per year which is statistically significant. The contrasts between single sex and mixed schools are also statistically significant, in favour of single sex schools. Voluntary denominational schools' examination performance is significantly better than that of county schools, especially for the Roman Catholic schools.

The final two coefficients describe the relationship between the examination score and the proportion of the 16-year-olds in each school who were eligible for free school meals. Thus the average score difference between students in schools where 10 per cent of 16-year-olds are eligible for free school meals and those with 30 per cent eligible is about six points.

In the case of all these coefficients it should be remembered that the estimates are not estimates of the actual differences (say, between the performance of girls and boys) but the difference *after* taking the other factors into account, in particular after adjusting for VR band at intake. The differences therefore reflect progress made during secondary schooling.

Table 2 shows the random effects, that is, the variation between students and within schools and, at level 3, the extent to which the differences between the sub-groups (as shown in table 1) vary between schools, and relate to each other: more technically, the variances and covariances of the differences. There are potentially very many of these difference parameters and not all of them can be fitted in a single model. Moreover, there are only small correlations between the 'year trend' coefficient and the other coefficients that vary across schools, and it was not therefore necessary to fit these covariances; hence the appearance of 'parameter not fitted' in the bottom row.

In table 2 it can be seen that differences in the performance of VR Band 1 and Band 3 students vary substantially between schools: these differences have a variance of 17.4 (and therefore a standard deviation of 4.2), around an average of 19.0 (from table 1). So in some schools the difference is as small as 11 points and others as large as 28. The difference in the performance of VR Band 2 and Band 3 students however has a variance of only 2.8 (i.e., a standard deviation of 1.7) around a mean of 8.2. The sex difference (in mixed schools) has a standard deviation of 1.4 around a mean of 2.5, implying that

Table 2: Random parameter estimates

Between students (level 1) variance	96.7
Within schools, between years (level 2) variance	1.2
Between schools (level 3)	

	Intercept	VR1/VR3	VR2/VR3	Sex	Caribbean/ESW	Year
Intercept	2.9					
VR1/VR3	−1.9	17.4				
	(0.0)					
VR2/VR3	−0.1	6.1	2.8			
	(0.0)	(0.9)				
Sex[a]	−1.5	2.4	0.6	2.1		
	(−0.6)	(0.4)	(0.2)			
Caribbean/ESW	−0.4	−1.8	−0.5	−0.3	1.1	
	(−0.2)	(−0.4)	(−0.3)	(−0.2)		
Year	0.1	NF[b]	NF	NF	NF	0.5
	(0.0)					

Note: Variances and covariances, with correlations shown below covariances and in brackets.
[a] The sex coefficient varies only across mixed schools.
[b] NF = parameter not fitted.

there are a few schools where boys actually do better than girls. The difference in the performance of Caribbean and ESW students has a standard deviation of about 1 score point, around a mean of −0.4.

Discussion

The differences shown in table 1, for example between the sexes and between different kinds of schools, are well established and come as no surprise. The differences between ethnic groups have also been reported earlier (ILEA Research and Statistics, 1987b) both before adjustment and after adjustment for other factors. They are of great concern to the ILEA and are being investigated by schools, teachers and inspectors. An important limitation of the present analyses is that data about the socioeconomic level of the students' families are unavailable. It should be recognized that the ESWI population of inner London is not representative, socially or economically, of the total ESWI population of the United Kingdom and Eire, and there could be confounding of the ethnic differences with socioeconomic differences.

One kind of effect shown in table 1 is of particular interest, exemplified by the proportion of the 16-year-old age group in each school eligible for free school meals. This kind of effect is termed a *compositional* effect and it has often been hypothesized that, over and above the expected differences in performance attributable to differences between individuals attending each school, greater *concentrations* of underperforming groups will further depress performance (or vice versa). The finding that the performance declines as the proportion of students eligible for free school meals increases is a potential example of such a compositional effect (but it is not a true example because data were only available at the aggregate level for this variable and not at the individual level as well). (A few preliminary analyses within a single year (Nuttall, 1989), using proportions in VR Bands 1 and 3, and the proportion of students of Caribbean background, have shown no significant compositional effects, but this topic is being studied further.)

The results in table 2 are of great interest and bear out the hypothesis that schools' performance varies along several dimensions associated with sub-groups, some schools narrowing the gap between boys and girls or between students of high and low attainment on entry, and some widening the gap, relatively speaking. Furthermore, other analyses (not reported here in detail) indicate that other ethnic group differences vary across schools, even more than the Caribbean–ESW difference. For example, the Pakistani–ESW difference has a standard deviation of some 3 score points across schools. It is, of course, those schools that narrow the gap by raising the performance of the lower achieving group (rather than by lowering the performance of the higher achieving group) that are of special interest. It would be valuable to study such schools in depth in cooperation with expert observers, such as ILEA inspectors, to explore possible reasons for their differential performance.

As with compositional effects, the number of possible differences that could be explored (for example, all the ethnic group differences) is too large to include sensibly within one model. Further study of the statistical and practical significance of particular differences and compositional effects is being carried out.

The stability of the efforts over time is an important consideration. The standard deviation of the year trend coefficient is 0.7, indicating that the performance of some schools increases by about 5 points, and that of others not at all over the period 1985 to 1987. In addition there is an unexplained between-year standard deviation of about 1 score point. The reasons for this may be partly to do with an inadequate statistical adjustment. In particular, attainment on entry is available only in the three broad VR bands; it is being replaced by a continuous variable in 1988 (derived from a reading comprehension test). The lack of stability may also be partly to do with the unreliability and lack of comparability of the examination scores. This analysis nevertheless gives rise to a note of caution about any study of school effectiveness that relies on measures of outcome in just a single year, or of just a single cohort of students. Long time series are essential for a proper study of stability over time.

Finally, the relatively small correlations in table 2 should be noted. For example, the school difference between the performance of VR Band 1 and 3 students is not very strongly correlated with the sex or Caribbean–ESW difference. Furthermore, the Band 1–3 differences are virtually uncorrelated with the intercept, i.e., the effect for the students in VR Band 3. This implies that knowing which schools widen or decrease the Band 1–3 *difference* tells one nothing about whether those schools do well or badly for those in VR Band 3. There is, however, a relatively small variation for the intercept which means that the variability in performance of VR Band 3 students between schools is small; hence the variability of VR Band 1 students' performance between schools must be substantial.

A number of the further analyses and investigations that are required have been referred to above. Other further analyses will investigate sensitivity to the specification of the model employed and to the scaling of the outcome variables, as previous work (Goldstein, 1987) has drawn attention to the variation in results as a consequence of variation in model specification. It is also hoped to use the results of examinations in specific subjects (for example, in English or in mathematics), rather than a composite outcome measure, to explore differential effectiveness in different parts of the curriculum, as Mortimore *et al.* (1988) using an even wider range of outcome measures (both cognitive and non-cognitive) found evidence of differential effectiveness.

Concluding Comments

In summary, this research has found that school effectiveness varies in terms of the relative performance of different sub-groups. To attempt to summarize school differences, even after adjusting for intake, sex and ethnic background of the students and fixed characteristics of the schools, in a single quantity is misleading.

The findings are not consistent with those of Smith and Tomlinson (1989) who argue that, because they found that the overall variation between schools in examination performance was much greater than the variations in the differences between ethnic groups, it is appropriate to conceive of a single dimension of school effectiveness. Our research indicates, with three years' data in 140 schools as opposed to one year's data in twenty schools, that it is more meaningful to describe differences between schools for different sub-groups: the concept of overall effectiveness is not useful.

Finally, we wish to stress that the implicit definition of school effectiveness in terms of examination performance used here is limited, since examinations represent only a partial, albeit important, measure of 'output'. The results cannot necessarily be generalized to other measures.

Acknowledgments

We would like to thank colleagues in ILEA Research and Statistics Branch, particularly Steve Greenhill and Sona Chumun, for their help in preparing the data for analysis.

References

AITKIN, M., and LONGFORD, N. (1986) 'Statistical modelling in school effectiveness studies', *Journal of the Royal Statistical Society A*, 149, pp. 1–43.

BRYK, A.S. and RAUDENBUSH, S. (1987) 'Application of the hierarchical linear model to assessing change', *Psychological Bulletin*, 101, pp. 147–58.

CUTTANCE, P. (1988a) 'Intra-system variation in the effectiveness of schools', *Research Papers in Education*, 3, 3, pp. 180–216.

CUTTANCE, P. (1988b) *Modelling Variation in the Effectiveness of Schooling*, Edinburgh, Centre for Educational Sociology.

GRAY, J., JESSON, D. and JONES, B. (1986) 'The search for a fairer way of comparing schools' examination results', *Research Papers in Education*, 1, 2, pp. 91–122.

GOLDSTEIN, H. (1987) *Multilevel Models in Educational and Social Research*, London, Charles Griffin.

HALLINGER, P. and MURPHY, J.F. (1986) 'The social context of effective schools', *American Journal of Education*, May, pp. 328–55.

ILEA RESEARCH AND STATISTICS (1986) *Looking at School Performance* (RS 1058/86), London, ILEA Research and Statistics.

ILEA RESEARCH AND STATISTICS (1987a) *Actual and Predicted Examination Scores in Schools*, (RS 1129/87), London, ILEA Research and Statistics.

ILEA RESEARCH AND STATISTICS (1987b) *Ethnic Background and Examination Results — 1985 and 1986*, (RS 1120/87), London, ILEA Research and Statistics.

MORTIMORE, P., SAMMONS, P., STOLL, L., LEWIS, D. and ECOB, R. (1988) *School Matters*, London, Open Books.

NUTTALL, D.L. (1989) 'Differential school effectiveness', paper presented at the annual meeting of the American Educational Research Association, April, San Francisco.

RASBASH, J., PROSSER, R. and GOLDSTEIN, H. (1989) *ML2: Software for Two-level Analysis (three-level upgrade)*. London, Institute of Education.

RUTTER, M., MAUGHAN, B., MORTIMORE, P. and OUSTON, J. (1979) *Fifteen Thousand Hours*, London, Open Books.

SMITH, D.J. and TOMLINSON, S. (1989) *The School Effect: A Study of Multi-racial Comprehensives*, London, Policy Studies Institute.

TASK GROUP ON ASSESSMENT AND TESTING (1988a) *A Report*, London and Cardiff, Department of Education and Science and the Welsh Office.

TASK GROUP ON ASSESSMENT AND TESTING (1988b) *Three Supplementary Reports*, London and Cardiff, Department of Education and Science and the Welsh Office.

TEDDLIE, C., STRINGFIELD, S., WIMPELBERG, R. and KIRBY, P. (1989) 'Contextual differences in models for effective schooling in the USA', paper presented at the Second International Congress for School Effectiveness, January, Rotterdam.

WOODHOUSE, G. and GOLDSTEIN, H. (1988) 'Educational performance indicators and LEA league tables', *Oxford Review of Education*, 14, 3, pp. 301–20.

Nuttall, D.L. (1989c) 'National assessment: Complacency or misinterpretation?' in Lawton, D. (Ed) *The Educational Reform Act: Choice and Control*, London, Hodder and Stoughton.

Introduction

This next paper was delivered as a lecture at the University of London Institute of Education in March 1988, when the National Curriculum assessment framework in England and Wales was very new. The Task Group on Assessment and Testing (TGAT) model — the main elements of which are described in this paper — was still untried and unchanged. Indeed, the fact that the model was still at a very preliminary stage of implementation is well demonstrated by the fact that Desmond Nuttall felt obliged to add a substantial postscript to his original text, with the publication of the three supplementary TGAT reports in June 1988.

Desmond Nuttall's comments as he observes the evolution of national assessment arrangements and the Education Bill's passage through Parliament, show clearly his aversion to narrowly mechanistic forms of assessment which he knew from experience with GCSE and earlier to be both educationally undesirable and technically unworkable. In this article he calls for curriculum objectives to 'embody the spirit of education in the round'; for a curriculum and assessment structure which is flexible and capable of recognizing individual progress and achievement *whatever* its direction. Desmond Nuttall contrasts the likely effects of the TGAT model in practice with those of records of achievement and the latter's emphasis on '*ipsative*', *self*-referenced achievement.

The contribution heralds many of the themes which would inform Desmond Nuttall's active involvement in the debates over national assessment policy during the last years of his life — the need to involve teachers and pupils in the creative practice of assessment and its development; the need for a 'value-added' measure in any national reporting of school results; the need for extensive programmes of research and development *before* the implementation of such a massive and costly programme of national assessment.

Desmond Nuttall knew that what the Government was seeking to do at that time in terms of implementing national assessment called for assessment technologies that did not then exist — how to get valid individual scores from group tasks, for example or how to manage extended, naturalistic assessment activities in the classroom; how best to moderate the results — and so on. At this stage Desmond Nuttall was already anticipating the problems which were indeed to dog the Government's national assessment programme. Many of them are still unresolved today as the last contribution to this collection (Paper 20) — Desmond Nuttall's speech to the Centre for Policy Studies in September 1993 — so clearly demonstrates. In the meantime he had also substantially revised his view of the effectiveness of the implementation of the TGAT proposals (see Paper 17), and called for a radical change in national curriculum assessments.

NATIONAL ASSESSMENT: COMPLACENCY OR MISINTERPRETATION?

In the first chapter, Stuart Maclure called the Education Reform Act 'the most far-reaching and important piece of education legislation since 1944'. Many, like me, feel uneasy about the underlying philosophy of the Act; it is designed to encourage competition between schools and implicitly between pupils, and to reduce the power of the local education authorities. In this chapter I will be addressing the topic of national assessment, a topic which is not covered in any great detail in the Act. Indeed there are only one or two passing references in the context of the provisions for the National Curriculum. In particular, Section 4 says that:

> The Secretary of State may, by orders, specify in relation to each of the foundation subjects such attainment targets, such programmes of study and such assessment arrangements as he considers appropriate for that subject.

— and that's about it on national assessment. Later sections of the Act give the details of the constitution of the School Examinations and Assessment Council (SEAC) but say little of its duties. It is noticeable that there is no requirement upon SEAC to consult, though in contrast the National Curriculum Council does have to consult about the nature of the curriculum proposals.

Thus, we cannot look to the Act itself to find out how the assessment system will work; we must look to the Report of the Task Group on Assessment and Testing (TGAT, 1988a). In this chapter I want to examine the TGAT proposals critically; but here I face a dilemma. On the one hand I am very unhappy about the underlying philosophy not only of the Act but also of an elaborate and untried system of national assessment in up to ten subjects of the curriculum at four different ages. I am also very critical of the negligible amount of time for consultation over the proposals. Nor would I find it difficult to find fault with a number of the arguments put forward in the Report. Moreover, like the leader writer of *The Times* (14 January 1988), I am somewhat suspicious of the reaction to the Report: he or she wrote:

> Something curious is surely happening in the education world when the big teacher unions and the Labour Party joined Mr Kenneth Baker in welcoming a report that shows exactly how children can be tested at the ages of 7, 11, 14 and 16.

On the other hand, I have a feeling that being a whingeing academic does not help in the present climate. The Government wants national assessment, parents want national assessment;[1] they have become very impatient with education professionals who bring up nothing but objections and difficulties. We are going to get national assessment and the TGAT proposals are not as oppressive and anti-educational as many feared. Paul Black himself said at a BERA Conference that:

> It is easy enough to construct as an Aunt Sally some simplistic and oppressive alternatives and then to show the virtues of the TGAT Report by comparison — perhaps the Report received more than its deserved share of welcome by this very process.[2]

We must recognize that Mr Baker is under pressure from the Prime Minister and the right wing of the Conservative Party to adopt a much simpler and tougher method of testing, but it does seem that by publication of the summary of the TGAT proposals (1988b) the Secretary of State, in the words of *Education*, 'has won a significant victory over his right wing critics' and further that 'Mr Baker's approval of the DES propaganda mission is being viewed as a sign of his unconditional endorsement of the Report' (*Education*, 12 February 1988). So the political realities suggest that, at the present time, if one destroys the TGAT proposals one is more likely to find in their place a more oppressive system; if on the other hand one largely accepts them, and seeks ways of improving and implementing them sensitively, one is likely to arrive at the least bad solution. So I take the view that the balance of

Figure 1

Current initiatives are striving to make assessment

- more comprehensive
- provide better and quicker feedback
- more positive
- give more responsibility to the student
- create flexibility and adaptability in the student
- more valid

Figure 2

The Four Criteria

- The assessment results should give direct information about pupils' achievement in relation to objectives: they should be *criterion-referenced*;
- The results should provide a basis for decisions about pupils' further learning needs: they should be *formative*;
- The scale or grades should be capable of comparison across classes and schools, if teachers and parents are to share a common language and common standards: so the assessments should be *calibrated* or *moderated*;
- The ways in which criteria and scales are set up and used should relate to expected routes of educational development, giving some continuity to a pupil's assessment at different ages: the assessments should *relate to progression*.

---

advantage lies in being constructively critical about the Report — a report that offers the best set of national assessment proposals that we are likely to get.

What I would like to do is to evaluate them against the background of my own appreciation of current initiatives to improve assessment (figure 1), and TGAT's own criteria (figure 2). The key words are *criterion-referenced, formative, moderated* and *relating to progression*.

The essence of the proposals is that the attainment targets should be clustered into ten levels spanning the age range 7–16. The norm would be progress by one level every two years, as figure 3 shows. At age 7 one would expect that most pupils would achieve either level 1, 2 or 3; level 2 being the expected level, and level 1 indicating that a student might need considerable extra help.

These levels are designed to apply not to subjects as a whole but to a number of profile components within each subject. A profile component is a cluster of related attainment targets that have some intellectual coherence (though it is likely that different principles will be used to devise the profile

Figure 3

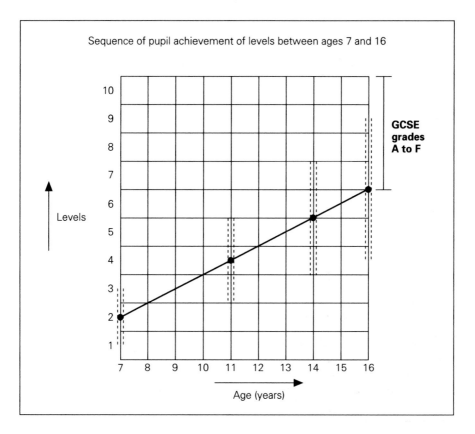

components in different subjects — incidentally they were called domains when similar work was being done for the GCSE). The TGAT proposal is that each subject should comprise up to *six* profile components by the age of 16, though as figure 4 shows they are expecting some profile components to emerge by a process either of bifurcation or by insertion, so that at age 7 there will not be nearly as many profile components within a subject as there will be by the age of 16. Indeed one could expect up to *forty* profile components by the age of 16 on the assumption that there are seven subjects that are going to be defined in terms of attainment targets, while art, music and PE will simply have guidelines.

The assessment will actually be done by a combination of assessment by teachers and nationally standardized assessment tasks. The teachers' assessment will be moderated by groups of teachers who meet to discuss the work of students on the standardized tasks and their own assessments. For 7-year-olds the proposals are, I think, very sensitive: the assessment tasks are to be as naturalistic as possible, that is, part of the normal work in the classroom

Figure 4

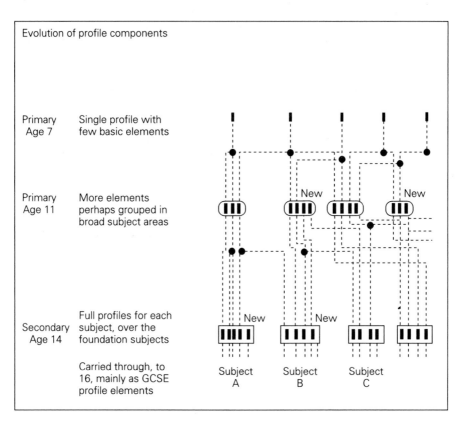

Evolution of profile components

Primary Age 7	Single profile with few basic elements	
Primary Age 11	More elements perhaps grouped in broad subject areas	
Secondary Age 14	Full profiles for each subject, over the foundation subjects	
	Carried through, to 16, mainly as GCSE profile elements	

Subject A   Subject B   Subject C

rather than specially set-up situations. Tasks or assignments should be chosen by teachers from a bank that will allow the assessment of a wide range of diverse skills, so that instead of having a test for English, a test for maths, and a test for science there will be tasks which should allow the assessment of attainment targets and profile components covering maths, English and science. One of the examples given in the Report is of 'winter through to spring': language work comes from discussing the question 'how do we keep warm in the winter?' For maths there could be a survey of the clothes worn by children in the classroom, and later some science experiments looking at heating and cooling, and insulation.

On special educational needs the Report is again very sensitive; it allows schools to exempt such students from sitting the tasks at the discretion of the headteacher but, on the other hand, it does allow the possibility of such students attempting the tasks and, if necessary, being provided with help and assistance (with the fact that such assistance has been given to be recorded). That proposal signals a way of assessment that is good for *all* students. Feuerstein has pioneered this approach primarily with children with special

educational needs but the Russian psychologist Vygotski also looked at ways
of assessing normal children that compared what they could do unaided with
what they could do with the help of an adult or a peer — 'the zone of next
development'.[3] The Report also recognizes the dangers of gender and ethnic
bias in assessment, but I think that we need to be more positive and to explore
ways of investigating such bias much more vigorously. And finally, but no
means least, the Report organizes the importance of teachers in the process of
assessment. Mr Baker, himself, acknowledged that:

> The task ahead will not be done, nor done well, without the initia-
> tive, effort and commitment of the education profession, in particular
> the teachers in the classroom. (DES/WO, 1987)

The TGAT Report expands that notion and indicates the many ways in
which teacher involvement is a condition for the success of the venture. Among
their proposals are stress on the formative aims, a realistic timescale for phas-
ing in the new system, adequate resources including in-service provision, and
widespread consultation and discussion.

In this chapter, I examine four issues in particular. They are not by any
means the only four that either cause me concern or are starting points for
further development, but they do crystallize, for me, some of the possibilities
within the TGAT Report. The four issues are:

1   The nature of attainment targets
2   Moderation
3   The publication and reporting of results
4   Implementation

The Nature of Attainment Targets

What are attainment targets, or benchmarks as Mr Baker sometimes calls
them? We have had goals and we have had objectives for many years; attainment targets seem to be a new version of those. We also know from the
experience of industry and commerce that clarifying goals both for the organization and for the individual appears to be motivating and helpful (see, for
example, Trethowan, 1987). But in education attainment targets are perhaps
more difficult to formulate. To illustrate the nature of attainment targets I like
to quote from Ted Wragg's column in *The Times Educational Supplement*. In
the context of GCSE he illustrated grade criteria as follows. He felt, incidentally, that it was necessary to add three further grades to the bottom of the
grading scale, those three grades to be reserved for Chelsea supporters. The
criteria for those three grades were 'J' to put a thumb print on the paper, 'I'
to put a neat thumb print on the paper, 'H' to colour the thumb print in
Chelsea's colours. Then, rejoining the official grading scale, 'G' to spell

history, 'F' to tell a history book from a maths book, 'E' to be able to put a history book under the shortest leg of a rickety table, 'D' to *understand* why they put a history book under the rickety table, 'C' to be able to pass 'O' level history, 'B' to know at least thirty useless dates and thirty meaningless facts and 'A' to recite the names of the whole of Wellington's army.

To prepare grade criteria for the GCSE, dozens of teachers were locked away in Newcombe House, the headquarters of the Secondary Examinations Council (SEC), to see if they could come up with improvements on Ted Wragg's proposals. I have looked through the accounts and annual reports of the SEC to try to work out how much the exercise cost, but unfortunately they do not analyse expenditure by individual projects. Nevertheless, I can confidently say that hundreds of thousands of pounds went in this venture to develop grade criteria. But that exercise has run into the sand in terms of producing *national* grade criteria. The current effort is devoted to something called performance matrices, that is, a presentation of criteria for assessing different grades that is derived from *particular* syllabuses, and from the work of candidates on examination papers and other forms of assessment on those syllabuses. Considerable work is scheduled for the development of performance matrices over the next three or four years. I think that it is too early to say whether performance matrices will be of any benefit — what they certainly will not do is to create a system of *national* attainment targets. Similar difficulties were experienced in Scotland where in their Standard Grade examination (which is, of course, a national examination operated by their only examination board) the grade criteria ran into severe problems. Within a matter of months of the new system being introduced, a committee had to be established to seek ways of simplifying the examination and the grade criteria. In particular, that committee recommended that grade criteria should *not* be used as devices for framing and organizing assessment. They were excellent for clarifying goals and objectives for *teaching* but as *an assessment framework* it was felt that they were far too elaborate and complicated. One of the main problems in public examinations is undoubtedly the fact that there may be hundreds of different attainment targets but they still have to be aggregated and reported on a single scale for each subject. The multiplicity of targets is therefore the first problem. As Margaret Brown has pointed out, if you set up committees with the best of intentions, you can still find that attainment targets multiply like white mice.[4]

One of the high priests of the movement for the clear specification of educational objectives is the American, Jim Popham. In a recent article he has made it clear that too many goals (or too many attainment targets) can confuse people:

> Simply stated the most important lesson we have learned about the use of behaviourally stated objectives is that *less* is most definitely *more*. Too many objectives, because the decision makers will not attend to them, are completely dysfunctional. (Popham, 1987)

Figure 5

Attitudes

Attainment Target: Curiosity in relation to the activities undertaken, materials studied and used and issues discussed in the classroom.

The pupil:

- Shows interest in things which are new or familiar ones which are pointed out.
- Spontaneously questions new and familiar things even though interest may be shortlived.
- Seeks by questioning or action to find out about new and familiar things in the environment.

The Mathematics Working Group has taken this lesson to heart, at least in theory. Its criteria for the development of attainment targets are that they should be broad-based, accessible to all pupils, recognizable outputs of the educational process and in some cases taught in a cross-curricular context. They go on to say that 'our intention is that attainment targets should be relatively few in number' (National Curriculum Mathematics Working Group, 1987). All the signs are that there will be more than a hundred for each age group. I would argue that we should look for *far fewer* than that: keep them few, keep them broad. In the Scottish Action Plan post-16, and a lot of work being done on modules and units here in London, the number of different defined targets is small: four or five — that is the sort of number that you would reasonably expect young people to keep in mind to frame their work. If you want only a few, you must have them broad. Above, I give an example of those being proposed in a context of science (figure 5). I have deliberately chosen examples from the area of attitudes rather than more conventional and perhaps more easily devised objectives in the area of knowledge and understanding. They are interesting, but too specific in my view.

The TGAT Report proposes that one profile component (that is, one cluster of attainment targets) should be cross-curricular and therefore should reappear in other subject areas, but some modern approaches to the curriculum, for example in TVEI and pre-vocational courses, are much more fundamental in the sort of cross-curricular skills they foster — both intellectual, such as the use of literacy and numeracy across the curriculum, and in the realm of social and personal skills — above all in cooperative learning rather than competitive learning. So I think that we must find ways of allowing those courses that provide interesting, helpful challenges to young people to survive within a National Curriculum. I would suggest that it is in the way in which one formulates attainment targets that this is best achieved.

Attainment targets are based on the objectives model of education and there is substantial literature from the 1960s and 1970s — notably the work of

Lawrence Stenhouse — which has much to say about the limitations of objectives (see, for example, Stenhouse, 1975). I think that those limitations have been implicitly recognized by the Government when they indicate that there are not to be attainment targets in PE, art and music but just guidelines. We must avoid the mechanistic approach and the reductionism that the objectives model can easily lead to. In the words of Maurice Holt (1987) commenting on the National Consultation Document:

> The entire document is steeped in the mechanistic assumption that schools can be run like biscuit factories. Providing the skills and technology are there, backed by clear objectives and precise assessment, the right product will roll off the assembly line.

Objectives need to embody the spirit of education in the round. Some people might challenge me and say that juxtaposing education in the round with the very word 'objectives' is a mistake and a contradiction. Perhaps then we must look for broad aims (rather than objectives), aims stated in such a way that one can find ways of assessing them.

My next point about attainment targets concerns the degree to which they should be regarded as fixed. The whole of the National Curriculum proposals are based on fixed, age-related targets. The model underlying national assessment is clearly that of graded assessment, but most graded assessment systems are not rigidly age-related but flexible. The idea is that you enter for the test or assessment *when you are ready*. This is certainly true in music and ballet. In graded assessment in mathematics in London (the GAIM Project), they too have broken away from age-related assessment. The student collects targets one by one and accumulates them for certification. There is no fixed route implied. Indeed the research of Margaret Brown and her colleagues, though indicating some common patterns, shows that pupils develop and learn in different ways (Denvir, Brown and Eve, 1987). More importantly, Rosalind Driver's work in science shows how many different ways and different routes there are to learning according to the concepts or, indeed, the misconceptions that young people bring with them to the classroom.[5] GAIM and other graded assessment projects have moved away from the notion that all fourth-year students take a test on a given day in June; rather, teachers monitor progress by the steady accumulation of targets. When the student has collected a defined group of targets then he or she can receive a certificate indicating the achievement of the corresponding level.

A second aspect to fixedness is the *pre-ordained nature* of attainment targets implied by the National Curriculum. This is at variance with the powerful notion within records of achievement that students and teachers should negotiate, and set a limited number of future targets, in the light of the progress made and in the short term.[6] Perhaps that sort of negotiation of short-term targets will still be possible within a system that defines targets at only four stages separated by several years, but I nevertheless think that TGAT should encourage much more recognition of the value of pupil self-assessment and teacher/pupil review, that is, a discussion of whether targets have been reached as well as what targets are appropriate for the future. The model of assessment is not clearly defined within the TGAT Report. The use of terms like 'standard assessment task' rather than 'test' is still implying that assessment is done *to* the pupil rather than done *by* the pupil in cooperation with the teacher. I am suggesting, however, that there are ways, even within a system of fixed and age-related targets, to develop a more responsive system. In the longer term I suspect that the age-relatedness of the targets may disappear and that we may move to a system of graded assessment or assessment when ready. Such a system would still allow us to report that, by the age of 14, some 10 per cent of young people had reached level 5, 50 per cent had reached level 6 and so forth, so that a system of *reporting* at fixed ages does not necessarily mean a system of *testing* at fixed ages.

My final point about fixedness arises from the very nature of criterion-referencing. Current rhetoric has painted a picture of norm-referencing as bad and criterion-referencing as good. But in fact criterion-referencing reflects an impersonal abstract social need whereas norm-referencing recognizes that 'the measure of mankind is man'. (Incidentally, I thought hard about how to make that last remark non-sexist but failed.) There is also a feeling that criterion-referencing and norm-referencing are the only two models available. In fact ipsative assessment, that is, assessment of the person against his or her own performance on a prior occasion — something which many many teachers do naturally in their assessment in the classroom — is a third powerful framework for assessment. The very notion of progress through levels implies an ipsative framework as much as it does a criterion-referenced one.

I have addressed at some length the issue of attainment targets, and their problems and possibilities, not least because there is still a massive amount of work to be done on attainment targets, not just by TGAT, but a task that will continue for many years to come as the curriculum working groups do their job. I think that there is much more scope for change and development in that field than the TGAT Report acknowledges.

Moderation

TGAT propose that results from national assessments (the standard assessment tasks) and the teachers' own assessments of individuals should be discussed in a process of group moderation, and any differences reconciled. In CSE, to some extent in GCE, and certainly in GCSE, the staff development role of group moderation has long been recognized, as well as its potency for promoting consultation and feedback to examining boards. Indeed, in one of the original CSE boards, the West Yorkshire and Lindsey Board, the model was of standards being determined locally by teacher groups and being fed *up* the system to the examining board, rather than imposed centrally and disseminated through the system of groups. The proposals for moderation within the TGAT Report are demanding professionally (but, as I have indicated, also rewarding professionally) and very time-consuming. I consider that the teachers' contract imposed by Mr Baker should be revised to reflect the amount of time that would be needed to do this part of the job adequately. I support the basic model of moderation; what I am unhappy about is the TGAT argument that, since the system will be time-consuming, there may have to be an acceptance that moderation in this group fashion does not take place for all profile components every year, and that, where there is no group moderation, test results should override the teacher assessment if there is any discrepancy.[7] That, in my view, is anti-teacher. I would suggest that there are other ways of using the test results, for example, with test results functioning as a moderating instrument as used by the Business and Technician Education Council (arising from work that my colleagues and I did at the beginning of 1980s), showing how a test coupled with other information can be used as a device to indicate where teacher-based assessment might be out of line with national standards (Nuttall and Armitage, 1985). That seems to me to be using tests to support and monitor teacher judgments rather than to supplant them.

The Publication and Reporting of Results

The TGAT Report distinguishes between those two words, proposing that the results of assessments should be *reported* to parents, to pupils and to others that have the right to know (though, of course, they also propose that an individual's results should be confidential to that individual and his or her parents). They then go on to recommend that the results should be *published* only in aggregated form and in context. It is interesting to note that the proposals for national assessment in Scotland have a much lighter touch — in other words, not only will the testing be just in literacy and numeracy rather than across the curriculum as a whole, but the results are to be given *only* to children and their parents; there is no proposal in Scotland that the results should be aggregated and published for each school and each classroom (as reported in *The Independent*, 20 November 1987). In England and Wales, though, the Government has every intention of publishing results for individual schools. On this matter the TGAT Report is in my view rather confused. It is the confusion between reporting and publication, and the naivety of the TGAT proposals, that I would like to comment upon especially. They recommend that national assessment results from a class as a whole and a school as a whole should be available to the parents of its pupils; they also recommend that there should be no requirement to *publish* aggregated results of the pupils at age 7. But then they say that these results should be made available to parents, governors and providers (presumably the LEAs and the DES). I believe that, with a system of nationally standardized assessment results, *reporting* to such groups will be equivalent to *publishing* the results, and publishing them classroom by classroom. Many parents will be tempted to provide that information to many other people, for example to prospective parents and the local press. The TGAT proposals have, therefore, to be viewed as proposals for *publication* even at the age of 7.

My second worry concerns their proposal that the results for each school should be published without statistical adjustment, but in the context of a written account of socioeconomic and other influences that are known to affect attainment. They argue that the publication of such results and the use of such results to compare schools' performance 'would be liable to lead to complacency if results were adjusted and to misinterpretation if they were not' (TGAT, 1988a, para. 133). And it is that quotation that provides the title for this chapter.

I cannot understand why they feel that adjusted results should lead to complacency. The ILEA received considerable publicity because of the figures published in answer to a Parliamentary Question in January 1988 that showed that the proportion of leavers from ILEA with five or more 'O' level grades A to C (or equivalent) put the Authority in eighty-sixth place out of ninety-six LEAs. Whereas we know, from all the research done by the DES and others such as Gray and Jesson, that once one takes into account background factors such as the level of deprivation in London (for example, the number of one-parent families, and the number of children eligible for free school meals) ILEA examination results are very much in line with expectation.[8] That doesn't make the Authority complacent; nobody is saying that examination results in inner London are good enough. There are several important initiatives like the London Compact and the London Record of Achievement that provide a framework for all the work on assessment in secondary schools. These initiatives are designed to raise standards in the Authority's schools, and to give more young people the opportunity to achieve examination results and hence jobs. To suggest that our adjusted examination results make us complacent is a nonsense. I think that headteachers and governors are quite capable of looking at the actual results alongside the adjusted results school by school, and of seeking ways of improving them. I also think that complacency about adjusted examination results is no more likely than it is among schools who get good results just because they have favoured catchment areas. If I may quote again the same leader from *The Times* (14 January 1988) commenting on the unadjusted local authority league table; rather scathingly, it said:

That Harrow's results are four times better than Barking's for an extra £70 a head reveals very little more than that middle class children tend to do rather better at school than working class children.

This supports TGAT's own argument that results with no adjustment are liable to be misinterpreted. I cannot understand why, having made that statement, they then go on to propose that no adjustment should be made. They are inviting the very misinterpretation to which they draw attention.

I concede that the ways that we have of adjusting school examination results are not perfect. Now is the time to do more research; indeed, I am working with Harvey Goldstein of the Institute of Education to improve our methods. Verbal comments explaining why pupils in particular schools do not get as good examination results as pupils in more favoured schools are likely to be ignored. With national assessment, we must therefore adjust results, as we do in the ILEA, to reflect the intake of each school.

Implementation

The TGAT Report is excellent in the way that it recognizes the time, the preparation and the in-service work needed to implement such a complex and innovative system. They have learned lessons from GCSE INSET where phase 1 of the INSET had to be done *before* there were any syllabuses and specimen materials, which made the materials rather abstract and divorced from classroom practice. TGAT should note the work of Michael Fullan who shows, through his extensive research and development in Canada, the sorts of support systems that are needed for schools when major innovations are proposed (Fullan, 1982). In looking for a strategy to implement the London Record of Achievement and graded assessment in ILEA schools, we have drawn on Fullan's work and provided development officers who work in about four schools, spending a day each week in each school to help in a variety of ways — in in-service, in general classroom support, and in commenting on and helping to define goals; on the fifth day, they return to County Hall to share their experience with their fellow development officers. They provide support within the context and the ethos of the school, and they provide it on a regular basis that keeps people working to a timetable of development. I would suggest that one needs such assessment missionaries like the famous Cockcroft mathematics missionaries. I am not sure that TGAT has really taken delivery of the sorts of support and training that are going to be needed for what is, for many, a really new venture. Primary schools have no tradition of group moderation in the same way that secondary schools have, and must allow time and all sorts of trials to prepare them.

Also, to prepare for the implementation we need research and development. The Report seems to rest on the notion of item banking or task banking. Like the history of grade criteria, the history of item banking has many casualties along the way and we need to review those experiences. Extensive work is needed on test and task development, and I would highlight especially the need to develop ways of assessing bias within tests and indeed within teacher assessment, bias, that is, on the grounds of gender, race and social class.

Assessment is often seen as the culprit, the cause of many of our problems in schools. The 11+ is always held up as example of an assessment system that had (and still has in some areas) tremendous backwash not only on the curriculum of primary schools but on the attitudes and motivation of young people and their parents. But of course it wasn't the act of assessment that was the true problem, it was the act of selection, the fact that we decided that young people at the age of 11 should be sorted into sheep and goats. What is important is that we do not use national assessment as a new system for sorting and sifting as some fear it might be, particularly at age 11 when there are to be new kinds of institutions like city technology colleges and grant-maintained schools. Nevertheless, I would urge that in the discussion of assessment we distinguish between the effects of assessment itself and the reasons why we have assessment.

Summary

I would like to end with a summary of my major points. In chapter 1, Stuart Maclure called the Act 'allergic to systems', particularly local education authorities, arguing that that is why there were proposals for opting out and for market choice. Within the context for National Curriculum and national assessment, though, elaborate new systems are being created, systems that will make the bureaucracy of GCSE look small by comparison. The system will not be like that of TVEI, which was established under broad criteria that offered money for local creativity and local development; the system will not, therefore, allow teachers to 'take the money and run' as they have with a number of devolved developments like Technical and Vocational Education Initiative (TVEI) and Lower Achieving Pupils Programme (LAPP) in recent years. Nevertheless, within the national framework of the TGAT system, I believe that there is plenty of scope for improvement and autonomy. In particular, it is not too late to see pupils as active partners in the process of assessment and able to be assisted during assessment in the manner of Vygotski. It is not too late to limit the number of attainment targets, to widen their range and their scope, and to promote cooperative learning and assessment. It is not too late to move nearer a system of assessment at stages rather than ages (though the implications for the organisation of schools and classrooms still have to be thought about). It is not too late to look for publication of adjusted results; indeed, I am told that even if this is not recommended nationally it is still open to LEAs to publish adjusted results. Nor is it too late, of course, to do the research and development that would improve some of these proposals considerably — first, to look at the issue of bias and, second, to look at moderation using the national test as a post-hoc monitoring device rather than as an imposed device.

So I would urge those of you who face the same dilemma as I did to apply one of the criteria that I proposed in figure 1, one that underpins the GCSE, that is, to look for *positive achievement*. I *can* make a positive assessment of the TGAT Report, particularly if I am allowed to renegotiate some of Mr Baker's targets and to develop them further. There is some complacency in the Report; there is some misinterpretation; but by and large the proposals make assessment the servant of the curriculum rather than its dominating master.

Postscript

At the time this paper was originally given as a lecture, the Task Group on Assessment and Testing was still at work, and some of the points made were designed to influence their deliberations. The three supplementary Reports of TGAT were published in June 1988.[1] The first supplementary Report reviews the reactions and comments that they had received in response to the original Report; it is defensive in tone, but clarifies one or two points, though making no significant changes. The second Report describes the consultations with subject associations. The third Report is the longest and the most significant. It elaborates the support structure needed for the system of national assessment and fleshes out the proposal for group moderation and INSET. In response to a Parliamentary Question on 7 June 1988, the Secretary of State for Education and Science accepted the basic framework of the TGAT proposals, including the notion of ten levels, and the need for teacher assessment. He felt, however, that the suggestions on the moderation system appeared 'complicated and costly'. He therefore asked the School Examinations and Assessment Council and the National Curriculum Council to review the issues with interested parties and, by implication, to propose a simpler and cheaper solution. He also agreed that there should be no legal requirement for schools to publish aggregated results for 7-year-olds, but strongly recommended that schools should do so.

No significant amendments were made to the Education Reform Bill before enactment in relation to national assessment. Many people, including myself, had not noticed, however, that section 2 specified that the arrangements for assessing pupils should be 'at or near the end of each key stage'. This provision means that it would be difficult to have assessment on demand, in the fashion of graded assessment, and consequently more difficult to move towards a system of grouping pupils by stage rather than by age. In addition, this section makes it less likely that results of assessment at age 11 will be used in the process of selection for different kinds of school, since the results will be known only after most of the transfer decisions will have been made.

If the passing of the Act shed little further light on the detail of national assessment, the detailed proposals for the National Curriculum in mathematics and science certainly did. The working groups reported in the summer of 1988, and the National Curriculum Council consulted widely over their proposals.[2] The Secretary of State made his views known as well, and the National Curriculum Council published a revised set of proposals for attainment targets and programmes of study.[3] The nature of attainment targets has thus begun to become clear. In mathematics, fourteen attainment targets are proposed, closely resembling educational objectives in phraseology. For example, Attainment Target 2: Number is 'understand number and number notation', while Attainment Target 13: Handling Data is 'represent and interpret data'. Each target is then broken down into ten levels (often illustrated with sample questions). For example, level 1 of Attainment Target 2: Number is 'count, read, write and order numbers to at least 10, and know that the size of a set is given by the last number in the count; understand the conservation of number', while level 9 has the description 'distinguish between rational and irrational numbers'. (The other part of the level 9 description that appeared in the original proposal, namely 'be able to express a positive integer as a product of primes' has disappeared from the National Curriculum Council's proposals.) Not all targets have ten levels; indeed level 10 is not specified for Attainment Target 2. The 14 attainment targets are to be grouped, for reporting and assessment, into two profile components: the first comprises 'knowledge, skills, understanding and use of number, algebra and measures', while the second comprises 'knowledge, skills, understanding and use of shape and space and handling data'. Neither of these titles for the profile components seems designed for clear communication to parents and the public.

In science, seventeen attainment targets are proposed. As in mathematics, each attainment target is differentiated, usually but not always with ten levels. For reporting and assessment, the attainment targets are to be grouped into two profile components. The first, consisting only of Attainment Target 1, covers 'exploration of science, communication and the application of knowledge and understanding'. The second, covering the remaining sixteen attainment targets, comprises 'knowledge and understanding of science, communication, and the applications and implications of science'.

The working groups originally proposed rather more attainment targets (fifteen in mathematics and twenty-two in science) and more profile components (three in mathematics and four in science). Some of the attainment targets were non-cognitive in nature reaching as far as 'personal qualities' in mathematics. The structure of attainment targets and profile components for each subject was generally welcomed during the consultation exercise, but the Secretary of State was not happy with these more affective targets. Flying in the face of majority opinion, but consistent with the preferences of the Secretary of State, the National Curriculum Council eliminated such targets and simplified the structure of profile components. There must consequently be some doubt as to the independence of the National Curriculum Council.

Finally, the reports of the working parties shed further light on the notion of Standard Assessment Tasks (SATs). Both reports indicate that they expect assessment to be carried out using naturalistic tasks arising from the normal work in the classroom, often occupying several hours of activity, exclusively at age 7 and substantially at other ages. The only example given of such a SAT appears in the mathematics report (para. 9.13): 'work in a group to plan, schedule and run a trip for your class'. This is considered suitable from age 11 upwards. No advice is given about the problem of assessing pupils in a group while at the same time assigning the achievement of each individual pupil to a specific level in each of a number of different attainment targets. The suggestions on assessment made so far confirm my opinion that a massive research and development exercise is required, and in many cases will have to solve as yet unsolved problems in educational measurement.

Notes to Postscript

1 National Curriculum: Task Group on Assessment and Testing, *Three Supplementary Reports*, DES Welsh Office, 1988.
2 *National Curriculum: Mathematics for ages 5 to 16*, DES/Welsh Office, 1988, *National Curriculum: Science for ages 5 to 16*, DES/Welsh Office, 1988.
3 National Curriculum Council, *Mathematics in the National Curriculum*, York, National Curriculum Council, December 1988.
   National Curriculum Council, *Science in the National Curriculum*, York, National Curriculum Council, December 1988.

Notes

1 A Gallup Opinion Poll in September 1987 (reported in the Daily Telegraph, 7 October 1987) showed that 71 per cent of parents supported written tests with 24 per cent against.
2 National Assessment and Testing — A Research Responses, papers presented to the BERA Conference on Benchmark Testing, Kendal, BERA, 1988.
3 See, for example, Sternberg (1982).
4 See note 2.
5 The Children's Learning in Science Project at the University of Leeds.
6 The national evaluation of records of achievement supports the significance of pupil-teacher negotiation in improving classroom relationships and enhancing pupil motivation (Broadfoot *et al.*, 1988).
7 The use of statistical moderation in this manner would be permissible under the General Criteria of the GCSE National Criteria only in rare circumstances.
8 DES Statistical Bulletins 16/83 and 13/84; Gray and Jesson (1987).

References

BROADFOOT, P.M., JAMES, M.E., McMEEKING, S., NUTTALL, D.L. and STIERER, B.M. (1988) *Records of Achievement: Report of the National Curriculum*, London, HMSO.
DES/WO (1987) *The National Curriculum 5–16: A Consultation Document*, London, DES/WO.
FULLAN, M. (1982) *The Meaning of Educational Change*, New York, Teachers' College Press.
GRAY, J. and JESSON, D. (1987) 'Exam results and local authority league tables', *Education and Training UK*.

HOLT, M. (1987) 'Bureaucratic benefits', The Times Educational Supplement, 18 September, p. 30.

NATIONAL CURRICULUM MATHEMATICS WORKING GROUP (1987) *Interim Report*, para. 4.4.

NUTTALL, D.L. and ARMITAGE, P. (1985) *Moderating Instrument Research Project: A Summary*, London, BTEC.

POPHAM, J. (1987) 'Two decades of educational objectives', *International Journal of Educational Research*, 11, 1, pp. 31–41.

STENHOUSE, L. (1975) *An Introduction to Curriculum Research and Development*, London, Heinemann Educational.

STERNBERG, R.J. (Ed) (1992) *The Handbook of Human Intelligence*, Cambridge, Cambridge University Press.

TASK GROUP ON ASSESSMENT and TESTING (1988a) *A Report*, London, DES/Welsh Office.

TASK GROUP ON ASSESSMENT and TESTING (1988b) *A Digest for Schools*, London, DES/ Welsh Office.

TRETHOWAN, D. (1987) *Appraisal and Target Setting*, London, Harper and Row.

Nuttall, D.L. (1989a) 'National assessment — Will reality match aspirations?', *BPS Education Section Review*, 13, 1/2, pp. 6–19.

Introduction

It was characteristic of Desmond Nuttall that he was always open to arguments, especially those based upon research evidence, which could cause him to change his mind. It is, of course, the ultimate objective of research to challenge existing thinking and to have the potential to produce evidence to support alternative ideas, theories and policies. A striking example of this occurred on 8 March 1989 when Desmond Nuttall was invited to address a 'Testing Times' conference, organized by Macmillan Education, which provided a forum for reviewing developments in National Curriculum assessments in England and Wales. This address was given roughly one year after the previous paper (Paper 16) in which he had given qualified support for the TGAT proposals, referring to them as 'the best set of national assessment proposals that we are likely to get' (see p. 172).

In his 1988 lecture (Paper 16) he had upset a number of his colleagues and university-based friends, by taking a swipe at 'whingeing academics', who were raising numerous objections to the National Curriculum proposals. He once again hit the headlines with this 1989 lecture (Paper 17) by pronouncing that the TGAT National Curriculum assessment proposals had been 'seriously distorted in the implementation stage' leaving a 'monster of an external assessment system'. This final phrase became a front page headline in the *Times Educational Supplement* (10 March 1989) later that week for an article which reported Desmond Nuttall's revised view that the National Curriculum assessment stakes should be lowered by replacing the complex assessment procedures, which were emerging, by a simpler system of short tests in reading, maths and science. On this occasion then Desmond

Nuttall was to be found advocating a view favoured by the right-wing of the Conservative party, but for different reasons. They wished to pull back the National Curriculum to concentrate on 'basic skills', whereas Desmond Nuttall wanted a strategy that would clearly separate the requirement for national assessments from his desire to 'leave plenty of space for the rest of the curriculum to blossom and flower'. He was also keen to see school-based formative assessment given a worthwhile role alongside, but distinct from, national testing.

This paper highlights once again some of the key dilemmas involved in developing assessment procedures in harmony with educational curricula. Learning is often best supported by detailed systems of formative assessment, which can be oriented to the individual characteristics of the learners and the course that they are following. Such detail can rarely be reproduced in national assessment systems, which are designed for the purposes of national monitoring and accreditation of standards in education. However where external assessment systems focus on limited, rather than comprehensive curriculum areas, then the danger is always that, if the assessment stakes are high, then the backwash effects on the way that the curriculum is then taught in schools can be damaging and at odds with the curricula intentions.

These were not Desmond Nuttall's final thoughts on National Curriculum assessment, and this is a topic to which we will return in the final paper in this collection (Paper 20). That was his contribution to the Dearing review, which some five years on from this paper was attempting to slim down the National Curriculum and simplify the assessment arrangements!

NATIONAL ASSESSMENT — WILL REALITY MATCH ASPIRATIONS?[1]

The TGAT Proposals

First of all, I must make it clear that I am giving my own opinions not necessarily those of the ILEA.

A year ago, almost to the day, I spoke about national assessment in the light of the first TGAT report published a few weeks before. I suggested that they had put forward the best model of national assessment that we were likely to get. I offended many of my friends in universities by referring to whingeing academics who were complaining on the sidelines, when what we needed to do was accept the TGAT model and to see if we could get it to work, refining it in some important areas like equal opportunities and the reporting of results. I have to confess today that I am not sure if I was right.

I still admire the clever way in which TGAT nearly reconciled the irreconcilable, that is the various conflicting purposes of assessment, the formative, the summative and the evaluative. Nevertheless, I think that their developmental model was over-simplified and that they failed to recognize adequately the good practice in self-assessment and target-setting, and more recently in individual action planning, that we see in the records of achievement movement. They left many unsolved problems, particularly I think in the field of aggregation, that is aggregating performance on different attainment targets into a single score for a profile component, aggregating profile components into subjects and aggregating the results of standard assessment tasks and teacher assessment. They used, and the National Curriculum Council have followed them in using, percentage weightings for profile components; percentages really don't work when you are dealing with a criterion-referenced and simple system of ten levels. They only work when you are dealing with fine-grained mark distributions as we do in public examinations.

They viewed criterion-referencing as unproblematic and they didn't reflect on the sad history of criterion-referencing in the GCSE examination. First we had grade-related criteria, then we had grade criteria. The SEC didn't get far with those and dropped them quickly, feeling that performance matrices were the new philosopher's stone that was going to make our base norm-referenced measurement into the gold of criterion-referencing. But one of the first acts of the School Examinations Council was to freeze all work on performance matrices. As far as I know, they haven't resuscitated performance matrices and so criterion-referencing in GCSE has fallen by the wayside.

TGAT also didn't recognize the problems and dangers of breaking knowledge and understanding down into small pieces, into atoms devoid of the context of learning. As Lauren Resnick pointed out in her Presidential Address to the AERA in 1987, school learning is disconnected enough from real life, as it is, without fragmenting the decontextualized skills as well. In my view the National Council for Vocational Qualifications has fallen into the same trap and is rapidly trying to pull themselves out of it by talking about things called generic units, and finding ways of getting breadth, for example, through overarching skills and competences.

Above all, TGAT failed to address the relationship (or possible lack of relationship) between assessment and the raising of standards, as Harvey Goldstein has pointed out.

But despite these criticisms, I still think that TGAT made a brave attempt. They were constrained, of course, by their terms of reference and, in particular, they were constrained to design a system that had to compare school and school. In some ways, I pity them; I rather feel that they were like the rustic person asked the way to the big city by tourists, who scratched his head and said 'Well, if I were you, I wouldn't start from here'.

Developments Since the TGAT Reports were Published

But I did like the way in which TGAT gave prominence to assessment of normal class work by teachers and the involvement of *all* teachers in the process of moderation. My concern is that in the year or so that has passed since TGAT's ideas were published, we have seen some considerable dilution of their ideas. Indeed one could argue that they themselves diluted some of the original ideas about teacher assessment. In the red Consultation Document about the National Curriculum issued in the summer of 1987, the Secretaries of State said that they envisaged that '*most* of the assessment at ages 7, 11 and 14 and at 16 in non-examined subjects will be done by teachers as an integral part of normal classroom work'. Then they went on: 'But at the heart of the assessment process there will be nationally prescribed tests done by all pupils to *supplement* the individual teacher assessments'. TGAT simply argued that the external tasks and the internal assessment were of equal importance. I quote: 'we wish to emphasize that both forms of assessment are important and have distinctive contributions to make; neither should reign supreme'.

For those young people embarking on the National Curriculum this September, one would have hoped that formative assessment would be there from the very beginning. The standard assessment tasks, you will remember, are needed only for the summer of 1991 and even then the results won't be made public; the teacher assessment, as I say, is needed from this coming September. But, I ask, what work has started on specifying guidelines and ideas for teacher assessment against the new system of levels and targets, and on giving support to teachers in the same way as was necessary for course-work in GCSE despite the long tradition of coursework in CSE and many 'O' level examinations? The answer, I fear, is that practically no guidance is being offered on teacher assessment for this autumn. The tender document put out by SEAC in October was for the development of standard assessment tasks for pupils at the end of the first key stage. The document makes it quite clear that the developers' central task is to develop SATs.

TGAT's moderation proposals look like being another casualty. When in June 1988 the Secretary of State for Education and Science accepted TGAT's framework, he accepted the need for moderation but did however indicate that he felt that their proposals for moderation combined with the model of INSET was 'costly and complicated'. When he charged SEAC with a whole range, indeed an unbelievable workload, of tasks he divorced INSET from moderation. He gave SEAC until October 1988 to come up with preliminary ideas on INSET, and to the end of February to give much more information about the moderation system. As I speak it is, of course, only a few days after the end of February, but I am not aware of any emerging advice from SEAC. Indeed it looks as though they have turned to the consortia charged with the development of SATs to get help from them. The tender document says, for example, that it will be part of the task of development agencies to assist

SEAC to come to a view on how the moderation process might best be conducted. Other parts of that document indicate that moderation is changing from something that applies to teacher assessment into something that might apply to the SATs themselves, that is, part of the process of standardizing assessment by literally hundreds of thousands of different teachers up and down the country. In the tender document there are only one or two passing references to teacher assessment. In relation to INSET the document suggests that the INSET material 'may be expected to include guidance to teachers as to how information from their own assessments might be combined with that of SATs so as to produce evidence of their pupils' attainments for moderation purposes'. Note, though, it is not about the design of teacher assessment, it's how you conflate it and possibly moderate it.

I am therefore arguing that teacher assessment and moderation are being pushed further down the agenda despite the desperate need for early guidance on their nature. In the summaries of the work of the SATs development consortia, as far as I can see, only one consortium, that is the STAIR consortium based in the North West, recognizes the significance of teacher assessment. They say that only by working on teacher assessment and SATs at the same time can each inform the other and the formative use of assessment be realized. They have taken the point but everyone else seems to have forgotten teacher assessment. I would observe, too, that other issues of great importance seem to have been pushed to the side. I am thinking in particular of the clear presentation of results from national assessment both for the individual and for aggregated assessments applying to classrooms, schools and local authorities. Admittedly there is a fair amount of time to do work about aggregating to the level of the school, but the presentation of results should go hand in hand with the design of the task itself. About £6 million has been awarded for the development of SATs at Key Stage 1. Where, I ask, are the £6 million projects for teacher assessment, for the design of moderation systems and for reporting?

Equal Opportunities

Although the TGAT report reprinted evidence in full both from the Records of Achievement National Steering Committee and the Equal Opportunities Commission, I always felt that TGAT had not taken the ideas of both these bodies fully into their own thinking and their own proposals. TGAT paid lip service to bias in assessment but didn't grapple with its true nature. Similarly, the tender document on SATs requires developmental agencies to make every effort to ensure that the SATs which they produce avoid ethnic or cultural bias, that their use would not be inhibited by translation into a foreign language, and that they do not contain material that would disadvantage pupils from the ethnic minorities. Likewise they will need to make every effort to ensure that the tests they produce are free from overt or covert gender bias.

So far, so good — but it is very much easier said than done. I think we must in the first place follow the Code of Fair Testing Practices in Education that all the major testing agencies in the United States now abide by. For example the code requires agencies to indicate 'for all assessment material the evidence obtained concerning the appropriateness of each test for groups of different racial, ethnic or linguistic background'. We cannot just leave it to the good offices of the test designers, they must show us the evidence. But more than that, they must continue to monitor for what is known as adverse impact. In a study of school district testing practices in the United States, Mary Catharine Ellwein shows that in the beginning test developers took every precaution to avoid biased items but they failed to monitor test results after the application of tests to look for differences between groups and to justify them. As you know, the ILEA is leading the way in monitoring public examination results by sex and by ethnic group. Monitoring is only a start, of course, but at least it begins to allow us to devise sensible strategies to eradicate racism from the curriculum and from our institutions. Designing unbiased tests, and using all the technologically sophisticated item analysis procedures, are not enough.

Returning to the design of assessment I would stress that there are, in any case, many problems in devising tasks that are equally fair to different groups. Partly this is because of the different experiences, for example, of girls and boys as they grow up and the way in which they attend to different cues in the task. Patricia Murphy has shown, from her work for the Assessment of Performance Unit, how a problem can be perceived in different ways by boys and girls. Boys tend to abstract the problem from the context while girls attend to the totality of the problem context including what I, as a male, might describe as extraneous and irrelevant cues. She surmises that it is perhaps this characteristic of girls that makes them do less well than boys in multiple-choice tests, when the reader is bombarded with irrelevant and often erroneous information. She didn't, I am afraid, go on to speculate what it is about essay examinations that allow girls to do so much better on them!

In designing appropriate tasks one also has to take account of learning styles and different cultural traditions. Two examples highlight some of the issues. Patricia Murphy gives the example of a design task set both to primary and secondary pupils. It was for a vehicle and a boat to go round the world. The boys' designs tended to concentrate on army-type vehicles, sports cars, power boats and battleships. The boys varied the details but the majority had elaborate weaponry and next-to-no living facilities; they also took account of mechanisms of movement and navigation and so forth. In contrast, the girls' boats were generally leisure cruisers. The vehicles were family transport, agricultural machines or children's play vehicles. There was a total absence of weaponry in the girls' designs and a great deal of detail about living quarters and requirements, including food supplies and cleaning materials (which were noticeably absent in the boys' design). Very few of the girls' designs included any form of mechanical detail.

The second example comes from comments by my ILEA colleague, Liz Gerschel, on the draft attainment targets for speaking and listening in English, which include the frequent formula 'speak freely', and, at Level 2, specify that the pupil should speak freely to the teacher. First of all, we have a problem for the bilingual child with little command of English. It is a great challenge for her or him to speak freely to the teacher. But for some ethnic minorities there will be cultural rather than linguistic inhibitions; after all, there are a good many parents who hesitate to speak freely to teachers. Social, cultural, class factors, and indeed the effects of racism, mean that speaking freely to teachers is not something that comes easily to a large part of the population.

These are examples of what might more broadly be termed the effect of context and circumstances on performance. There is a growing literature now which indicates the conditions which can either inhibit or facilitate the bringing out of the student's best performance. When I reviewed this literature in a published article, I drew out three key factors. First of all, the motivation to do the task and interest in it, which of course will be influenced by the personal experience of the student and the instrumental value of performing the task. Secondly, the relationship between the assessor and the individual being assessed and generally the physical conditions under which the assessment is made. And thirdly, the way in which the task is presented, the language used to describe it and the degree to which it is within the personal experience of the individual being assessed.

Smaller contextual factors can also have an influence. When John Eggleston reviewed the first APU Mathematics findings, he drew attention to the way in which the exact formulation of the problem and the layout could influence the results. He came to the conclusion that 'the success rate is in general diminished when the mathematical performance is embedded in an everyday problem formulation'.

For the work of the Cockcroft Committee, Bell and his colleagues reviewed similar factors in mathematics, and identified five: (a) the context, whether it was familiar or unfamiliar; (b) readability, which includes all sorts of linguistic factors; (c) the size and complexity of the numbers appearing in the task, mentioning the striking feature that complicated numbers appear to make it more difficult to recognize which operation is actually needed, let alone to manipulate the numbers using that operation; (d) the number and type of operations and the stages involved, and (e) the distractions, including superfluous information.

All of this adds up to saying that the context of assessment can exert a marked influence on children's performance; in some situations one might conclude that a pupil was perfectly capable of doing a task but under other circumstances that she or he was unable to do it. This makes the proposals of the Science Working Group extremely problematic when they suggest that one might give only the shell of a task plus assessment criteria to teachers and allow them to develop the details of the task according to their current activities in the classroom. In that way one would stimulate tremendous variation of tasks from classroom to classroom.

The fact that TGAT suggested that there should be a choice of standard assessment tasks (again to get some match with the curricular activities in any particular school) also increases the problem of comparability — and it is, of course, comparison and comparability that are the true problems. If one was concerned only with the progress of an individual student, one could make sure that the circumstances of assessment and the task were designed to facilitate the best performance of that individual, but when one wants to compare student with student, and classroom with classroom, one cannot afford that luxury.

The Impact of Testing

That leads me to my last theme, the impact of testing and assessment upon the curriculum and the behaviour of the young people and their teachers. I do not deny, of course, that assessment can be a force for good, a force for improvement, as well as a stultifying constricting brake on the curriculum. We all know the horror stories from the days of the 11+ about what a narrowing effect it had. Only a decade ago, Her Majesty's Inspectorate wrote a damning indictment of the effects of 16+ examinations. I quote: 'The effect of the dominating pursuit of examination results was to narrow learning opportunities . . . sustained exposition of the teacher and extensive note-taking by the pupil intended to limit oral work . . . in many subjects writing tended to be stereotyped and voluminous — the result of the widespread practice of dictated or copied notes'. Their conclusions about GCSE were, of course, far more favourable; they have pointed on several occasions to the improvement in learning and teaching styles from the wider range of objectives assessed in GCSE and the wider variety of tasks, especially coursework tasks, that are used as part of GCSE assessment.

And in those areas where the 11+ continues (notably Northern Ireland), we are now getting evidence that again not all is as black as it has been painted. Indeed there appears to be no greater concentration on the basics and the skills tested in 11+ in those areas where the tests are still used than there is in those areas where there is comprehensive education and no selection through testing.

It has become the practice in the United States to distinguish between two kinds of testing. One, designed to support learning, is known as low stakes testing and the other, involving comparison between school and school, or a testing requirement as part of high school graduation requirements, is known as high stakes. In the context of low stakes testing programs there are various evaluations continuing or completed that show positive results. For example, the evaluation by Dick Corbett and Bruce Wilson, of Research for Better Schools, shows that the state-wide testing programs in Maryland and

Pennsylvania had clarified the curriculum, provided additional information about students and indeed created a belief that student skills in some areas were improving. The evaluation in four districts by Bob Stake and his colleagues also shows some positive benefits of low stakes testing procedures: in particular, the promotion of high level skills and greater beneficial differentiation of teaching and the curriculum.

But when the stakes are raised we seem to move very suddenly — perhaps, an example of catastrophe theory — from positive to negative: the researchers report that concentration on raising scores conflicts with sound educational practice. Corbett and Wilson found that as local perception of the stakes went up, districts increasingly gave 'single-minded devotion to specific, almost game-like ways to raise test scores'. Administrators acknowledged that they did so for political reasons, not to improve instructional programmes but to look good; this cosmetic strategy overran existing efforts to improve curricula and eroded the many good effects attributed to testing.

Ellwein, in her evaluation, also came to the conclusion that competency tests and standards function as symbolic and political gestures, not as instrumental reforms.

I am sure that no one here is under any illusion that the stakes are very high indeed in our system of national assessment. The pay-off for schools with good results in terms of their marketing and recruitment will be enormous because, upon open enrolment, more pupils means more cash. I fear that we will see many 'game-like ways' — and some that won't be games but tragedies — in which schools attempt to launder their results. One of the most worrying ways people might do this, I think, is to disapply temporarily the National Curriculum at testing times for some students, particularly perhaps the bilingual, to make sure that their results (which may be poor because of lack of familiarity with English rather than any underlying learning difficulties) will not contribute to the school's overall results. The suggestion that tests can be translated into other languages is laudable, but in my view completely impractical when you realize that over 170 different languages are spoken in the homes of children in the ILEA area alone. I know, of course, that one has to be careful about generalizing from the experience in a foreign country to our own experience but I think that we all fear the effects of competition, particularly when coupled with the prospect of unfair comparison, that is, comparison of raw test results rather than the value added by the individual school.

Conclusions

In an article published around last Halloween, Caroline Gipps reflected on whether the TGAT report was a trick or treat. She felt that TGAT's real trick had been to adopt educative forms of assessment such as graded assessment and all the other kinds of assessments that contribute to records of achievement, and to harness such formative assessment to the highly competitive arrangements required by the Education Reform Act. I now take the same view. You cannot combine formative, summative and evaluative purposes in the same assessment system and expect them all to function unaffected by each other. By making the stakes so high we are making sure that the evaluative function predominates and that the pressure for comparability and rigid systems of moderation (which will make the system as cheat-proof as possible) will drive out good formative practice and the facilitating conditions that allow pupils to put forward their best performance.

How could we lower the stakes? Well, one way is to adopt the strategy of the APU and simply to *sample* pupils, but I fear that would not meet with the approval of those people who feel that the very act of testing individual pupils does indeed, in some magic way, raise standards.

I think that we can lower the pressure a little by attending far more to the presentation of results clearly and fairly, but even those states like California that have tried to present test results of similar schools in a variety of ways, in order to take the heat off the league tables that might appear in estate agents' windows, have not been fully successful.

My argument is that the developments since the TGAT reports were published, especially the upgrading of SATs and the downgrading of teacher assessment and moderation, mean that most of what was good about the TGAT reports has been driven out. The design wasn't bad, but its realization has seriously distorted the design. We are being left with a monster of an external assessment system. I don't think that we can tinker round the edges, we have got to seek a more radical solution to lower the stakes. My own solution would be a very much simpler system of tests — and I mean tests. A short reading test, a short maths test and perhaps a test of science. Yes, of course, that sort of system would have its effect on the curriculum but at least it wouldn't be a pretence. It would leave plenty of space for the rest of the curriculum to blossom and flower, for true formative assessment to underpin and help children's learning, and for individualized assessment and individualized action planning to contribute to the creation of a full and worthwhile record of achievement.

The accountability of the education system would be amply demonstrated by these records of achievement. Schools themselves could develop their own records of achievement. Testing, and I use that word advisedly, testing rather than assessment, could be relegated to a small but still very important place. Only by a radical solution like that can we ensure that the curriculum, and our teaching and learning strategies, are not irreparably harmed.

Note

1   Professor Desmond Nuttall presented the Opening Address to the Education Section Annual Conference on the theme *Assessment*. The present paper is a further contribution to the same theme.

Paper 18

Nuttall, D.L. (1991) *Assessment in England*, Report prepared for Pelavin Associates.

Introduction

Any paper which includes as one of its principal aims a description of the detailed requirements of a particular education policy, will, inevitably, become rapidly dated. Re-reading *Assessment in England* four or more years after it was published, it is clear that very considerable changes in national assessment requirements have taken place since that time — not least as a result of the Dearing Review of 1993/94. Nevertheless, this paper is an important one both in itself and as an illustration of the work of Desmond Nuttall.

It is important in itself as an historical document, since it encapsulates comprehensively the 'tensions and dilemmas' which were informing national assessment policy and implementation in England in its early stages. The quotation from Prime Minister John Major on page 208 in which he dismisses 'some weird experiment in a corner' in favour of more conventional paper and pencil testing, also implicitly dismisses the now very substantial international interest in performance assessment and the search for, more valid assessment approaches.

The Prime Minister's uncritical acceptance of the power of testing truly to represent 'how people are doing', is symptomatic of the central problem in the conception of English national assessment in that it reflects a belief in the possibility of crude and limited measures to provide accurate and meaningful data concerning learning outcomes and school quality which can legitimately be sued for a whole range of purposes from league tables to teachers' curriculum decisions. This in turn reflects the current Government's more general unwillingness to listen to the evidence from research and the advice of professionals. The paper's analysis of the way in which the original, professionally-informed proposals from the Task Group on Assessment and Testing were systematically eroded by successive Government changes is a telling lesson in this respect.

This paper is also an important illustration of Desmond Nuttall's work in that it encapsulates so many of the preoccupations which informed it. The concern with the need for validity in assessment, for example, and the need for integrity of purpose have been themes which informed a great deal of his writing, re-emerging here in the particular context of national assessment. The explicit concern with equity issues and with the more general effects of assessment requirements on curriculum and teaching, are equally definitive of Desmond Nuttall's work. Thus 'Assessment in England' provides a good example not only of Desmond Nuttall's capacity to apply his comprehensive understanding of technical and policy issues in assessment to any particular policy context, but also of how often he sought to do this whether the subject was CSE, GCSE, national monitoring, teacher appraisal, records of achievement or performance indicators. The capacity to communicate clearly and synoptically the complex details of a particular policy was an enduring hallmark of Desmond Nuttall's presentations both orally and in writing and one that, together with his willingness not to flinch from the consequences of outspoken criticism when he felt it to be necessary — made him much in demand as a contributor to the media.

ASSESSMENT IN ENGLAND

Introduction

Assessment has never been so prominent a topic of public and professional debate as it is in England at present,[1] and its power to influence teaching and learning has never been recognized so publicly.

Until recently, although schools used commercially published tests, sometimes at the request of their local education authority, the individual or aggregate results were not made public but used mainly for screening and to inform professionals about performance.

For over 100 years, there have been public examinations both at age 16 (formerly the General Certificate of Education at Ordinary level, now the General Certificate of Secondary Education — GCSE) and at age 18 (since 1951, the General Certificate of Education at Advanced level), the latter for university entrance. Only since 1981, though, have the results had to be published in an aggregated form for each school as a means of accountability, and to give parents more information on which to base their choice of secondary school. In 1991 new regulations have been introduced to oblige schools not only to continue to publish this information but also to aggregate it in such a way that a league table of schools' performance could readily be created (for example, by local newspapers).[2]

The Education Reform Act 1988 was one of the most substantial pieces of English legislation on education this century. One of its most significant parts mandated the creation of a National Curriculum and an associated assessment system, again primarily designed to give information to parents to help them in their choice of school, both primary and secondary, but also to increase the accountability of schools. The remainder of this paper examines these ideas as they are being developed in practice; it ignores the public examination systems for 18-year-olds, though these too are likely to change within the next few years in an attempt to give vocational education equal status with academic education.

The National Curriculum

The National Curriculum comprises three core subjects (English, mathematics and science) and six other foundation subjects (technology, geography, history, art, music and physical education). Religious education also remains a compulsory subject (to age 16, the end of compulsory schooling); in addition (for age 11, the normal age for starting secondary education), a modern foreign language becomes part of the National Curriculum. The detailed content of each subject is prescribed (in the manner described below) and further guidance about suitable teaching and learning activities is also given at national and local level. No time allocation for teaching each subject is given, but the original proposals envisaged National Curriculum subjects occupying about 75–80 per cent of the school week. In practice schools have found that it occupies almost all of the time, so that subjects like economics and classical studies are being squeezed out. There are also concerns about how little time can be given to personal and social education (including health education and sex education).

The manner in which the National Curriculum is specified was established by the Government-appointed Task Group on Assessment and Testing (TGAT), who realized that the principles of the curriculum specification and of the assessment specification had to be devised simultaneously. One of their cardinal principles was that the system should be criterion-reference, and that the curriculum should therefore be in terms of an explicit definition of what a student should be able to know, understand and do. The group drew on the experience of graded testing, a ladder of grades up which a student could progress at his or her own pace, common in music, ballet and other physical activities, and imported into the mainstream curriculum for subjects like modern languages, mathematics and science in the last fifteen years or so (see, for example, Pennycuick and Murphy, 1988). They recommended that, for each subject, there should be ten levels of attainment spanning the ages of compulsory schooling (5–16). These would be anchored such that the

Figure 1: Mathematics attainment target 2: number

Pupils should understand number and number notation

LEVEL   STATEMENTS OF ATTAINMENT

Pupils should:

1
- count, read, write and order numbers to at least 10; know that the size of a set is given by the last number in the count
- understand the conservation of number

2
- read, write and order numbers to at least 100; use the knowledge that the tens-digit indicates the number of tens
- understand the meaning of 'a half' and 'a quarter'

3
- read, write and order numbers to at least 1000; use the knowledge that the position of a digit indicates its value
- use decimal notation as the conventional way of recording in money
- appreciate the meaning of negative whole numbers in familiar contexts

4
- read, write and order whole numbers
- understand the effects of multiplying a whole number by 10 or 100
- use, with understanding, decimal notation to two decimal places in the context of measurement
- recognize and understand simple everyday fractions
- understand and use the relationship between place values in whole numbers

5
- use index notation to express powers of whole numbers
- use unitary ratios

6
- read, write and order decimals; appreciate the relationship between place values
- understand and use equivalence of fractions and of ratios; relate these to decimals and percentages

7
- express a positive integer as a product of primes

8
- express numbers in standard index form using positive and negative integer powers of 10
- use index notation to represent powers and roots

9
- distinguish between rational and irrational numbers

10
- use the knowledge, skills and understanding attained at lower levels in a wider range of contexts

performance of a 'typical' 7-year-old would be at Level 2 and would improve by one level every two years.

Figure 3 in Paper 16 (p. 173) shows the framework of this model. National Curriculum Assessment (NCA) will take place at the end of each key stage of education (i.e., at ages 7, 11, 14 and 16). The black circles in the figure indicate the expected performance of the typical student at that age; the dotted lines indicate the range of levels that would embrace about 80 per cent of the age group.

Working parties, consisting largely of educationists, were set up in each subject to develop a curriculum adhering to the framework above. The subject was to be conceived of as comprising a series of major domains (usually about five), known as *attainment targets*. Within each attainment target, ten performance levels were defined (by the best judgment of the group) in the form of *statements of attainment*. An example is shown in figure 1 for Mathematics Attainment Target No 2: Number.

Attainment targets can also be grouped into *profile components* (for example, English Profile Component 3 comprises three attainment targets,

Writing, Spelling and Handwriting) below the level of the subject. At age 16, the General Certificate of Secondary Education (for which the first examinations were taken in 1988 after nearly twenty years of trials and discussion) is having to be changed radically, to conform to this specification. Its grading scheme is also having to be changed to conform to the ten-level structure.

Given that grading is carried out mainly by consensus agreement of an examining team, rather than statistically, considerable work and training will have to take place before 1994. The training is even more necessary because, for historical reasons, the key boundary in the current system is between grades C and D, which has no equivalent in the new scale.

National Curriculum Assessment

The Task Group on Assessment and Testing stressed the value of *formative* assessment (to guide teaching and learning on a day-to-day basis) but was charged to design a system that would also provide *summative* assessment at the end of key stages (the Government later adding *informative* assessment, i.e. providing information to parents about their child's progress), and *evaluative* assessment by aggregating students' performance to the level of the classroom or the school, to allow class and class or school and school to be compared. As a consequence some mechanism of ensuring that standards were comparable across the nation was needed. The task of ensuring nationwide comparability in examinations has been the preserve of the GCE examining boards for generations.[3] It has usually been accomplished through the professional judgment of experienced teachers and examiners — they are believed to have a 'feel' for the difference between a grade C and a grade D. They can rarely put this 'feeling' into words, but they can reach reasonable empirical consensus, and the public seems to have confidence in this 'professional' approach.

There is in England no history of litigation, no such organization as fair test and virtually no understanding of the commonly used equating methods used routinely in the USA. My opinion is that the examination boards would be very vulnerable to legal challenge; the Government has recently introduced a special appeal body to be the final arbiter of disputes between examining bodies and their clients. This is an important step forward, but cynically one might feel that it was done in the hope of fending off litigation, at least until the next century.

For National Curriculum Assessment, the obvious way to ensure comparability was to use 'tried and trusted' techniques of the examining bodies. Every teacher of children aged 7, 11 and 14 would be trained, sometimes within the school, sometimes in large meetings for schools from a wide area, to acquire this 'feel' for standards, and to discuss the criteria for assessment, so that ultimately the teacher becomes trusted to assess in line with national standards (subject to external audit). (Quotation marks are employed to indicate the unscientific nature of this approach to standardization of grading.)

This belief — that every teacher can assess to national standards, after appropriate training and experience — allowed TGAT to propose that the bulk of National Curriculum Assessment could be carried out by teachers in their own classrooms. This heralded the way to designing assessment tasks for children that could be naturalistic, part of the daily routine of the classroom rather than a special event, and thus not creating anxiety in children, especially those aged 7. This strategy therefore encouraged the creation of performance tasks (practical, oral or written). Thus was the Standard Assessment Task (SAT) born, building especially on the experience of the Assessment of Performance Unit (APU) (which was roughly equivalent to NAEP, assessing samples of students) in imaginative ways. The APU has now been closed down since the new National Curriculum Assessment is expected to give the same information and more.[4]

The SAT used in summer 1991 was made available to teachers several weeks before the administration period, to allow them to become familiar with the range of tasks required (both of them and of the children) and to encourage them to plan normal teaching activities that would make the SAT tasks arise naturally. It was estimated that three weeks would be needed to administer all the tasks to all the children in a typical class. The administration could be spread over a period of six weeks if the teacher desired, and the teacher was encouraged to introduce the tasks in his or her own words.

The tasks themselves varied in mode of presentation and response, though orally was most common. Many tasks were specific to a level (Levels 1 to 3, and 'working towards level 1') and instructions were given on how children could enter at a high level, or be routed back to normal teaching if a particular task was clearly beyond them. There were writing tasks in English. In mathematics, one of the tasks (for a group of four children) was to devise their own game (dice and counters were provided). Another activity ('shopping') allowed assessment of basic number skills. In science, there was assessment of basic knowledge and understanding (for example, names of parts of the body, life cycle). There was also a substantial practical activity on floating and sinking.

During the trials of SATs in summer 1990, and in a full-scale pilot run in summer 1991, SATs at Key Stage 1 (i.e. for 7-year-olds) were found interesting for teaching, learning and assessment purposes, but totally unmanageable in the practical sense. Making a careful assessment by observation of the practical and intellectual behaviour of a group of six children aged 7, while at the same time keeping the other twenty-four children usefully occupied, was clearly impossible. In the national pilot, many teachers were fortunate to get extra help in the classroom from support teachers (often at considerable financial cost), from the headteacher/principal and sometimes from parents; the helper would look after the other children while the teacher devoted her attention to the assessment of a small number of children or to an individual child. Without such a helper, assessment by SATs was very difficult indeed, even with the 1991 version, which had been drastically slimmed down from the SATs tried out in 1990.

TGAT saw the SATs as being the lynchpin of the National Curriculum Assessment system, especially as a device for spreading good practice about ways of assessing students and as a device for helping teachers to understand the criteria and to interpret them uniformly. But the SATs could only sample the achievements of individual children, and a more rounded, more valid and perhaps more reliable assessment of the child could be derived from the teacher's own accumulated experience of the child's achievements over a period of nearly one year. This assessment is known as Teacher Assessment (TA). While TA is arguably much more valid and comprehensive than a SAT, it is perhaps more prone to unwitting bias, unreliability and divergence from national standards. So the Government decide that the SAT, the standardized sample of achievements, should overrule the teacher's cumulative assessment (subject to an appeal by the teacher to a moderator in certain prescribed circumstances).

Complex rules have been devised to help in the variety of ways of combining scores. First, the TA score and the SAT score, each reported in the form of a level on the ten-level scale, have to be combined. The rule is simple: the SAT score stands, over-ruling the TA score (subject to an appeal procedure). Why, then, is it worth having the TA at all? At first glance it would seem that the TA is useless, but on reflection it is clear that there is some value in the process, because it operates as a standardizing mechanism in improving the comparability of TA nationwide. Moreover, the 1990 trials at Key Stage 1 required SAT assessment of some thirty separate attainment targets — categorically impossible, said the teachers after their experience in the trials. So the SAT has been simplified to assess only *nine* of the targets; the remainder are assessed *only* by TA.

The next combination is of the attainment target levels (produced where necessary by combining SAT and TA) into a level for the Profile Component. So a Profile Component consisting of four attainment targets will have its level determined by a simple algorithm: for example, a student at Level 1 in three of the targets and at Level 2 in the fourth will be judged a Level 1 in the profile component; another with two Level 1s and 2s is judged as Level 2 on the profile component. Then, finally as far as the individual child is concerned, the profile component levels have to be combined to provide a level for the subject as a whole (using rules similar to those for combining attainment targets to profile components). So if a 7-year-old is at Level 2 in English, what can be deduced? She is certainly a typical 7-year-old, since some 70 per cent of her peers will also be Level 2. What more? The criterion-referencing at the level of statements of attainment within attainment targets may be a little crude but still useful to the teacher. All other criterion-referencing has been lost: our 7-year-old might be at Level 1 in one profile component, and at Level 3 in another, and within a profile component at Level 1 in one attainment target and at Level 3 in another. There is no way that we can deduce the standard she has achieved in writing or in reading. She could be at least two years (one level equals two years of normal progress) ahead of a typical 7-year-old in reading, and two years behind the typical 7-year-old in writing, despite the fact that she was a typical 7-year-old in terms of her English attainment. So, as was the case with attempts at criterion-referencing the GCSE examination during the 1980s, the attempts to build criterion-referencing into all aspects of NCA have failed, since criterion-referencing cannot be reconciled with score aggregation.[5]

Reporting the Results

The primary purpose of NCA is to provide more information about education and educational progress to the public in general and particularly to parents of children at school. The previous section demonstrated the variety of information available (at the level of attainment target, profile component and subject). Teachers and many parents would want information at the attainment target level or even at the statement of attainment level (where, arguably at least, criterion-referencing is achieved, and provides information useful to planning the next stages in teaching, be they remedial, just a matter of more practice, or moving on to a more advanced topic). Others, such as most parents and the public, would want more of a summary of the information. There is no shortage of information available: levels for fourteen attainment targets in mathematics alone, plus seventeen in science (covering perhaps double or triple the number of statements of attainment). These thirty-one attainment targets provided so much information and, more significantly, required so much assessment and testing that after only two years of trials the Government ordered that they should be reduced to about five for each subject. The draft detailed proposals for the structures and definitions of the five attainment targets were circulated for comment in mid-1991 and were immediately criticized for their significant errors (such as a confusion between 'mass' and 'weight' in the science proposals).[6] On the assumption that, after amendment, the new structures for mathematics and science will come into force, the information available will be as follows: scores on 5 attainment targets, 2 profile components and 1 subject score in mathematics, 5, 2 and 1 in science, 5, 3 and 1 in English, 5, 2 and 1 in technology, 3, 1 and 1 in history and 5, 1 and 1 in geography (the exact structures of the other subjects and their assessment arrangements not having been agreed at the time of writing).

There are few people who would require all this information, the teachers and the head teacher at the child's school possibly being the only ones. The parents will receive the profile component and subject levels achieved by their child, and are entitled to be given the attainment target levels on request. All this information about an individual child is confidential to the child, his or her parents/guardians and the teachers. These arrangements for providing information about individuals are supported by all except the most eccentric dissident, but the same consensus is not apparent for the aggregated information. The details have not yet been agreed, but the Government has made it clear that aggregated scores will be reported publicly both for classrooms (a convenient euphemism for 'teachers') and for schools. This immediately transforms assessment with ostensibly the primary purpose of supporting learning in individuals to assessment with very high stakes for teachers. In the pilot runs, no aggregated scores have been reported (and for schools with 7-year-olds there is likely to be no compulsion to report aggregated scores), so that formal and universal publication is likely not to happen before 1993 (for Key Stage 3) at the earliest. The exception is at Key Stage 4: scores, i.e. the school's GCSE results, have to be published, as noted in the Introduction; reporting by classroom is not required. As a result, experience and behaviour in the pilot runs are not necessarily a good guide to what will happen once results have to be reported publicly.

One of the major debates about NCA surrounds this issue of publishing the results. The Government is adamant that the publication of results is fully justified so that parents and the public have access to a better way of judging the effectiveness of their local schools. Coupled with the right of parents to choose the school that they want their child to attend, the publication of results is seen as a spur to encourage (some would say 'force') schools with poor results to improve their performance (as an alternative to withering away as parents desert them). A large part of the educational establishment does not accept the view that market forces are an appropriate tool of school improvement but, given the Government's views on the matter, is obliged to seek ways of complying in a way that is as constructive as possible. Current thinking is building upon the experience during the 1980s of local education authorities that have tried to minimize the extent to which the mandatory publication of aggregated examination results (for school students aged 16, 17 and 18) mislead the public or their own employees. Following the methodology of the school effectiveness movement (see, for example, Mortimore *et al.*, 1988), the examination results have been inspected in the context of the kinds of student that attends the school: information on their prior achievements, their social class, their sex, or their ethnicity (or usually some combination of these) has been used most frequently.[7] The most commonly used technique has been multiple regression, now in the form of multi-level modelling,[8] which provides an estimated examination score for each school, based on the characteristics of the students that attend it. This statistically estimated score can be compared with the score achieved in practice. If the estimated score exceeds the actual score, the school is considered to be not performing up to its potential — there will be another school with very similar students somewhere in the county who perform much better in their examinations. If the actual score of a school consistently exceeds its estimated one, the school should be congratulated for the success of its efforts to maximize the attainment of its pupils. Conceptually, it has added more value to the students' attainment than could reasonably be expected.

The structure of the National Curriculum provides a vivid and comprehensible way of demonstrating the progress that students make while attending a particular school. For each subject (and indeed each profile component and attainment target), an assessment of the students' attainment is available on their entry to the school, and a few years later there will also be an assessment of the students' attainment as they leave the school. These assessments will both be in the same metric, namely the levels of each attainment target. A school can thus estimate the value added to each student's attainment while the student was in its care, and aggregate such information across classrooms and the school as a whole. Preliminary thinking has been done on possible ways of presenting the information.

As indicated above, no decisions have yet been made on the mode of presentation, but the Government has recently acknowledged that the value added method has merit.[9]

Evaluation and Critique

This paper thus far has described the design of NCA and the arrangements for it, as they were in July 1991. Since the proposals of TGAT were published, and accepted (almost as written) by the Government in mid-1988, substantial changes to the design have been made, largely because of the major practical problems in realizing the original design; indeed, many would argue that the changes have altered the design beyond recognition. The changes to the attainment targets in mathematics and science (the first two National Curriculum subjects that went on stream) have been noted above. In 1989, it was realized that formal external assessment via SATs in nine subjects at Key Stage 1 (and possibly at other key stages) was wholly impractical using the TGAT model. The decision was therefore made to confine the assessment that used both SATs and TA to the three core subjects (English, mathematics and science). Assessment in other subjects is likely to be solely by TA, supported in some subjects by non-statutory SATs that teachers can use if and when they please.[10] The latest, and the most significant, change was announced by the Prime Minister in July 1991: the expensive SATs, concentrating on naturalism and creating problems of time and class management, were to be drastically simplified and abbreviated. Most of the tasks for students, certainly at Key Stage 2 and above, will be 'pen-and-paper', i.e. presented in the written mode and answered by students in writing, usually as short, even one-word, answers and occasionally in a more extended written manner. It is unlikely that multiple-choice questions will be employed, though.[11] The further simplification can, in the light of experience, be justified in terms of the cost and complexity of the SATs. There has, however, been from the outset a lobby arguing for short written tests on the grounds that such tests are objective, whereas SATs and TA are unlikely to be. This view is encapsulated in the comments of the Prime Minister, John Major, to a Sunday newspaper in July 1991:

> By testing I do not mean some weird experiment in a corner. What
> I mean is paper and pencil testing for a classroom so that people have
> a measure of how they are doing — see if there is a problem so that
> you put it right.

The development contracts for assessment material at Key Stage 3 were immediately cancelled, and a new specification for this work was issued, indicating that the assessment was to be made largely with group written tests
lasting no longer than four hours and usually less, the tests to be scored by
the students' own teachers. At the same time it was announced that GCSE
examinations should rely less on work done during the course and more on
standard written tests at the end of the course. The implications of these
decisions for assessment at Key Stage 1 are not yet clear.

This rehearsal of just a small number (though admittedly the most important) of the changes that have taken place in three years demonstrates
immediately why it is difficult to evaluate the assessment proposals: by the
time any evaluation is published, the proposals have been modified yet again.
It is therefore important to note that this critique was written in July 1991; it
focuses on three interrelated themes: conflict of purpose, the likely effects of
NCA and equity. Moreover, there is little technical information available
about the assessments, for example, through generalizability studies, (in keeping with the British custom of scrutinizing all assessments far less rigorously
than is the custom in the US).

Conflict of Purpose

In an imaginative and trail-blazing set of proposals, TGAT almost managed
to find a way to combine assessment for formative, summative and evaluative
purposes into a single system that gave equal status to each of the purposes.
Subsequent developments have squashed this notion irrevocably (if, indeed, it
was ever achievable): the system that is being developed is incontrovertibly
'high stakes' — much will ride on the assessment results when they are published each year. Issues of standardization and comparability immediately
become paramount, as does the need for assessment to be *external* to the
school, so that there is much less likelihood that the results can be 'laundered'
within the school. Assessment techniques that can be tailored by the teacher
to the needs of whole classes or individual students, to ensure that assessment
truly supports and follows learning, become out of the question.

The real nature and effects of this conflict of purposes cannot yet be
known, as no aggregated results have yet been made public, but experiences
of this conflict in other times and places demonstrate that its resolution leads
inevitably towards the dominance of the evaluative and summative purposes
to the detriment — or even the disappearance — of the formative one.[12]

Likely Effects

One likely effect — the dominance of the evaluative purpose — has already been discussed above. Almost all the other effects flow from it. First, the dominant quality that the assessment/results should possess now has to be comparability: parental choice between schools cannot be properly enhanced if a child's performance were to be judged as Level 2 in one school and as Level 3 in another. Comparability is, of course, an essential ingredient of fairness, as is reliability, but to a lesser extent in these circumstances (because the emphasis is on aggregated results rather than those of individuals). Practicality has also to be a major consideration: it is inappropriate to divert excessive resources, most notably the time of teachers, to assessment at the expense of learning and teaching.

The SAT administered in the 1991 national pilot to 7-year-olds (by their own teachers) was designed to occupy some thirty hours of teaching time (for all the children, not for each individual), but most teachers found this optimistic — forty-five to fifty hours was nearer the mark. Moreover they had to spend a similar amount of time outside school hours in preparing themselves for the assessments, and in recording and calculating each student's results.

Practical and educational objections were made by teachers on all these grounds. In short, the SAT was seen and experienced as unmanageable. This has legitimated the Government's switch to 'pen-and-paper' tests.

The real casualties are validity and 'authenticity'. The tasks will no longer be the sort of activities that children engage in the normal course of schooling (and that therefore fit easily into the curriculum and cause the children no anxiety) and in a naturalistic manner; they will be artificial tasks that bear no relation to normal activities in school or out. (Herein lies the primary justification for performance assessment, aka authentic assessment. All the psychometric textbooks stress that validity should be the most sought-after quality in any kind of assessment, whereas most psychometricians would admit that reliability and utility are more commonly valued in practice.)

Because the assessment is high-stakes, a premium is placed upon maximizing scores. There are a plethora of suitable techniques available (most being unethical and some illegal), but the one most commonly employed is 'teaching to the test', in terms both of its likely content and of its known format. Advocates of performance testing see this as a virtue, because the attainment of high levels of performance in appropriate activities is a principal goal of education. But if the high performances are on trivial and irrelevant activities, the point of education becomes distorted. This is graphically demonstrated in a brief extract from an account of a nationwide evaluation of secondary education conducted by Her Majesty's Inspectorate of Schools in the late 1970s:

> . . . the effect of the dominating pursuit of examination results was to narrow learning opportunities, especially when work was concentrated

on topics thought to be favoured by examiners. Sustained exposition by the teacher and extensive note-taking by the pupil tended to limit oral work; this was especially likely to happen when the attainment of candidates had made them borderline performers. Even preparation for oral examinations became too dependent on the formal requirements of the examination. In at least one-fifth of the schools the demands of public examinations appeared to be an important factor in the impoverishment of reading, with the least able pupils suffering most, even though the school had often successfully helped them over their initial difficulties. In many subjects writing tended to be stereotyped and voluminous — the result of the widespread practice of dictated or copied notes, instead of encouragement to engage in a variety of kinds of writing for different purposes. In mathematics, examinations were one factor in encouraging narrow, repetitive practice and standard routines divorced from application to real situations, making it difficult to arouse interest and to deepen and broaden understanding. Similarly in science, the emphasis on content and concepts unrelated to the pupil's experience, again characterized by intensive note-taking, was precluding investigational activity even where examinations required assessment of such skills. (DES, 1979)

The distortion of education by testing and assessment procedures is, of course, also well documented in the USA and with earlier examinations (notably the 11+) in England. It is not an exaggeration to say that the effects of NCA could be educationally disastrous if the assessment takes the form only of 'pen-and-paper' tests.

Equity

The intention that the assessment should reveal what every individual knows, understands and can do, is motivated by the desire to improve Britain's economic performance; if realized, it would also be a major achievement in the struggle for greater equity in British society. There is now growing evidence, however, that valid and authentic assessment does not automatically lead to greater equity. By common consent, the GCSE (introduced in 1988) is regarded as an examination that tapped a wider range of skills and attainments and used a wider range of assessment techniques than its predecessors. The examination results show, however, that the performance gap between the performance of males and females has widened even further in favour of females, and the gaps among the performance of different ethnic groups have also widened (see ILEA, 1970, and Nuttall and Goldstein, 1991). What the position will be when the full National Curriculum Assessment is finally in place (which will certainly not be before 1994 and possibly later) remains to be seen; it must be recognized, though, that equity may have suffered rather than have been promoted.

Conclusions

The British Government sees well-educated and well-trained people as vital to Britain's future development, and to the maintenance of its position as one of the 'great powers'; not many British people would dissent. There is, however, far less agreement about the best ways to achieve this goal, though assessment and testing are usually acknowledged to have an important, if not a critical, role. The members of TGAT were hand-picked by the Government (though mainly from the education establishment). TGAT's proposals were elaborate, complex and imaginative, in an attempt to ensure that the formative function of assessment predominated, or at least had equal status with the function of evaluating schools and teachers. During the development of the detailed structure of NCA and from the trials themselves, it has become apparent that the proposals, well-intentioned as they were, were nevertheless unrealizable. The system of NCA that is currently being created is a pale, almost unrecognizable, likeness of TGAT's original proposals; it has few of their virtues and most of their drawbacks (plus more than a few new ones). Fewer people in Britain in 1991 than in 1988 regard NCA as a tool to improve education; many now regard it as a serious threat to the quality of education.

These conclusions should be set against the general trend in England in the 1980s for a wide range of initiatives attempting to make assessment:

- more comprehensive (i.e. covering a wide range of skills)
- provide better and quicker feedback
- more positive
- give more responsibility to the student
- more valid (see Nuttall, 1987)

One of the major vehicles to support these attempts were Records of Achievement (similar to some portfolio projects in the US), and it is Government policy that every school-leaver in 1992 should take with them such a record. In future, the aim is that this National Record of Achievement would also embrace all post-school qualifications whether vocational or academic. Mixed messages about assessment thus continue to be sent out by the Government.[13]

Notes

1   The arrangements for examinations and national assessment in England are slightly different from those in Wales, somewhat different from those in Northern Ireland, and substantially different from those in Scotland. This paper is, therefore,

limited to the arrangements in England. The Policy Task Group on Assessment of the British Educational Research Association has prepared a paper entitled 'A comparison of the proposals for national assessment in England and Wales, Scotland and Northern Ireland' which will become public in late August 1991.

2 *The Citizen's Charter*, published by the Government in July 1991, implies that there will be a requirement to publish such league tables in future.

3 The way in which the examining boards attempt to maintain nationwide standards is best described in Christie and Forrest (1981).

4 The genesis and functioning of the APU are well described and analyzed in Gipps and Goldstein (1983).

5 The failure of the attempts to build criterion-referencing into examinations in England and Wales has never been properly documented.

6 A summary of the criticisms of the new proposals appears in *The Times Educational Supplement*, 26 July 1991, p. 3.

7 The Inner London Education Authority carried out these analyses on a routine basis (see, for example, ILEA, 1990) and they are now being carried out by a large number of local education authorities. Salganik has reviewed the similar procedures that are used by several states in the USA in a paper for the NCES Panel on Indicators.

8 Multi-level modelling theory and procedures are described in Goldstein (1987). Multi-level modelling is also known as hierarchical linear modelling.

9 Letter dated 18 July 1991 from Lord Cavendish of Furness to Lady David.

10 This idea of SATs as support material for teachers carrying out their own assessments appears likely to be widely used in England and Wales in subjects other than English, mathematics and science. This is the approach to be used in Scotland for all their national assessment.

11 The term 'pen-and-paper' is used to indicate that performance tasks are still likely to be used (with students responding in continuous prose), rather than multiple-choice questions which normally require pencil marks (which can be erased).

12 There is an extensive US literature on the effect of 'high stakes' assessment, for example Corbett and Wilson (1988).

13 Some tables and figures have been omitted from this versions of the Paper.

References

CHRISTIE, T. and FORREST, G.M. (1981) *Defining Public Examination Standards*, London, Macmillan Education.

CORBETT, R. and WILSON, B. (1988) 'Raising the stakes in state-wide mandatory minimum competency testing', *Politics of Education Association Yearbook*, Lewes, Falmer Press.

DEPARTMENT OF EDUCATION and SCIENCE (1979) *Aspects of Secondary Education*, London, HMSO, p. 248.

GIPPS, C.V. and GOLDSTEIN, H. (1983) *Monitoring Children: An Evaluation of the Assessment of Performance Unit*, London, Heinemann Educational Books.

GOLDSTEIN, H. (1987) *Multi-level Models in Educational and Social Research*, New York, Oxford University Press.

ILEA (1990) *Differences in Examination Performance*, London ILEA Research and Statistics Branch.

MORTIMORE, P. *et al.* (1988) *School Matters*, London, Open Books.

NUTTALL, D.L. (1987) 'The current assessment scene', *Coombe Lodge Reports*, 19, 7.

NUTTALL, D.L. and GOLDSTEIN, H. (1991) *The 1988 Examination Results for ILEA*, London, ILEA.

PENNYCUICK, D. and MURPHY, R. (1988) *The Impact of Graded Tests*, Lewes, Falmer Press.

Nuttall, D.L. (1994) 'Choosing indicators' in Riley, K. and Nuttall, D.L. (Eds) *Measuring Quality: Education Indicators United Kingdom and International Perspectives*, London, Falmer Press.

Introduction

The OECD indicators project marks a massive international effort to define common key variables which can be used to monitor and compare the quality of individual education systems. Desmond Nuttall played a key role in the first stage of this project contributing, in particular, to the task of conceptualizing the nature of the indicators that would be appropriate for this purpose. This article is another typical example of Desmond Nuttall's work characterized as it is by a desire to address a pressing and important practical problem for policy-makers: how can educational systems be assessed for how *good* they are? How can indicators be developed that are really useful? In his attempt to answer these questions Desmond Nuttall's account identifies some of the criteria for identifying a good indicator, a task which involves him in turn in discussing the different uses to which such measures might profitably be put.

It is clear from this paper that Desmond Nuttall himself had no doubts about how indicators might usefully be used and their limitations. As a researcher he was well aware of the inevitably partial character of all such data and recognized that it could only ever be suggestive, indicative and diagnostic. He was himself clear what the 'instructions for use' should be if indicators were to become a useful implement in the educational planning tool kit. Readers may in consequence judge there to be an unusual degree of naivety in this article. There is no discussion of the very great potential for abuse when policy-makers, especially politicians, are provided with ready-made league tables. The essentially scientific quest in which Desmond Nuttall was, with others, engaged, to find useful, reliable and practicable indicators of quality had little in common with subsequent crude initiatives to impose similar ideas on schools. The league tables of truancy rates and student post-school destinations which are now required of schools in England have little in common with the subtle and sensitive arguments concerning what indicators should be chosen and how they should be used, which are put forward in this article.

This text was first published as part of *Making Education Count: Developing and Using International Indicators*, an OECD publication based on papers presented to the General Assembly of the International Indicators of Education Systems (INES) project in Lugano, Switzerland in September 1991. It was one of a collection of contributions that explored fundamental conceptual, ethical and practical problems in the use of such indicators. This volume, and Desmond Nuttall's contribution to it, is likely to endure as one of the more authoritative texts in this area. The text of Desmond Nuttall's contribution has recently been republished by Falmer Press in a book he edited with Professor Kathryn Riley entitled *Measuring Quality*. This posthumous publication was, sadly, Desmond Nuttall's last word on the subject. It is clear, however, from the article that Desmond Nuttall had only just begun to mine a rich seam of potential insight concerning how educational quality might effectively be conceptualized and measured. His achievements were sufficient however to make a major contribution to firmly establishing the importance of this topic on both policy and research agendas.

CHOOSING INDICATORS

The aim of this chapter is to examine the factors that influence the selection of particular indicators as components of an indicator system, and to derive a general set of principles that would make the selection process more systematic. The chapter therefore starts with a clarification of the term 'indicator', and then considers what may be learnt from the history of indicator systems in other fields. In the light of this analysis, the chapter looks at the major considerations that govern the selection process and at how they have been embodied in lists of criteria proposed by workers in the filed, before proposing such a set for use with educational indicators.

What are Indicators?

There is general consensus that indicators are designed to provide information about the state of an educational (or, more generally, a social) system. They act as an early-warning system that something may be going wrong, in the same way that the instruments on the dashboard of a car can alert the driver to a problem or reassure him or her that everything is functioning smoothly. A dial pointer moving into the red zone is only a symptom of some malfunction and further investigation is needed to establish the cause. Viewed as reassuring or warning devices, indicators conform to the dictionary definition; for example, the Oxford dictionary defines an indicator as 'that which points out or directs attention to something' (quoted by Johnstone, 1981, p. 2). If something is wrong, the indicators themselves do not provide the diagnosis or prescribe the remedy; they are simply suggestive of the need for action.

The consensus over the broad purpose of indicators does not extend to the precise definition of what an indicator is. Some reserve the definition to a narrowly quantitative one; thus,

> A third feature of an indicator is that it is something which is quantifiable. It is not a statement describing the state of a system. Instead it must be a real number to be interpreted according to the rules governing its formation. (*ibid.*, p. 4)

Others take a much wider view, and would include descriptive or even evaluative statements within the scope of indicators (for example, Chartered Institute of Public Finance and Accountancy (CIPFA), 1988). Almost always, though, even the widest definition limits the concept to information, and excludes analysis or discussion.

The fears of those who adopt a wider view are that the limiting of the concept to just the quantitative will mean that indicators cannot portray the full richness and diversity of the educational process, and that, at worst, they will indicate merely the trivial and focus attention on the unimportant. This is similar to one of the major criticisms of quantitative research in education and the social sciences by those who espouse the qualitative approach, and as such goes beyond the scope of this chapter. Nevertheless, it is incumbent on those who propose indicators to demonstrate that they are not too reductionist, and will not divert attention from equally important (or even more important) goals.

It would seem that the more common view of indicators is of the quantitative variety. For example, in the survey carried out under the OECD Institutional Management in Higher Education programme, an indicator is defined as 'a numerical value . . .' and the OECD Indicators Project has tacitly taken the same view. The line between management statistics and indicators is not easily drawn, however. Some suggest that indicators imply a comparison against a reference point (as in a time series or an average), while by implication statistics do not, but in fact it is rare that the interpretation of even descriptive statistics dispenses with comparison. Others limit the term to composite statistics such as a student-teacher ratio, so that the number of students enrolled in a particular phase of education would not be considered an indicator (though it could well be an important item of management information).

A somewhat broader definition was adopted by Shavelson *et al.* (1987): 'An indicator is an individual or a composite statistic that relates to a basic construct in education and is useful in a policy context' (p. 5). They deny that all statistics are indicators, though: 'Statistics qualify as indicators only if they serve as yardsticks (of the quality of education)' (*ibid.*, p. 5).

The confusion over definition was noted by Jaeger (1978), who proposed that:

> all variables that (1) represent the aggregate status or change in status of any group of persons, objects, institutions, or elements under study, and that (2) are essential to a report of status or change of status of the entities under study or to an understanding of the condition of the entities under study, should be termed indicators. I would not require that reports of status or change in status be in quantitative form, for narrative is often a better aid to comprehension and understanding of phenomena than is a numeric report. (pp. 285–7)

It therefore seems that there is no clear agreement on exactly what an indicator is or is not; Selden (1991) cuts the Gordian knot by proposing that we should drop preconceptions about what 'indicators' are and recognize that it is their *use* that makes them 'indicators'. For the purposes of this chapter, an indicator is taken to be *quantitative*, recognizing that it could stretch to a quantification of a professional subjective judgment (as in the rating of the quality of teaching); an indicator would *also be quoted alongside other similar indicators to allow comparison* (usually over time, but also with an average or norm, or with values from other institutions, regions or nations). Above all, indicators are seen *as part of a set or system of indicators* that together provide information designed to be greater than the sum of its parts, rather than something displayed in isolation (as test scores have been in some international comparisons of achievement in the past). This idea of an indicator system is discussed further below.

Indicators in the Policy-making Process

If there is no agreement on the definition of indicators, there is a large measure of agreement over their purpose, namely that they are designed to give information to policy-makers about the state of the educational system, either to demonstrate its accountability or, more commonly, to help in policy analysis, policy evaluation and policy formulation. The policy-makers can be at the national, regional or district level, within the institution itself (as senior managers or faculty managers), or even at a classroom level, where, in effect, the teacher is always reacting to information about the pupils' progress to adjust the pacing or focus of his/her teaching.

Indicators will naturally be only one of the aids in policy analysis, alongside such techniques as cost-benefit analysis and futures research, but nevertheless they are seen as an increasingly important contribution to *rational* policy analysis (Carley, 1980; Hogwood and Gunn, 1984). Moreover, indicators tend to send signals about what is or should be important, and thus contribute to the public identification of policy issues and concerns — the stream of public problems seen as important, as Kingdon (1984) put it. Indeed, Innes (1990) argued that 'social indicators ultimately have their most important role to play in framing the terms of policy discourse' (p. 431). She proposed an interpretative or phenomenological view of knowledge to help the recognition and comprehension of the badly needed integration of indicator concepts with the understandings of the public.

Others also take the view that research knowledge is not used directly by the policy-maker. Partly this is because there are limits to the rationality of the policy-making process, as argued by Cohen and Spillane, and partly because knowledge is only one of the influences upon policy-making, which is inevitably a political process (McDonnell, 1989). Indeed, the only function of knowledge in the policy-making process may be to alter the general climate of opinion (Nisbet and Broadfoot, 1980) or the *Zeitgeist*. Weiss (1979) sees its function as general 'enlightenment':

> Here it is not the findings of a single study nor even of related studies that directly affect policy. Rather it is the concepts and theoretical perspectives that social science research has engendered that permeate the policymaking process. (p. 429, cited by McDonnell, 1989, p. 244)

The history in the USA of social indicators (which came to prominence in the 1960s and 1970s but faded away in the 1980s) shows that several factors contributed to their decline (analyzed in detail by Rockwell (1989) and in a symposium published in the *Journal of Public Policy* [Rose, 1990]).

The first factor was essentially political. Any indicator system embodies value judgments about what is meant by quality or desirable outcomes in education, nor is any underlying model or framework objective. The review by van Herpen (1989) demonstrates that such frameworks or models almost always have a bias towards one particular epistemological perspective of the education system (for example, the economic or the sociological). The meaning of the indicators (and their changes over time) thus becomes contentious, and there is a 'tendency for indicators to become vindicators' (Bulmer, 1990, p. 410) and for the reports to be 'rather bland compromises, deliberately presented without text that might link the data to policy' (Innes, 1990, p. 430).

Secondly, the system became divorced from the policy context and too theoretical and abstruse, run essentially for and by the social scientific community. Innes (1990) suggested that the social scientists had an overly simplistic and overly optimistic view of how and in what circumstances knowledge is used in the process of policy analysis, and of how straightforward it would be to develop indicators:

> They focussed energy on the measurement task, often to the exclusion of the political and institutional one. They did not recognize how the political and institutional issues would interact with decisions about methodology. (p. 431)

Bulmer (1990), attributed the lack of success of the social indicator movement to the failure of social science to become institutionalized in the governments of industrial societies, something that is particularly difficult to achieve under conservative administrations. MacRae (1985) concurred, suggesting a need for a 'technical community':

> an expert group that conducts and monitors research, but directs its work at concerns of citizens and public officials, not merely at improving its own theories (in the manner of a 'scientific community'). (p. 437)

Such groups have become more common in the last few years as policy analysts or researchers in the direct employ of national or local government.

The third and, according to Bulmer (1990), the most important factor lying behind relative failure of social indicators was the lack of general social scientific theories of a specificity that allowed the development of indicators to measure the theoretical constructs. Economic theories have been worked out in much more detail, and economic indicators have the advantage of a common measure of value (i.e. money), though they will sometimes include other kinds of numbers (for example, the unemployment rate). Notwithstanding the largely common measure, there are rival economic theories and much contention over the interpretation and explanation of indicators that spills into the media. But in other social sciences, Bulmer (*ibid.*) considered that 'the absence of theory does not preclude the construction of indicators, but it means that when this happens, they often lack a clear rationale and conceptual justification' (p. 409).

How are Indicators Chosen?

There is clearly much to be learnt from the recent past about the factors that ought to be taken into consideration in creating an indicator system in education. There appear to be three basic sources of influence that interact in the creation of indicators: policy considerations, scientific/technical considerations, and practical ones. These are considered in turn in this section.

Policy Considerations

In the case of a general interest about the state of the educational system, some principle will govern the choice of indicators, but it may be as simple as the use of information already available. This seems to have been the case with the Wallchart in the USA, where only data that were routinely collected (for a variety of different purposes) were displayed in the Wallchart; they were chosen for their perceived relevance to appraise the educational performance of the fifty states. Some of the indicators in the Wallchart have been criticized on the grounds that they do not permit fair comparison between states. For example, the average SAT scores need to be corrected for the different proportions (largely due to self-selection) of the student population that take the test in each state, if comparison is to be meaningful (Wainer, 1986). Others would argue that socioeconomic differences between state populations also ought to be taken into account if the comparisons are to be fair (in the way that they have in school or school district comparisons in some US states [Salganik, 1990], and in school comparisons in the Inner London Education Authority in the UK [ILEA, 1990]). The publication of the Wallchart has stimulated a number of activities designed to improve upon the set of indicators displayed, and for that reason alone may be considered to have been a valuable impetus to improvement.

A more systematic approach is being followed by the Panel on Indicators established by the National Center for Educational Statistics in the USA. They are likely to recommend a thematic approach, with possibly different periodicities for updating; possible themes include: the acquisition of knowledge and the engagement of the student in the learning process, readiness for entry to the school, and equity. Within the set of indicators for each theme, the indicators may be arranged in a pyramid, with a few key indicators at the top and many more in tiers below for those who want or need a more thorough analysis.

Alternative systematic approaches that limit the number of indicators see them as being created to give information about current policy issues (for example, the effectiveness of particular educational reforms) or about the attainment of particular goals or explicit targets. The targets set by the US President jointly with the State governors in 1990 (such as drug-free schools and the elevation of the USA to first position in the international league tables of school students' performance in mathematics and science by the year 2000) lend themselves to the creation of particular indicators. This is also the approach advocated by the proponents of institutional development planning, who see indicators as being the primary tool for evaluating the degree to which the particular targets chosen for a given development cycle are attained (for example, Osborne, 1990; Hargreaves *et al.*, 1989).

A system of indicators based on the policy concerns of the day runs the risk, as Carley (1981) put it, 'of faddism, and over-concentration on social factors of passing interest at the expense of those not currently subject to influence and debate' (p. 126). Hogwood and Gunn (1984) took a similar view, advocating a more comprehensive approach, including indicators which, though they may not seem very important or subject to much change over time at the present time, may turn out to be 'sleepers' which suddenly become of more significance ten years into the future. Darling-Hammond also stresses the importance of creating indicators independent of the current policy agenda.

While understanding the desire of busy policy-makers and managers for a limited and simple set of indicators, and the researchers' desire for a parsimonious one, there are dangers that arise from keeping the set small. The greatest danger is that of corruptibility of the behaviour of those whose performance is being monitored. The best-known example is 'teaching to the test', commonly seen when the stakes are high, that is, when an individual's future hinges on his or her test result. Broader, and possibly deeper, education suffers when almost all effort is devoted to changing the indicator values for the better. Darling-Hammond therefore argues for a measure of redundancy in the information conveyed by an indicator set, so that if behaviour changes in respect to one indicator it will also affect other indicators (not necessarily for the better).

This principle was taken considerably further by McEwen and Hau Chow (1991) to encompass different educational value systems and the different levels of education that each need different kinds of information. They argue for:

> the proposed strategy (that) might be called the multiplier effect:
> (i)   multiple goals of education, based on appropriate dimensions and domains of schooling;
> (ii) multiple indicators of each goal measured by multiple methods;
> (iii) multiple levels of analysis: student, class, school, system, province, (and potentially) country, the world; and
> (iv) multiple participants: government, administrators, teachers, academics, parents.
>
> (McEwan and Hau Chow, 1991, p. 81)

While it is easy to see the value of such a set of indicators, there are other factors (notably feasibility and cost) that curtail the possibility of its development — one of many examples of how the different kinds of considerations (policy, technical and practical) come into conflict.

Nevertheless, policy considerations — indeed, the whole policy context — will always remain salient if the indicator system is to continue to be useful (as the fate of the social indicator system discussed above demonstrates). As McDonnell (1989) sees it:

The policy context, then, plays two distinct roles in the design of an indicator system. First, it provides the major *rationale* for developing and operating such a system. Second, the policy context constitutes a key *component* of any educational indicator system, because specific policies can change the major domains of schooling in ways that affect educational outcomes. (pp. 241–2)

The Modelling Approach

The increased value of a system of indicators that reveals cause-and-effect relationships, that can therefore predict changes as a result of policy-makers' actions, is obvious, but not easy to achieve. Variables must be included in the model that are amenable to direct manipulation by the policy-maker and that link through some causal mechanism to effect the desired outcomes.

Social and educational research has, over the years, provided much evidence of relationships between variables, sometimes causally linked but more commonly just associated, but no general model of the educational process, including all phases from pre-school to recurrent education, and for all kinds of different outcomes (intellectual, social and behavioural), currently exists. The review by van Herpen (1989) demonstrated how many different models have been put forward in educational research, and how incomplete and biased (towards one epistemological perspective) they are. The OECD Indicators Project adopted a broad framework based essentially on an input-output (i.e. economic) model of education (see below) and commentators were quick to draw attention to competing models, for which different indicator sets would be derived. Moreover, Bulmer (1990) claims that the theories and models in the realm of social indicators are all too general to provide an adequate starting point for the development of indicators.

Only econometric models are sufficiently detailed to be used to predict future behaviour (of the economy), but even then models provide different results and reflect the theoretical positions of the modellers. The policy-makers' expectations of such models may then be too high, destined for disillusionment before long. As Greenberger, Crenson and Crissey (1976), who reviewed the use of models in the policy process, put it,

> . . . the effectiveness of policy modelling depends not only on the model and the modeller, but on the policymaker too. Increasing the usefulness of models as instrument for enlightening decision makers will require behavioral adjustments by the policymakers as well as by the modelers. (pp. 328–9)

If adequate models cannot be constructed, some organizing principles behind the indicator system are still needed, and the term 'framework' is commonly used to avoid implications of causes and effects. In the field of social indicators, for example, a structuring by programmes (for example, health, education, etc.) is often used. Carley (1980) views this approach as cost effective and straightforward but warns:

> The chief danger is that the sometimes tenuous cause and effect relationships implicit in the indicators might go unnoticed by administrators who may overvalue the explanatory power of the indicators. (p. 194)

This danger is seen in the framework put forward by the RAND study on indicators for mathematics and science (Shavelson *et al.*, 1987). It was constructed after study of the research literature, and appears to be a form of flowchart or model on account of the arrows. The text makes a very important caveat that might easily be missed:

> The relationships depicted in this figure, of course, do not constitute a model in either a strict predictive or causal sense. However, they can serve as a framework, showing logical linkages among elements of the schooling system. (*ibid.*, pp. 10–11)

The general consensus is that our understanding of the educational process is not yet sufficient for the postulation of a model, but that we are in a position to create a framework that embodies our limited knowledge of some empirical relationships, and that begins to relate malleable variables (that is, variables that can be readily altered by the policy-makers) to desirable outcomes, *without* appearing to promise too much. The INES Project has moved cautiously in its development of a framework, for this reason among others. In its first phase, a very basic framework was employed. In its second phase this has been elaborated considerably, but again without arrows between the boxes which might imply causal relationships.

Thus the two approaches (the one derived from policy considerations and the other from the modelling of the educational process) can be united in the form of a framework, as long as no strong cause-and-effect relationships are inferred and as long as it is recognized that values (both political and epistemological) will have influenced both the general design of the framework and the particular indicator categories used.

Technical Issues

If there are difficulties in arriving at a general framework or model embracing policy-relevant concepts such as 'achievement in science' and 'quality of teaching', there are also problems in defining the concepts sufficiently precisely to allow measures (indicators) to be taken. The problems in this move from concept to measure are well-known in the social sciences: one concept can

Figure 1: Linking elements of the educational system

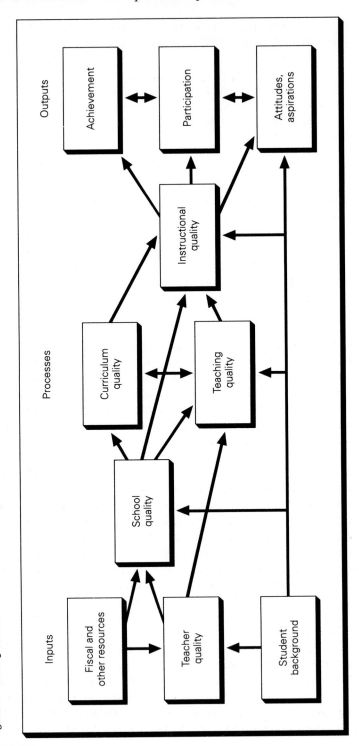

*Source:*Shavelson *et al.*, 1987, p. 10.

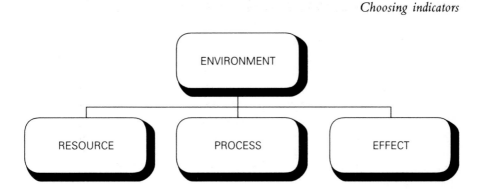

generate dozens of different indicators. Most concepts require detailed specification and clarification — for example, what sorts of skills (in what mix),
applied to what facts and concepts, constitute 'achievement in science'? Value
systems inevitably influence the choice. Given such a specification, it may
prove much easier to develop measures of some skills than it is of others, and
practical issues such as cost (discussed in more detail below) begin to assume
importance; and, moreover, it may be much easier to specify some skills than
others, such as the 'noble goals' that Shavelson (in press) suggests that we
should develop indicators for.

Given the subjectivity that can enter the process of developing indicators,
it is important to apply social scientific principles to their evaluation, especially to evaluate the reliability and validity of the measures used. There are
well-established techniques in the social sciences to do this (see, for example,
Messick, 1989; and Feldt and Brennan, 1989). There are two levels to the
validity questions: how do the measures relate to the concept, and how does
the framework linking the concepts relate to the reality of the educational
system? These two levels can often mean that the indicator set may be far
from being an adequate representation of reality. This is particularly so in the
case of international indicators, notably in the measurement of achievement.
It is almost impossible to devise a single test that is an equally valid measure
of each country's definition of achievement in mathematics, say.

In practice, the relationship between concepts and indicators is not all one
way. The development of indicators, and a study of their interrelationships,
can help to refine the concepts and the interrelationships between them as
represented in the framework or model. This interaction of theory and measurement has been particularly productive in the field of school effectiveness
(see, for example, the review by Scheerens, 1990) and frequently leads to the
development of composite or complex concepts. For example, the review of
the literature on the influence of school context by Oakes (1989) led her to
propose three general constructs of significance (all seen as *enablers* rather than
causes of student learning): access to knowledge, press for achievement, and
professional teaching conditions. All three are far from *simple*, and for each
Oakes suggests that it would be necessary to measure at least nine 'more
tangible school characteristics'. She does not propose whether or how the

separate measurements should be combined to form a single indicator, or how the validity of the measures would be established.

The creation of composite indicators is likely to be important in indicator systems, if only to avoid overloading the reader with numbers. Social science and statistics can again offer well-tried techniques for forming homogeneous composite measures (for example, using factor analysis or other approaches to multi-dimensional scaling — see, for example, Mardia, Kent and Bibby, 1979), but they have rarely been applied in indicator systems (except in achievement and attitude measurement). Some have gone so far as to suggest a single composite indicator of the success of the educational system, namely the Gross Educational Product (analogous to the Gross Domestic Product, which is itself composed of a multitude of smaller measures). The former is not, of course, as simple as the latter, since education lacks the sort of common measure that economics employs (dollars or pounds sterling). The creation of a composite would therefore require the application of scaling and weighting techniques (see, for example, Petersen, Kolen and Hoover, 1989). In any case, even econometric modelling runs into difficulties when there is no direct and simple way of generating a monetary indicator, for example, for intangibles such as environmental pollution or for non-monetized activities such as household chores.

Nevertheless, the general thrust of research in education suggests that it is complex concepts of the kind synthesized by Oakes that are likely to have explanatory power; many of these may have to be appraised and measured by experts, such as inspectors, who may be able to arrive at numerical judgments of the relative 'quality of the learning environment' or 'professional teaching conditions' across different institutions. With such judgments, not only is validity an important concern but the reliability or consistency of judgment, between experts and over time, also becomes of great significance. Reliability of lower level indicators such as pupil-teacher ratio is more easily achieved, but is still a vital quality.

To be useful to the policy-maker, indicators do not only have to be relevant but, experience shows, they must also be timely, comprehensible and few in number. Ensuring timeliness puts pressure on the indicator technicians who themselves may often be dependent on the actions of thousands of others in providing data (an activity to which those thousands may not attach much priority, not least because they often stand to gain little by carrying it out), and on the cost of the exercise: modern information technology and sampling both offer ways of streamlining procedures, but the cost of providing timely high quality information is likely to remain substantial. This is particularly true in the domain of student achievement measures.

Restricting the number of indicators probably assists in their gaining attention and being comprehensible, but may reduce the validity of the set of indicators as a framework representing the education system. Comprehensibility will be assisted by clear presentation, but many argue that the clearest-presented information still needs interpretative comment (for example, Odden,

1990) — the indicators do not 'speak for themselves'. Such interpretative comment will inevitably reflect the values of the commentator if it is to be other than bland, which can therefore lead to political difficulties over the provision of any comment. Social indicators fell into this trap in the USA which led to the commentaries being offered elsewhere (notably in the *Annals of the American Academy of Political and Social Sciences*) rather than beside the indicators, and they were therefore frequently not referred to.

Another desirable characteristic of indicators is that the data should be incorruptible, in other words not liable to deliberate alteration before they are collected. Achievement testing is particularly prone to such manipulation, for example, by schools' making sure that those of lower achievement are absent on the day of the test or by coaching the students for the test.

Who Chooses the Indicators?

The previous section has examined the various factors that might influence the way in which indicators and indicator systems might be chosen. It is apparent that these choices are inevitably influenced by the value systems of those making the choice, and need to reflect the interests of the policy-makers while also reflecting scientific understandings of how the educational system functions. This led MacRae to propose a 'technical community' that could bridge the gap between the policy-makers and the social scientists (see above). Others feel that the 'consumers' of education should also have a voice (see Riley, 1990). Pollitt (1986) warns that imposing a system of indicators from above will alienate those whose assistance and goodwill are needed in the enterprise, and advocates a pluralistic stance so that every interested party can contribute to the discussion before the system is finalized.

Thus the answer to the question 'Who chooses the indicators?' must be in large measure political (or reveal political values) and will inevitably be of significance to the process of the selection of indicators, and to the outcomes of that process. Many writers have attempted to recognize its importance, alongside political, technical and practical considerations, by creating a set of criteria that an indicator system, and individual indicators, should meet before they come into use.

Criteria for Choosing, Developing and Evaluating Indicators

These criteria differ according to political values, as well as according to the particular policy context, the particular educational system and to the particular level (for example, national, regional or local) under study. The principles that have been proposed for developing and evaluating indicators therefore vary, as do the safeguards against misinterpretation and misuse that have been advocated, but there is also much in common between the criteria proposed.

For the OECD INES Project, Nuttall (1989) proposed the following principles:

(a) indicators are diagnostic and suggestive of alternative actions, rather than judgmental;

(b) the implicit model underlying the indicators must be made explicit and acknowledged;

(c) the criteria for the selection of indicators must be made clear and related to the underlying model;

(d) individual indicators should be valid, reliable and useful;

(e) comparisons must be done fairly and in a variety of different ways (for example, with like groups, with self over time, and using dispersions and differences between sub-groups as well as averages);

(f) the various consumers of information must be educated about its use.

A further criterion, aimed at safeguarding against the punitive use of indicators, was originally proposed:

Control over data must remain with those who provide it. Desirable though such a criterion might ideally be, in the end it was not retained on the grounds that in an international project it could not be met. Apart from the more technical criteria, this list appears to be primarily concerned with lowering the expectations and increasing the sophistication of users.

Other criteria proposed by English writers have attempted to seek a pluralistic view of indicators to ensure that the community has a genuine stake in them. For example, Riley (1990) proposed the following set:

• The process of developing school indicators should ensure that all the partners in education have a sense of ownership in the indicators.
• Accessible to all the partners in education.
• Comparable throughout the authority (school district or local education authority).
• Linked to school ethos and objectives.
• Inclusive of both cognitive and non-cognitive outcomes.
• Implementable.
• Based on consumer evaluation of the education experience.

It is apparent that this set concentrates on school-level indicators, as does the set proposed by Gray and Jesson (1988):

1 The most important consideration relating to the construction of performance indicators is that they should directly measure or assess schools' performance. Many of the proposals we have encountered to date seem only directly related to actual performance.

2   They should be central to the processes of teaching and learning which we take to be schools' prize objectives.

3   They should cover significant parts of schools' activities but not necessarily (and certainly not to begin with) all or even most of them.

4   They should be chosen to reflect the existence of competing educational priorities; a school which did well in terms of one of them would not *necessarily* be expected (or found) to do well in terms of the others.

5   They should be capable of being assessed; we distinguish assessment here from measurement, which implies a greater degree of precision than we intend.

6   They should allow meaningful comparisons to be made over time and between schools.

7   They should be couched in terms that allow schools, by dint of their efforts and the ways in which they chose to organize themselves, to be seen to have changed their levels of performance; that is to have improved or, alternatively, to have deteriorated relative to previous performance and other schools.

8   They should be few in number; three or four might be enough to begin with. After some experimentation over a period of years one might end up with a few more.

Gray and Jesson went on to propose what those three indicators should in fact be, based on the research evidence from the school effectiveness literature:

Performance Indicator Focus	Key Questions to be Addressed	Answer Categories
1(a)	Taking the school as a whole, what proportion of pupils made expected levels of progress over the relevant time period.*	all or most well over half about half well under half few
1 Academic Progress		
1(b)	What proportion of pupils of: (i) below average (ii) average (iii) above average prior attainment made expected levels of progress over the relevant time period?*	all or most well over half about half well under half few
2(a)	What proportion of pupils in the school are satisfied with the education they are receiving?	all or most well over half about half well under half few

2 Pupil Satisfaction

	2(b)	What proportion of pupils of	all or most
		(i) below average	well over half
		(ii) average	about half
		(iii) above average	well under half
		attainment are satisfied with the	few
		education they are receiving?	
	3(a)	What proportion of pupils in the	all or most
		school have a good relationship	well over half
		with one or more teachers?	about half
			well under half
			few

3 Pupil-teacher Relationships

	3(b)	What proportion of pupils of:	all or most
		(i) below average	well over half
		(ii) average	about half
		(iii) above average	well under half
		attainment in the school have a	few
		good relationship with one or	
		more teachers?	

* Initially this question might be posed in terms of summary measures of pupil attainment; subsequently, more detailed breakdowns (subject-by-subject for example) might be attempted.

This set of indicators and the criteria that precede them see particular merit in the number of indicators being kept small, and the writers do not worry that the list only partially covers the goals of education (and certainly contains no redundancy). The indicators are chosen to focus on important goals, and pay no attention to processes and virtually none to context (only 1a and 1b, by using the term 'expected levels of progress', acknowledge the relativity of measures).

Criteria proposed in the USA tend to reflect primarily the concerns of policy-makers above the level of the school. Windham (1990) drew attention to the conclusions in the economic sphere that indicators should be 'accurate, relevant, timely, understandable and affordable'; Carley (1981) attributed the failure of the social indicators movement largely to the dominant influence of researchers who, in the search for accuracy, ignored relevance, timeliness and comprehensibility. Nevertheless, there had for some time been a recognition that these factors were important. For example, the US Urban Institute put forward the following criteria:

(1) *Appropriateness and validity*: indicators must be quantifiable, in line with goals and objectives for that service, and be oriented towards the meeting of citizen needs and minimizing detrimental effects;

(2) *Uniqueness, accuracy and reliability*: indicators generally need not overlap, double counting should be avoided, but some redundancy may be useful for testing the measure themselves;

(3) *Completeness and comprehensibility*: any list of indicators should cover the desired objectives and be understandable;

(4) *Controllability*: the conditions measured must be at least partially under government control;

(5) *Cost*: staff and data collection costs must be reasonable;

(6) *Feedback time*: information should become available within the time-frame necessary for decision-making.
(Hatry *et al.*, 1977, quoted by Carley, 1981, p. 166)

Rockwell (1989) offers a rather similar list: timeliness, providing 'handles for policy', covering both current and emerging policy issues, in a time series, measures adaptable to changing circumstances, valid, reliable and accurate.

The most influential US proposals for criteria emerged from the RAND work on indicator systems for monitoring mathematics and science education (Shavelson *et al.*, 1987, pp. 27–8). They were that indicators should:

- Provide information that *describes central features of the educational system* — for example, the amount of financial resources available, teachers' work load, and school curriculum offerings. Even though research has not as yet determined the relationship of some of these features to particular outcomes, information is needed about them to understand how the system works and because policy-makers and the general public care about factors such as per pupil expenditures and class size.

- Provide information that is *problem-oriented*. Indicators must provide information about current or potential problems — for example, factors linked to teacher supply and demand, or to the changing demographics of urban areas.

- Provide information that is *policy-relevant*. Indicators should describe educational conditions of particular concern to policy-makers and amenable to change by policy design. For example, indicators of teacher characteristics such as educational background and training are policy-relevant, since they can be changed through legislation or regulations governing teacher licensing.

- *Measure observed behaviour rather than perceptions*. Indicators will be more credible if they assess actual behaviour rather than participants' opinions or judgments. For example, the academic rigour of schools is better measured by course requirements and offerings than by principal, teacher, and student perceptions.

- *Provide analytical links among important components*. Indicators will be more useful if they permit the relationships among the different domains of schooling to be explored.

- Generate data from measures generally accepted as *valid and reliable*. Indicators should measure what they are intended to measure and should do so consistently.
- Provide information that can be *readily understood by a broad audience*. Indicators need to be easily comprehensible and meaningful to those beyond the immediate mathematics and science community — to policy-makers, press, and the general public.
- Be *feasible* in terms of timeliness, cost and expertise. Indicator data need to be produced within a time frame that is compatible with policy-makers' decision cycles and within given cost constraints; they should also be collectable, analyzable, and reportable within current levels of expertise.

On the more technical side, this list is similar to the others (several of which it influenced, no doubt) but it again sees the policy-maker as the main client for indicator information.

Some of the differences between the lists are a function of the particular audience that the indicators are designed to address (for example, national policy-makers or school personnel) but other differences are less easy to resolve. There is broad agreement about technical and practical matters (for example, validity, reliability, timeliness, comparability, feasibility and keeping costs reasonable) and little difference on the need for policy relevance and the importance of ensuring that the indicators are comprehensible to their audience(s).

The major areas of difference are the number and the focus of the indicators. While most commentators recognize that the indicators (or at least some of them) should be alterable or controllable (by the actions of the policy-makers), they differ about their number, the need for redundancy, and the extent to which the indicators should be comprehensive and organized by and into a framework that embodies the functioning of the educational system, with, where possible, known causal links. Where the set is not comprehensive, there is agreement that it should focus on the central features and outcomes of the educational process.

It is therefore unavoidable that indicators cannot meet all the different criteria that have been proposed. The developers of an indicator set must resolve whether they are going to lean more towards a small number of key indicators or more towards a comprehensive set, embodying context and process as well as outcome. They will have to trade off one criterion at the expense of another, for example greater comprehensiveness against greater cost.

Conclusions

The lessons from the fate of social indicators must be learnt and applied to the development of educational indicators, while recognizing that even in the field of economics there is not a single accepted framework and that the results of economic predictions, using econometric models, are still contentious.

Almost all the sets of criteria discussed above recognize the importance of policy-relevance and the inevitability of politicization.

This chapter has attempted to describe and analyze the cluster of interacting factors that influence the development of an indicator system. These factors are: (a) policy considerations, (b) research knowledge, (c) technical considerations, (d) practical considerations, and (e) the 'choosers' — those in a position to influence the choice and development of indicators.

Many have attempted to indicate, through the stating of criteria, how these factors can be translated into a set of principles for guiding the development of indicators, and the list below synthesizes some of the most important from among those discussed in the previous section:

- policy-relevant
- policy-friendly (timely, comprehensible and few in number)
- derived from framework (defensible in research terms, and including alterable variables, hence oriented towards action)
- technically sound (valid and reliable)
- feasible to measure at reasonable cost.

The nature and importance of these considerations will vary according to the locus or level of the action and the purpose of the system of indicators. For example, the framework and the potential action-points could be different for an indicator system led primarily by the concerns of national policy-makers from those for one designed for a local school system or an individual school site. The differences might be even more pronounced between a system designed to inform managers at the local level and a system designed for local accountability, which would tend to stress outcomes much more.

It also must be recognized that, whatever the level, these principles interact and sometimes conflict. Increases in validity rarely occur without increases in cost, and may well adversely affect timeliness. In the final analysis, then, the quality of the indicator system is likely to be crucially determined by those who hold the purse-strings, almost always the policy-makers on behalf of their constituents. It follows, first, that policy-relevance and policy-friendliness are likely to be of major significance, possibly at the expense of the 'scientific' validity of the framework. Second, fewer rather than more, indicators are likely to be preferred, again possibly at the expense of validity. *Finally, the technicians will have to work closely with the policy-makers, to ensure that expectations do not become so high that they are fated to turn into disillusionments, while nevertheless pointing to the potential, albeit limited, value of the development of an indicator system.*

Acknowledgment

This chapter originates from the International Education Indicators Project of the OECD and appears in the OECD publication from that Project 'Education Counts'.

References

BULMER, M. (1990) 'Problems of theory and measurement', *Journal of Public Policy*, 9, 4, pp. 407–12.

CARLEY, M. (1980) *Rational Techniques in Policy Analysis*, London, Heinemann Educational Books.

CARLEY, M. (1981) *Social Measurement and Social Indicators: Issues of Policy and Theory*, London, George Allen & Unwin.

CIPFA (1988) *Performance Indicators in Schools: A Contribution to the Debate*, London, CIPFA (The Chartered Institute of Public Finance and Accountancy).

FELDT, L.S. and BRENNAN, R.L. (1989) 'Reliability' in LINN, R.L. (Ed) *Educational Measurement*, New York, American Council of Education/Macmillan Publishing Company (3rd edn).

GRAY, J. and JESSON, D. (1988) Personal communication.

GREENBERGER, M., CRENSON, M.A. and CRISSEY, B.L. (1976) *Models in the Policy Process*, New York, Russell Sage Foundation.

HARGREAVES, D.H., HOPKINS, D., LEASK, M., CONNOLLY, J. and ROBINSON, P. (1989) *Planning for School Development: Advice to Governors, Headteachers and Teachers*, London, Department of Education and Science.

HATRY, H.P. *et al.* (1977) *How Effective are Your Community Services: Procedures for Monitoring the Effectiveness of Municipal Services*, Washington, DC, The Urban Institute.

HOGWOOD, B.W. and GUNN, L.A. (1984) *Policy Analysis for the Real World*, Oxford, Oxford University Press.

INNER LONDON EDUCATION AUTHORITY (1990) *Differences in Examination Performance* (RS 1277/90), London, ILEA Research & Statistics.

INNES, J.E. (1990) 'Disappointments and legacies of social indicators', *Journal of Public Policy*, 9, 4, pp. 429–32.

JAEGER, R.M. (1978) 'About educational indicators: Statistics on the conditions and trends in education', *Review of Research in Education*, 6, pp. 276–315.

JOHNSTONE, J.N. (1981) *Indicators of Education Systems*, London and Paris, Kogan Page and UNESCO.

KINGDON, J.W. (1984) *Agendas, Alternatives, and Public Policies*, Boston, MA, Little, Brown.

MACRAE, D. Jr (1985) *Policy Indicators: Links Between Social Science and Public Debate*, Chapel Hill, NC, University of North Carolina Press.

MARDIA, K.V., KENT, J.T. and BIBBY, J.M. (1979) *Multivariate Analysis*, London, Academic Press.

MCDONNELL, L.M. (1989) 'The policy context' in SHAVELSON, R.J., MCDONNELL, L.M. and OAKES, J. (Eds) *Indicators for Monitoring Mathematics and Science Education: A Sourcebook*, Santa Monica, CA, RAND Corporation.

MCEWAN, N. and HAU CHOW (1991) 'Issues in implementing indicator systems', *The Alberta Journal of Educational Research, XXXVII*, 1, pp. 65–86.

MESSICK, S. (1989) 'Validity' in LINN, R.L. (Ed) *Educational Measurement*, New York, American Council of Education/Macmillan Publishing Company (3rd edn).

NISBET, J. and BROADFOOT, P.M. (1980) *The Impact of Research on Policy and Practice in Education*, Aberdeen, Aberdeen University Press.

NUTTALL, D.L. (1989) 'The functions and limitations of international educational indicators', paper prepared for the OECD/CERI INES Project, Paris.

OAKES, J. (1989) 'What educational indicators? The case for assessing school context', *Educational Evaluation and Policy Analysis*, 11, 2, pp. 181–99.

ODDEN, A. (1990) 'Making sense of education indicators: 'The missing ingredient' in WYATT, T. and RUBY, A. (Eds) *Education Indicators for Quality, Accountability and Better Practice*, Sydney, Australian Conference of Directors-General of Education.

OSBORNE, D.A. (1990) 'The NSW school development and evaluation model' in WYATT, T. and RUBY, A. (Eds) *Education Indicators for Quality, Accountability and Better Practice*, Sydney, Australian Conference of Directors-General of Education.

PETERSEN, N.S., KOLEN, M.J. and HOOVER, H.D. (1989) 'Scaling, norming and equating' in LINN, R.L. (Ed) *Educational Measurement*, New York, American Council of Education/Macmillan Publishing Company (3rd edn).

POLLITT, C. (1986) 'Performance measurement in the public services: Some political implications', *Parliamentary Affairs*, 39, 3, pp. 315–29.

RILEY, K. (1990) 'Making indicators consumer-friendly', *Education*, 11 May, pp. 470–2.

ROCKWELL, R.C. (1989) 'Lessons from the history of the social indicators movement', paper prepared for the NCES Indicators Panel, Washington, DC.

ROSE, R. (Ed) (1990) 'Whatever happened to social indicators? A symposium', *Journal of Public Policy*, 9, 4, pp. 399–450.

RUBY, A. (1990) 'Do common values produce common indicators? An illustration from the CERI project on international education indicators' in WYATT, T. and RUBY, A. (Eds) *Education Indicators for Quality, Accountability and Better Practice*, Sydney, Australian Conference of Directors-General of Education.

SALGANIK, L.H. (1990) 'Adjusting educational outcome measures for student background: Strategies used by states and a national example', paper prepared for the NCES Indicators Panel, Washington, DC.

SCHEERENS, J. (1990) 'School effectiveness research and the development of process indicators of school functioning', *School Effectiveness and School Improvement*, 1, 1, pp. 61–80.

SELDEN, R. (1991) 'The INES framework', *The INES Handbook*, Paris, OECD.

SHAVELSON, R.J. (in press) 'Can indicator systems improve the effectiveness of mathematics and science education? The case of the US', *Evaluation and Research in Education*.

SHAVELSON, R.J., MCDONNELL, L., OAKES, J., CAREY, N. with PICUS, L. (1987) *Indicator Systems for Monitoring Mathematics and Science Education*, Santa Monica, CA, RAND Corporation.

VAN HERPEN, M. (1989) 'Conceptual models in use for educational indicators', paper prepared for the OECD/CERI INES Project, Paris.

WAINER, H. (1986) 'The SAT as a social indicator: A pretty bad idea' in WAINER, H. (Ed) *Drawing Inferences from Self-Selected Samples*, New York, Springer-Verlag.

WEISS, C.H. (1979) 'The many meanings of research utilization', *Public Administration Review*, 39, pp. 426–31.

WINDHAM, D. (1990) Personal communication (comments made as discussant at symposium on OECD/CERI INES Project at AERA Annual Meeting, April).

Nuttall, D.L. (1993b) 'Presentation at Centre for Policy Studies Conference, 21 September 1993'.

Introduction

In the summer of 1993, English teachers took the unprecedented step of boycotting National Curriculum assessment requirements. The last straw which broke the camel's back and prompted this extreme action was the design of the National Curriculum tests for English at Key Stage 3. Secondary teachers of the subject were incensed by the flagrant political interference in the content of the tests which would, inevitably, change the curriculum from that laid down, and broadly accepted, in the National Curriculum Orders. At heart, what was at issue was the question of who has the right to determine curriculum content and what that content should be. But this particular conflagration rapidly spread to fan the flames of smouldering discontent among other secondary teachers and the mass of primary teachers who had by then already been carrying the burden of what seemed to them unreasonable and unhelpful assessment requirements for several years. The political deadlock that this boycott created was in part resolved by the institution of a review of the content, structure, size and assessment arrangements of the National Curriculum. It was chaired by Sir Ron Dearing, then the newly-appointed Chairman of the newly-formed Schools Curriculum and Assessment Authority (SCAA).

This final contribution to our collection of Desmond Nuttall's papers is a speech he made, shortly before his death, to a conference on the Dearing Review of National Curriculum and Assessment arrangements which was organized by the right-wing Policy Studies Institute. This was Desmond Nuttall at his very best (see Michael Barber's comments quoted in the introduction to Paper 2). The argument is lucid, accessible and reasonable. It draws on national and international research to construct a rational argument concerning how policy should be developed, knowing Sir Ron Dearing's desire to resolve the issue of whether the 10-level scale should be allowed to continue, Desmond Nuttall's speech cuts through the plethora of words uttered and written on the subject during the course of the review, to make several simple and profound points. He argues in favour of a structure of curriculum expectations but against the proliferation of unassessable behavioural objectives; in favour of broad goals with teachers being helped to assess them through the provision of exemplar material and supportive moderation. He dares a more provocative call for the abolition of external examinations. Desmond Nuttall's 'shopping list' of proposals for the future with which he ended his speech, read also as the goals which would have informed his own work had he lived.

Sir Ron Dearing was apparently much impressed with Desmond Nuttall's speech and had invited him to write further briefing papers to inform the deliberations, briefing papers that, sadly, were never to be written. Thus this paper must stand as the final, definitive illustration of the particular character and quality of Desmond Nuttall's work — his ability to achieve a synoptic grasp of complex details, and his ability to communicate in a way that was meaningful and useful to policy-makers, politicians and practitioners as well as researchers. Above all though, the tone of this speech shows his own close involvement in the issues under discussion. For Desmond Nuttall these concerns were not the subject of academic detachment or intellectual conundrums. They were the focus of an intensely passionate commitment and the cause to which he devoted his life. This commitment was often too, for Desmond Nuttall, the source of great satisfaction when he felt a good decision had been achieved or his words had made an impact. Happily this was one such occasion.

PRESENTATION AT CPS CONFERENCE — 21 SEPTEMBER 1993

I have been invited here today to defend the model put forward by the Task Group on Assessment and Testing (TGAT) early in 1988. I have chosen to look at three fundamental aspects of their proposals, namely the 10-level scale, the place of teacher assessment and the purposes of assessment that they identified. But before I look at each of these I should just like to thank publicly all those who have helped to shape my views — though, of course, I take full personal responsibility for what I am about to say.

As Sir Ron Dearing has indicated, the 10-level scale or alternatives to it pose the most difficult issue that his review has to face. Finding the best way to specify the curriculum is an issue that has challenged educationists, philosophers and curriculum theorists for most of this century, and many nations are grappling with it at this moment. TGAT's 10-level scale was an exciting concept because of the way in which it made progression a fundamental component of the curriculum, viewing the curriculum as dynamic rather than static, relating it to learning. But learning is a very complex process and cannot be assumed to be linear even in subjects such as maths, science and modern languages, let alone in English and the humanities. Learning can, however, be sequenced in the same way across the nation. In my opinion, TGAT's vision was therefore appropriate — it is the manner and the haste in which that vision has been realized that have caused the problems identified in Sir Ron's review, especially the spurious precision in those dozens of Statements of Attainment (SoA) that fill the boxes at each level. The phrase 'Statements of Attainment' never appeared in the TGAT report.

I believe that we should keep the 10-level scale but change the way in which the levels for each Attainment Target are specified. Much as in Scotland, the levels should be exemplified through sample objectives and sample tasks, not exhaustively defined through SoAs. I make this recommendation very largely in the light of the experience of examining bodies throughout the world — they have tried and failed to employ strict criterion-referencing. Indeed, even the guru of criterion-referencing, James Popham, whose bumper sticker in the 1970s read 'Stamp out non-behavioural objectives' has recanted and now favours broad goals rather than detailed behavioural objectives. Examining bodies now favour grade descriptions or standards-based grade definitions, usually and most effectively exemplified through examples of student work. I would particularly refer you to the work of Royce Sadler in this field and to his article 'Specifying and promulgating achievement standards' in the *Oxford Review of Education* in 1987.

If we were to specify desired achievement at each level in these more general terms and exemplify it in terms of sample tasks and samples of student work (informed, wherever possible, by APU results), I believe that we would avoid the implication of a precise sequence of progression up a ladder with equal steps that, as Lord Skidelsky has argued, is manifestly at variance with educational reality. We would, however, preserve what is good in the 10-level proposal, namely a raising of horizons and expectations, a belief in progress (rather than condemning many pupils to grade D or E for their whole school careers — at least until they get grade F or G at GCSE) and a model for differentiation. Both the Scottish five levels and the Australian eight levels are defined much more generally; the former seem to work well, the latter though not yet having been tried.

If, however, the 10-level scale were to disappear and some other model were to be adopted, that defined desired achievement outcomes at the end of each Key Stage independently, I would urge the review team to examine experience in other countries: the US definitions of content and performance standards at three stages (grades 4, 8 and 12) linked to evidence from their national assessment (comparable to the Assessment of Performance Unit) which has defined three levels of performance (basic, proficient and advanced); the Dutch attempt to define foundation and advanced levels, which collapsed leaving a single level at each stage; and the current Ontario attempt to define benchmarks at three key stages using three levels at each stage: all students can . . . , most students can . . . , some students can . . . , exemplified through questions and tasks rather than objectives. None of these efforts to define a curriculum have been without problems and it is dangerous to assume that alternatives to the 10-level scale, which is of course becoming increasingly familiar to teachers, parents and children, would have any fewer problems.

This value of exemplification of levels and grades is supported by experience from around the world, as well as increasingly from England itself (see, for example, the evaluation by James and Conner of moderation at KS1, which shows how valuable the SEAC publication, *Pupils' Work Assessed* has been and how teachers have compiled their own portfolios to exemplify the levels). This experience shows that examples of student work, together with examples of tasks and questions, can hugely increase understanding of desired objectives and achievement outcomes. I would want to couple this knowledge of effective curriculum implementation practice with our more general knowledge of school effectiveness and school improvement: the giving of a measure of autonomy to individual teachers and to individual students, within the bounds of a clear framework, is a recipe for improvement.

Now I want to turn to teacher assessment. Like TGAT I believe that teacher assessment is bound to be richer, more varied and more comprehensive — in short, more valid — than any kind of externally set task or test, and that, moreover, only assessment by teachers on a continuous basis can provide real support for learning, that is formative assessment, the type of assessment that really matters in the classroom. Teachers clearly need help if they and their pupils are to gain the maximum from such formative assessment — though research (for example, by Gipps, Brown and their colleagues) is already showing how the experience of National Curriculum Assessment is helping teachers to improve their own assessment in the classroom. Further INSET and materials illustrating pupil work are clearly essential but above all I would argue for the power of consensus moderation across schools in enhancing teachers' understanding of the curriculum, in widening their horizons of teaching approaches, teaching materials and assessment approaches, and in bringing them to a common and shared understanding of levels or grades. Consensus moderation is a very powerful form of professional development, as the experience of CSE and 'O' level coursework schemes amply demonstrated in the 1960s and 1970s. It was, of course, TGAT's proposals for consensus moderation that the then Secretary of State, Kenneth Baker, rejected (on the grounds of excessive cost and complexity) thus immediately undermining the TGAT proposals.

So teacher assessment, backed by appropriate quality assurance of both the process of assessment and the product, can offer both high quality formative assessment and a contribution to summative assessment (as it has in CSE, 'O' level and GCSE for decades). These arguments are presented in much more detail in the work of the British Educational Research Association Assessment

Policy Task Group, whose papers on this subject were presented at BERA's Annual Conference earlier this month and are to be published in book form.

I believe that in the fullness of time, as foreseen by the Norwood Committee in 1943 and as happens in Queensland, Australia, in their equivalent of 'A' levels, we shall be able to rely solely on moderated internal assessment without the need for external tests. But I accept that we are probably not yet ready for that. If, to use the American term, the testing stakes are high — in other words, if an individual student's future (or indeed an individual teacher's future) is dependent upon the result, as in the 11+ or 'A' level, the test is bound to influence the behaviour of both student and teacher — leading to the potentially iniquitous teaching to the test. The Americans now realize the harm done by their extensive use of multiple-choice questions and are seeking to develop much broader assessment devices — portfolios, practical activities and so forth. This allows me to tell the story of the three Americans arriving at Heathrow. They had duly ticked the boxes on the immigration form, but the first had only been able to put a cross where the form required his signature. The second had put two crosses and, when questioned about this by the immigration officer, explained that the first cross stood for her first name and the second for her last name. The third had put three crosses and explained that the first stood for his first name, the second for his last name, and the third for PhD (Harvard).

The format and content of the tests can thus have a powerful effect on teaching and learning (positive in the way that, according to HMI and teachers, the GCSE has had a beneficial effect, or distorting and narrowing in the case of the 11+).

The fundamental mistake that TGAT made — now visible with the benefit of hindsight — was to try to design a single system of National Curriculum Assessment that was simultaneously *formative, summative* and *evaluative* (the last term referring to the Government's requirement that aggregated results for each school be published). The analysis by the BERA Assessment Policy Task Group demonstrates that in such a multipurpose system one purpose comes to dominate and the others wither. The casualty of the last few years has been formative assessment — the function of assessment that I argued earlier should be pre-eminent since it is about helping pupils to learn better.

I end then with my proposals for the future, some that I have been able to support with argument and evidence today and others that I have had no time to discuss but which are developed in colleagues' and my own writings.

First, the curriculum:

Plan the curriculum as a whole and the whole curriculum
Make Key Stage 4 span 14–19
Keep the 10-level scale
Define the levels in terms of broad objectives
(and provide examples of more specific objectives, of tasks and activities and of student work)

Second, assessment:

Establish separate systems:
1　Teacher assessment (and consensus moderation) for formative purposes
2　Core or cross-curricular skill tests/tasks for summative (and if necessary local evaluative) functions — but can we make such tests valid, and reliable, and avoid them distorting teaching and learning, and thus lowering standards?
3　APU-type system for national monitoring (samples of students, plus rich and varied tasks)
Abolish GCSE (an anachronism)
Reform 'A' levels radically

Finally, league tables:

1　Don't have them
2　If we do have to have them, publish raw *and* value-added tables

I conclude by saying 'Don't be frightened by a bit of complexity'. We've learnt to live with seasonally adjusted unemployment figures, a Retail Price Index that includes both rent and mortgages — how many of us pay both? — and incredibly complicated Rate Support Grant settlements using fiddled multiple regression. I believe that we can learn to live with appropriate complexity in value added.

References

BROADFOOT, P.M. *et al* (Eds) (1983) *Policy Issues in National Assessment* (BERA Dialogues No. 7), Clevedon, Multilingual Matters.

GIPPS, C.V. (1992) 'National Curriculum Assessment: A research agenda', *British Educational Research Journal*, 18, 2, pp. 277–86.

GIPPS, C.V. *et al.* (1992) 'National assessment at 7: Some emerging themes' in GIPPS, C.V. (Ed) *Developing Assessment for the National Curriculum*, London, Kogan Page.

JAMES, M.E. and CONNER, C (1993) 'Are reliability and validity achievable in National Curriculum Assessment? Some observations on moderation at Key Stage 1 in 1992', *The Curriculum Journal*, 4, 1, pp. 5–19.

MAW, J. (1993) 'The National Curriculum Council and the whole curriculum: Reconstruction of a discourse', *Curriculum Studies*, 1, 1, pp. 55–74.

SADLER, R. (1987) 'Specifying and promulgating achievement standards', *Oxford Review of Education*, 13, pp. 191–209.

SADLER, R. (1989) 'Formative assessment and the design of instructional systems', *Instructional Science*, 18, pp. 119–44.

An Unfinished Pilgrimage

An Unfinished Pilgrimage

The twenty papers that we have collected together in this volume tell the story not only of aspects of the work of an outstanding educational researcher, but also of a rapidly moving debate about educational issues and practices. This fascination with radical reforms in education has occurred not only in Britain but also around the world during the last quarter of the twentieth century. As we come close to the end of the millennium the awareness of ways in which educational opportunities and achievements could be and, indeed, need to be improved can rarely have been higher. Such changes are consistently prominent in the manifestos of the major political parties, and parents, community leaders, employers and industrialists regularly clamour themselves for changes and improvements. Education is a vital asset of any developed or developing society and it is perhaps an inevitable symptom of development that it leads to a greater awareness of the possibilities and challenges that can be considered. At the level of wealth creation, productivity, and economic development, education is big business. For this reason a significant number of governments are spending more than a fifth of their annual budget on providing education. Education is also big business in the sense that the stakes are high — the country that does not get the maximum productivity from its education system is likely to be the country that, despite massive investment, fails to compete successfully in the international marketplace.

The 'post-modern' era of technologically-based production now puts a premium on the creation of a highly-skilled and adaptable labour force. What would once have seemed unthinkable targets as mass levels of educational achievement — between 60 and 70 per cent of 19-year-olds achieving level three (two 'A' levels or its equivalent by the year 2000 in England for example)[1], in France and South Korea the equivalent target is 80 per cent achieving this level by the year 2000, — a level that Japan has already reached — are testimony to the profound conviction of both governments and employers that future economic competitiveness depends on developing to very much higher levels than in the past, the intellect and skills of the great majority of those entering the workforce. In the UK this argument has been repeatedly and explicitly made in publications from the Confederation of British Industry and the Royal Society of Arts and, most recently, the National Commission on Education (NCE, 1993).

At another level the debate about what education should include, and how access to it should be determined, is equally acute. Education has the potential to be used to defend traditional values and beliefs, to protect the interests of selected groups within any society, as well as being a means of challenging widely held assumptions, values and beliefs and being a vehicle for the promotion of social change. For these reasons education is bound to be politically sensitive, and a major focus for debate and the exercise of different forms of power. Thus the definition of the curriculum to be followed, and the way in which success is defined and measured, both for individual students, their teachers, the individual institutions or system wide, are likely to be contentious and at the centre of political debates. It follows that the debates about educational assessment and examinations, teacher appraisal, school evaluation and performance indicators, which we have revisited in the preceding chapters have been and will remain crucial in the debate about improving educational effectiveness. This debate involves considering both the technical issues involved in improving the quality of educational assessment and evaluation practices, and the political questions concerning the nature of the social reforms to which they can contribute. It is clear from this collection that Desmond Nuttall was fervently concerned with both sets of issues. He knew and cared about the quality of evidence gathering and reporting in education, and he also understood and felt deeply about the social consequences of adopting different strategies. In his case his own privileged background in the public school system of England seems to have fired his passion for seeking to combat social disadvantage by providing increased educational opportunities for all. Educational assessment, as he understood well, can act in different ways either as a barrier or as a gateway to educational success.

During the years of his life there was a burgeoning of mass educational provision in the UK and it was educational assessment procedures that provided the gears and the brakes of the new educational engine. With hindsight, it is now relatively easy to trace the way in which the social and economic changes of the industrial revolution led to the demand for all workers to have some level of basic schooling (Johnson, 1976). It is also relatively easy to understand the historical connection between these social and economic imperatives and the emergence of a parallel industry of tests and examinations which could provide an apparently rational, and so, fair and efficient way of regulating access to these newly-created educational opportunities. The development of examinations which accompanied the institution of national systems of mass educational provision reflected the overwhelming need — at that time — for an acceptable mechanism that could be used to select the relatively small numbers who would go on to acquire the knowledge and skills necessary to play managerial and other kinds of leadership role in the economy from the great majority who would undertake the necessary semi-skilled and unskilled jobs which an industrial society geared to manufacturing needed (Broadfoot, 1979).

For nearly 100 years educational assessment has been playing these key roles — providing for selection, attesting to competence and rendering the process of allocating life-chances through education acceptable. Examination systems in particular, have become progressively more refined and sophisticated in their capacity to measure student achievement and so, to be used by proxy, as a mechanism for judging the overall quality of the education system and indeed, a means of steering it.

One thing that traditional methods of educational assessment have not been designed to address and certainly would not be good at, is the quite different function of encouraging individuals to *continue* learning. One reason for this is the heavy reliance there has been upon psychometrics to provide the basic models for educational assessment and examinations (Wood, 1986). Given that the raison d'être of psychometrics is essentially the measurement of ability (which is assumed to be largely innate) as the basis for selection, its fundamental premises are at odds with an agenda which puts a priority on as many people as possible being able and willing to continue in their learning. Thus whilst we do not, as yet, have the benefit of hindsight in order to see the emerging 'post-modern' picture clearly, scholars around the world have begun to develop a quite different assessment paradigm in which it is *learning*, rather than *measurement* that is the prime concern (Broadfoot, 1994). One early indicator of this change was the growing concern with validity which in the 1980s came to be seen as being of equal important as the reliability of assessments (Murphy and Torrance, 1988). The growing concern with validity can be seen as a reflection of a diminishing emphasis on a selection agenda in assessment especially in those countries where keeping students *in* education, rather than progressively weeding students *out*, was becoming the imperative. In recent years this concern has expanded into various initiatives concerned with developing new techniques of assessing, recording and reporting performance which are capable of addressing the wide range of skills as well as knowledge that education systems are increasingly being required to develop and which are geared towards supporting continuing learning as much as for providing summative judgments.

The growth of interest in criterion-referenced, as opposed to norm-referenced, assessment since the early 1970s is another reflection of the growing concern to find approaches to assessment which are constructive and positive and which will therefore encourage students by their experience of success — rather than of the failure which is the inevitable outcome for the majority in a norm-referenced system — to want to continue learning.

Thus in the United States, for example, the birthplace of many psychometric assessment approaches, recent years have seen a powerful growth in alternative approaches such as 'performance assessment' and 'authentic assessment' in which the goal is to integrate assessment within the process of learning itself. Many other countries are developing integrated curriculum and assessment 'frameworks' which provide a learning ladder for students — a logical, integrated hierarchy of provision in which the achievement of each level is less likely to be the closing of a door than it is the encouragement to the next. The National Curriculum framework in England, the 5–14 Curriculum Guidelines in Scotland, the 'benchmarks' being developed in parts of Canada and Australia (Broadfoot, 1994) are just a few examples of the kind of integrated curriculum and assessment designs now becoming increasingly typical in countries wherever higher levels of overall educational achievement are the imperative.

The same pattern is also evident in further, higher and professional and vocational education. Sir Christopher Ball's vision of 'ladders and links' (Ball, 1992), of a world in which different levels of qualification are 'portable' across countries by an increasingly internationally-mobile labour force, is one currently being pursued in many countries. In the UK, the English systems of National Vocational Qualifications and General National Vocational Qualifications and the parallel Scottish systems are part of a framework of levels which will ultimately include all further, higher and professional qualifications. The associated developments of modularization, the accreditation of prior learning, and credit transfer and accumulation reflect the growing international realization of a world in which students are willing and able to navigate a personal learning career through systems of education and training provision that are sufficiently flexible and appropriate in the way they are delivered to meet the diverse intellectual and practical needs of a whole society committed to learning (Broadfoot, Murphy and Torrance, 1990).

Equally central to this vision is the need to equip individuals with the skills and resources they need to become self-reliant and self-motivated learners. The skill to assess what has and has not been learned; to evaluate personal learning needs and goals; to choose the appropriate route in order to achieve these goals — is vital to the vision of a learning society. It is for this reason that recent decades have seen an explosion of interest in developing new, student-centred forms of recording learning achievements, 'learning logs', 'portfolios', profiles, records of achievement and personal action plans which are typical of a host of different international initiatives which are geared towards this end. Though the original reasons behind these various initiatives were in some cases very diverse, a measure of hindsight now reveals a common rationale in the desire to empower learners with the skills and the motivation to maximize the quality and the quantity of their own learning in the way that is most appropriate for them.

This is indeed a bold vision, perhaps even a utopian one when set against the messy reality of contradictory practices, conservatism and conflicting ideologies. Whilst it is hard to climb high enough out of the present to see clearly the main defining features of the educational landscape laid out before us, it is even harder to know the best route to take to achieve our chosen goal of improving education. And even if we identify the route correctly, there are still many obstacles to overcome on the way — the obstacles of prejudice, of lack of resources, of political timidity, of inertia, of vested interests — to name but a few.

Desmond Nuttall believed that one of the principal routes towards improving education was the pursuit of more effective approaches to collecting evidence about educational achievement at the pupil, teacher, school and national level. He believed passionately in the need to explore possible routes to achieving this goal through educational research. Like Pilgrim in John Bunyan's famous allegory *Pilgrim's Progress*, he was willing to take on the forces of prejudice, inertia and self-interest, strengthened by his own faith in the rightness of the cause and the goal that would, ultimately be achieved. Like Pilgrim, Desmond Nuttall knew the slough of despond and the dangers of being diverted into easier, more immediately rewarding paths, but he rarely succumbed. There can indeed have been few pilgrims more steadfast in the quest for ways to make educational assessment and evaluation more effective.

The papers collected in this volume record that pilgrimage. His early work on the technical improvement of existing forms of assessment — especially examinations — reflected a time when the pursuit of reliability and quality in such procedures constituted the goal for more effective assessment. The gradual awakening of interest in examinations policy and, in particular, in the CSE and GCSE initiatives which in this country were the reflection of the desire for increased validity in assessment procedures for all pupils were the harbinger of the more radical initiatives which were to come later. Desmond Nuttall's growing interest in records of achievement in the 1980s represented the next stage in his reconceptualization of the goal of effective assessment. His continuing interest in modes of accreditation which would free schools and colleges from the stranglehold of external assessment, whilst retaining the necessary quality control, was another important part of the journey towards making it possible to integrate assessment within the teaching and learning process so that it could both properly reflect existing and encourage further achievements.

Desmond Nuttall recognized the international character of the developments taking place in education and was active both in furthering mutual knowledge between countries in order to facilitate progress and in working in a number of different countries himself to support significant initiatives. His initial interest in methods of assessing and reporting on pupil achievements grew naturally to encompass wider concerns for the evaluation of teachers, teaching, schools and national education systems. He believed passionately that in each case methods of evidence gathering could be developed and improved, and that this would in turn contribute to improvements in the overall effectiveness of education for all.

The last years of Desmond Nuttall's life were to be in the era when assessment research and development ceased to be a largely technical preserve and became rather a major policy issue; when the focus for assessment ceased to be largely that of the achievement of individual students but widened to include teachers, schools and indeed whole systems as part of the quality debate. Desmond Nuttall's own desire to harness the power of educational research to explore the ingredients that lead to quality and, more particularly, the ways in which such quality could most meaningfully be measured, was a mirror image of the assessment policy issues of the time. This centred on finding effective ways to identify individual and system performance with a view to using that knowledge to raise the overall level of achievement of individuals, schools and systems.

But if the quest was a common one, rooted in the changing priorities of the time, the choice of route was not. Desmond Nuttall found himself calling a different tune to those policy-makers in his own country who used ideology rather than evidence as their guide to action. His last public appearance typified his enduring stance in this respect as he used national and international evidence to counter the ideological assertions of his protagonists on a conference platform devoted to discussing how the National Curriculum assessment system might best be reformed.

Desmond Nuttall's chosen role as a pilgrim committed to the development of ever more effective educational assessment and evaluation meant that, inevitably, he was regularly confronted by obstacles and opposition. The fact that his work so closely matched the policy concerns of the day was a reflection of his capacity to seize on important new ideas and to milk them for their potential for educational improvement. The fact that so much of his later work was concerned with institutional, rather than student assessment as such, reflected a growing recognition of the potential of assessment, if recast in its focus to address the issue of quality in every part of the system. The formative-summative distinction which had long characterized debates concerning the priorities and practices of *student* assessment were recast in the debate over the assessment of teachers, schools and systems.

Desmond Nuttall's quest was essentially a rationalist one. The search for appropriate indicators with which to compare education systems for example (Paper 19) reflected his belief in the feasibility of the quest to find an empirical solution to the problem of effective assessment of system quality. The quest for an appropriate and valid index of school quality by identifying the 'value-added' by the school, was an equally powerful reflection of Desmond Nuttall's belief in the possibility of empirical, rationalist ways of meeting needs (Paper 15). His work also demonstrated a rationalist belief in the capacity of research to identify the ingredients of an effective school. Even in his concerns to promote social justice as part of the overall improvement of education this same commitment was apparent. Desmond Nuttall's strategy was to use evidence concerning differential rates of success as a way of convincing others of the reality of the problem (Papers 8 and 15).

Thus Desmond Nuttall leaves us with two major legacies from his work. The first is the nature of his own professional pilgrimage. The route that Desmond Nuttall followed was one that engaged him in all the principal assessment and evaluation debates that characterized a time of enormous change. Indeed, the samples of his work which have been presented in this volume, along with a fuller bibliography on pp. 253–57 provided important signposts to that route based on his own outstanding vision of what effective assessment and evaluation could truly become. The second major legacy that Desmond Nuttall leaves us from his work is the message concerning how we should go down that route. Coupled with that vision must be the patient, painstaking enquiry which yields the evidence to guide us through the maze of possible paths and to warn us of blind alleys.

In this book we have collected some of Desmond Nuttall's most significant contributions to the pursuit of effective assessment and the improvement of education. Their quality and timeliness speak for themselves. In years to come, with the benefit of hindsight, their unique significance may be even more apparent. For the present it will suffice that among countless readers who never knew Desmond Nuttall these articles will further the cause to which he devoted himself with such outstanding success.

Desmond Nuttall was a high achiever, who also knew all about failure and disappointment. Three of the organizations that he worked for (the Schools Council, the Middlesex Regional Examinations Board and the ILEA) closed down-in two cases while he was employed by them, and in the third case shortly after. There was in time a humorous side to this, prompting colleagues at the Open University and University of London Institute of Education to speculate on whether he was a latter day 'Jonah'. There was also, of course, a more sober confrontation with disappointment and distress, and for some of Desmond Nuttall's colleagues and friends, unemployment and the facing of uncertain futures. Thus in his professional life, as with his personal life, Desmond Nuttall knew sorrows as well as joys. He will, however, ultimately be remembered as an outstanding individual who in a professional career spanning some twenty-six years contributed much more to educational policy, practice and research than would seem humanly possible. He has left us all much to remember him by in his papers, his ideas and his achievements. A substantial tribute that we can pay him is to carry on with the work that was so dear to him building upon all that he left us, and working actively for the further improvement of education for all.

Note

1 Consultation Document of National Advisory Council for Education and Training Targets (*Times Educational Supplement*, 15 July 1994, p. 1).

A Bibliography of Desmond Nuttall's Major Publications

SKURNIK, L.S. and NUTTALL, D.L. (1968) 'Describing the reliability of examinations', *The Statistician*, 18, pp. 118–128.

NUTTALL, D.L. and SKURNIK, L.S. (1969) *Examination and Item Analysis Manual*, Slough, NFER (second edition), University of Nottingham Rediguide 33, 1987.

NUTTALL, D.L. (1971a) 'Modes of thinking and their measurement', unpublished PhD thesis, University of Cambridge.

NUTTALL, D.L. (1971b) *The 1968 CSE Monitoring Experiments* (Schools Council Working Paper 34), London, Evans/Methuen Educational.

NUTTALL, D.L. and WILLMOTT, A.S. (1972) *British Examinations: Techniques of Analysis*, Slough, NFER.

NUTTALL, D.L. (1973a) 'Convergent and divergent thinking' in BUTCHER, H.J. and PONT, H.B. (Eds) *Educational Research in Britain*, London, ULP (reproduced as Paper 1).

NUTTALL, D.L. (1973b) 'Practical aspects of data collection', *Open University Course E341, Block 3, Part 1*.

NUTTALL, D.L. (1973c) 'Principles of constructing a measuring instrument', *Open University Course E341, Block 3, Part 3*.

NUTTALL, D.L., BACKHOUSE, J.K. and WILLMOTT, A.S. (1974) *Comparability of Standards Between Subjects*, (Schools Council Examinations Bulletin 29) London, Evans/Methuen Educational.

TAYLOR, E.G. and NUTTALL, D.L. (1974) 'Question choice in examinations', *Educational Research*, 16, pp. 143–50.

NUTTALL, D.L. (1975) 'Examinations in education' in COX, P.R., MILES, H.B. and PEEL, J. *Equalities and Inequalities in Education*, London, Academic Press (reproduced as Paper 2).

WILLMOT, A.S. and NUTTALL, D.L. (1975) *Reliability of Examinations at 16+*, London, Macmillan.

NUTTALL, D.L. (1977) 'The context of CSE', Supplement to *Education*, 150, 15, p. ix.

NUTTALL, D.L. (1978) 'The case against examinations', Supplement to *Education*, 152, 2, pp. v–vi (reproduced as Paper 3).

NUTTALL, D.L. (1979a) 'A rash attempt to measure standards', Supplement to *Education*, 154, 12, pp. ii–iii (reproduced as Paper 4).

NUTTALL, D.L. (1979b) 'The myth of comparability', *Journal of the National Association of Inspectors and Advisers*, 11, pp. 16–18 (reproduced as Paper 5).

NUTTALL, D.L. (1979c) 'Principles of measurement', *Open University Course DE304, Block 5, Part 2*.

NUTTALL, D.L. (1980a) 'Will the APU rule the curriculum?', Supplement to *Education*, 155, 21, pp. ix–x (reproduced as Paper 6).

NUTTALL, D.L. (1980b) 'Did the secondary schools get a fair trial?' *Education*, 155, 2, pp. 46–51 (reproduced as Paper 7).

NUTTALL, D.L. (1981a) 'Criteria for successful combination of teacher assessed and external elements' in *Combining Teacher Assessment With Examining Board Assessment*, AEB, Aldershot.

NUTTALL, D.L. (1981b) *School Self-Evaluation: Accountability with a Human Face?*, York, Longman.

MACINTOSH, H., NUTTALL, D.L., CLIFT, P. and BYNNER, J. (1981) 'Measuring learning outcomes', *Open University Course E364, Block 4*.

NUTTALL, D.L. and BARNES, P. (1981) 'Examinations and assessment', *Open University Course E200, Block 4, Part 3*.

NUTTALL, D.L. (1982a) 'Problems in the measurement of change', *Educational Analysis*, 4, 3, pp. 97–105.

NUTTALL, D.L. (1982b) 'Prospects for a common system of examining at 16+', *Forum*, 24, 3, pp. 60–1.

NUTTALL, D.L. (1982c) 'Accountability and evaluation', *Open University Course E364, Block 1*.

BYNNER, J., McCORMICK, R. and NUTTALL, D.L. (1982) 'Organisation and use of evaluation', *Open University Course E364, Block 6*.

NUTTALL, D.L. (1983a) 'Unnatural selection?', *The Times Educational Supplement*, 18 November (reproduced as Paper 8).

NUTTALL, D.L. (1983b) 'Monitoring in North America', *Westminster Studies in Education*, 6, pp. 63–90.

NUTTALL, D.L. and McCORMICK, R. (1983) 'Inspections', *Open University Course E364, Block 2, Part 3*.

ORR, L. and NUTTALL, D.L. (1983) *Determining Standards in the Proposed Single System of Examining at 16+*, Comparability in Examinations Occasional Paper 2, London, Schools Council.

NUTTALL, D.L. (1984a) 'Doomsday or a new dawn? The prospects for a common system of examining at 16+' in BROADFOOT, P. (Ed) *Selection, Certification and Control*, Lewes, Falmer Press (reproduced as Paper 9).

NUTTALL, D.L. and GOLDSTEIN, H. (1984) 'Profiles and graded tests: the technical issues', *Profiles in Action*, London, Further Education Unit (reproduced as Paper 10).

NUTTALL, D.L. (1984b) 'Alternative assessments: Only connect . . .', *New Approaches in Assessment*, London, Secondary Examinations Council.

NUTTALL, D.L. and ARMITAGE, P. (1985) *The Feasibility of a Moderating Instrument*, Summary Report published by Business and Technician Education Council, main report mimeo by Open University.

PYLE, D.W. and NUTTALL, D.L. (1985) 'The nature of intelligence', *Open University Course E206, Block 2, Unit 11.*

NUTTALL, D.L. (1986a) 'What can we learn from research on testing and appraisal?', *Appraising Appraisal*, BERA, Kendal (reproduced as Paper 11).

NUTTALL, D.L. (1986b) *Assessing Educational Achievement*, Lewes, Falmer Press.

NUTTALL, D.L., TURNER, G. and CLIFT, P.S. (1986) 'Staff appraisal' in HOYLE, E. and McMAHON, A. *The Management of Schools* (World Yearbook of Education), London, Kogan Page.

NUTTALL, D.L. (1986c) 'Problems in the measurement of change' in NUTTALL, D.L. (Ed) *Assessing Educational Achievement*, Lewes, Falmer Press (reproduced as Paper 12).

GOLDSTEIN, H. and NUTTALL, D.L. (1986) 'Can graded assessments, records of achievement, modular assessment and the GCSE co-exist?' in GIPPS, C.V. (Ed) *The GCSE: An Uncommon Exam*, London, Institute of Education/Heinemann (reproduced as Paper 13).

NUTTALL, D.L. (1987a) 'The current assessment scene', *Action on Assessment in BTEC. Coombe Lodge Report*, 19, 7, pp. 375–92.

NUTTALL, D.L. (1987b) 'The validity of assessments', *European Journal of Psychology of Education*, II, 2, pp. 109–118 (reproduced as Paper 14).

NUTTALL, D.L., CLIFT, P.S. and McCORMICK, R. (Eds) (1987) *Studies in School Self-Evaluation*, Lewes, Falmer Press.

NUTTALL, D.L. (1987c) 'Testing, testing, testing . . .', *Education Review*, 1, 2, pp. 32–5.

NUTTALL, D.L., GOLDSTEIN, H., PRESSER, R. and RASBASH, H. (1988) 'Differential school effectiveness', *International Journal of Educational Research*, 13, 7, pp. 769–76 (reproduced as Paper 15).

NUTTALL, D.L., BROADFOOT, P.M., JAMES, M.E., McMEEKING, S. and STIERER, B.M. (1988) *Records of Achievement: Report of the National Evaluation of Pilot Schemes*, London, HMSO.

NUTTALL, D.L. (1988) 'The implications of National Curriculum assessment', *Educational Psychology*, 8, 4, pp. 229–36.

NUTTALL, D.L. (1989a) 'National assessment — Will reality match aspirations?', *BPS Education Section Review*, 13, 1/2, pp. 6–19 (reproduced as Paper 17).

NUTTALL, D.L., BAINES, B.M. and BROADFOOT, P.M. (1989) *Profiling in TVEI*, London, Training Agency.

NUTTALL, D.L. (1989b) 'How the ILEA approaches school effectiveness' in CREEMERS, B., PETERS, T. and REYNOLDS, D. (Eds) *School Effectiveness and School Improvement*, Amsterdam, Swets and Zeitlinger.

NUTTALL, D.L. (1989c) 'National assessment: Complacency or misinterpretation?' in LAWTON, D. (Ed) *The Educational Reform Act: Choice and Control*, London, Hodder and Stoughton (reproduced as Paper 16).

NUTTALL, D.L. (1989d) 'The assessment of learning', *Open University course EP228, Unit 14*.

NUTTALL, D.L. (1990a) *Differences in Examination Performance* (RS 1277/90), London, ILEA Research and Statistics Branch.

NUTTALL, D.L. (1990b) 'The GCSE: Promise vs reality' in BROADFOOT, P., MURPHY, R.J.L. and TORRANCE, H. (Eds) *Changing Educational Assessment. International Perspectives and Trends*, London, Routledge.

NUTTALL, D.L. (1990c) 'The functions and limitations of international educational indicators', *International Journal of Educational Research*, 14, 4, pp. 327–33.

NUTTALL, D.L. (1990d) 'Proposals for a national system of assessment in England and Wales', *International Journal of Educational Research*, 14, 4, pp. 373–81.

NUTTALL, D.L. (1990e) 'Measuring social justice in education', *Victoria State Board of Education Working Papers on Public Education, Vol. 2*, Melbourne, Australia.

NUTTALL, D.L., BROADFOOT, P.M., GRANT, M., JAMES, M.E. and STIERER, B.M. (1991) *Records of Achievement: Report of the National Evaluation of Extension Work in Pilot Schemes*, London, HMSO.

NUTTALL, D.L. (1991a) *Assessment in England*, Report prepared for Pelavin Associates (reproduced as Paper 18).

NUTTALL, D.L. (1991b) 'Measuring standards', *Education Review*, 5, 2, pp. 21–5.

NUTTALL, D.L., BROADFOOT, P., DOCKRELL, B., GIPPS, C. and HARLEN, W. (Eds) (1992) *Policy Issues in National Assessment* (BERA Dialogues No. 7), Clevedon, Avon, Multilingual Matters.

WEST, A. and NUTTALL, D.L. (1992) *Choice at 11: Secondary School's Admissions Policies in Inner London*, London, LSE Centre for Educational Research, Clare Market papers No. 2.

NUTTALL, D.L., VARLAAM, A. and WALKER, A. (1992) *What Makes Teachers Tick? A Survey of Teacher Morale and Motivation*, London, LSE Centre for Educational Research, Clare Market Papers No. 4.

NUTTALL, D.L., PENNELL, H. and WEST, A. (1992) *After ILEA: Education Services in Inner London*, London, LSE Centre for Education Research, Clare Market Papers No. 5.

HARLEN, W., GIPPS, C., BROADFOOT, P. and NUTTALL, D.L. (1992) Assessment and the improvement of education', *The Curriculum Journal*, 3, 3, pp. 215–30.

NUTTALL, D.L. (1992) 'Performance assessment: The message from England', *Educational Leadership*, pp. 54–7.

NUTTALL, D.L. (1992b) 'Performance indicators for equal opportunities', *Genderwatch*, Cambridge University Press.

NUTTALL, D.L. and THOMAS, S. (1993) *Monitoring Procedures Based on Centre Performance Variables*, Employment Department (Methods Strategy Unit Research and Development Series Report No. 11).

NUTTALL, D.L., SAMMONS, P. and CUTTANCE, P. (1993) 'Differential school effectiveness: Results from a reanalysis of the Inner London Education Authority's Junior School Project data', *British Educational Research Journal*, 19, 4, pp. 381–405.

NUTTALL, D.L. (1993a) 'Response by the BERA Policy Task Group on Assessment', *The Curriculum Journal*, 4, 1, pp. 125–6.

NUTTALL, D.L. (1993b) 'Presentation at Centre for Policy Studies Conference — 21 September 1993' (reproduced as Paper 20).

GOLDSTEIN, H., RASBASH, J., YANG, M., WOODHOUSE, G., PAN, HQ., NUTTALL, D. and THOMAS, S. (1993) 'A multilevel analysis of school examination results', *Oxford Review of Education*, 19, 4, pp. 425–33.

RILEY, K. and NUTTALL, D.L. (1994) *Measuring Quality: Education Indicators United Kingdom and International Perspectives*, Lewes, Falmer Press (reproduced as Paper 19).

References

BALL, C. (1992) 'Ladders and links: Prerequisites for the discussion of an international framework of qualifications', in New Zealand Qualifications Authority (Ed) *Qualifications for the 21st Century: Conference Papers*, Wellington, New Zealand.

BARBER, M. (1993) Obituary to Desmond Nuttall, *Education*, 29 October, p. 327.

BROADFOOT, P., MURPHY, R.J.L. and TORRANCE, H. (1990) *Changing Educational Assessment: International Perspectives and Trends*, London, Routledge.

BROADFOOT, P. (1979) *Assessment, Schools and Society*, London, Methuen.

BROADFOOT, P. (1994) 'Approaches to quality assurance and control in six countries', in HARLEN, W. (Ed) *Enhancing Quality in Assessment*, London, Paul Chapman Publishing.

DES REPORT (1979) Local Authority Arrangements for the School Curriculum: Report on Circular 14/77 Review, London, HMSO.

DONALDSON, M. (1978) *Children's Minds*, London, Fontana.

GIPPS, C. (1994) *Beyond Testing: Towards a Theory of Educational Assessment*, London, Falmer Press.

GIPPS, C. and MURPHY, P. (1994) *A Fair Test? Assessment, Achievement and Equity*, Buckingham, Open University Press.

GOLDSTEIN, H. (1987) *Multilevel Models in Educational and Social Research*, London, Charles Griffin Co.

GOLDSTEIN, H. (1993) Obituary to Desmond Nuttall, *Research Intelligence*, 48, p. 40.

HARTLEY, L. and BROADFOOT, P. (1986) 'Assessing teacher performance', *Journal of Education Policy*, 3, 1, pp. 39–50.

LAWTON, D. (1992) *Education and Politics in the 1990s: Conflict or Consensus?*, Lewes, Falmer Press.

JOHNSON, R. (1976) 'Notes on the schooling of the English working class 1780–1850', in DALE *et al.* (Eds) *Schooling and Capitalism*, London, Routledge and Kegan Paul.

MURPHY, R.J.L. (1987) 'Assessing a national curriculum', *Journal of Education Policy*, 2, 4, pp. 317–23.

MURPHY, R.J.L. (1989) 'National assessment proposals: Analyzing the debate' in FLUDE, M. and HAMMER, M. (Eds) *The Education Reform Act 1988: Its Origins and Implications*, Lewes, Falmer Press.

MURPHY, R.J.L. (1994) 'Desmond Nuttall: A great record of educational achievement', *British Journal of Curriculum and Assessment*, 4(2), 20–23 and 40.

MURPHY, R.J.L. and TORRANCE, H. (1988) *The Changing Face of Educational Assessment*, Milton Keynes, Open University Press.

NCE (1993) *Learning to Succeed*, Report of the National Commission on Education, London, Heinemann.

NISBET, J. and BROADFOOT, P. (1980) *The Impact of Research on Policy and Practice in Education*, Aberdeen University Press.

PLASKOW, M. (Ed) (1985) *Life and Death of the Schools Council*, Lewes, Falmer Press.

SMITH, D.J. and TOMLINSON, S. (1989) *The School Effect: A Study of Multi-racial Comprehensives*, London, Policy Studies Institute.

WHITE, W.M. (1974) 'Examinations in relation to the curriculum', *Report of a Conference on Examinations and Assessment*, Chelsea College, London, mimeo.

WOOD, R. (1976) 'Your chemistry equals my French', *Times Educational Supplement*, 30 July.

WOOD, R. (1986) 'The agenda for educational measurement' in NUTTALL, D.L. (Ed) *Assessing Educational Achievement*, Lewes, Falmer Press.

Index

R